Educating Rita and her sisters

Women and continuing education

Edited by Roseanne Benn,
Jane Elliott and Pat Whaley

NIACE

THE NATIONAL ORGANISATION
FOR ADULT LEARNING

Published by the National Institute of Adult Continuing Education
(England and Wales)
21 De Montfort Street, Leicester, LE1 7GE
Company registration no. 2603322
Charity registration no. 1002775

First published 1998
© NIACE

CATALOGUING IN PUBLICATION DATA
A CIP record for this title is available from the British Library
ISBN 1 86201 055 2

Typeset by The Midlands Book Typesetting Company, Loughborough
Text design by Virman Man
Cover design by Boldface
Printed in Great Britain by Biddles, King's Lynn

Educating Rita and her sisters

Women and continuing education

Acknowledgements

This book has arisen largely out of a series of seminar papers presented to the Universities Association for Continuing Education (UACE) Women and Continuing Education Professional Network. The members' contributions, discussions and moral support were fundamental to the completion of this book and we thank everyone who attended. We would like to thank UACE for its financial and other support and particularly its willingness to address gender issues; individual members of the Network who made a contribution but are not listed amongst the authors; and Elizabeth Gerver of the University of Dundee who, as Chair of the UACE Research Sub-Committee, worked with us on the research aspects of Genderwatch. We wish to record our thanks to our Departments for their encouragement and for enabling us to complete this book; Kieran Lewis for the use of his office in London; and members of our families for their forbearance. Finally we thank Virman Man of NIACE for his assistance in publishing this book.

Dedication

This book is dedicated to all the members of the UACE Women and Continuing Education Professional Network.

Contents

Chapter One

Introduction: Women and continuing education – where are we now?

Roseanne Benn, Jane Elliott and Pat Whaley

This book emerges during a period of far-reaching social and economic change from which the world of adult continuing education has not escaped. These changes have impacted on all aspects of women's lives: household, employment, culture and educational opportunities. The purpose of this book is to focus specifically on women's experiences of continuing education as both students and tutors in the context of a rapidly changing continuing education (CE) and further and higher education environment.

Social and economic changes

We cannot begin to understand the vast changes occurring in our continuing education world without a sense of the radical social and economic changes in the wider society which we inhabit. During the post-war period we have witnessed a major economic restructuring leading to the demise of heavy industries such as coal and steel. At the same time there has been a growth in the service and light manufacturing industries. These changes have been examined in the context of the notion of a 'post-industrial society' (Bell, 1976). Bell identifies some of the elements of 'post-industrial society' which include: 'the creation of a new intellectual technology'; the growth of the technological and professional classes; a change of emphasis from goods to service industries; and an emphasis on the production of knowledge.

This important economic shift has two major implications which are of relevance to this book. First, it is clear that with an emphasis on the production of knowledge, the growth of the technological and professional classes and a technology which is almost in a state of permanent revolution, there is a demand for a flexible and adaptable education service that is committed to lifelong learning. Second, the shift to service industries has facilitated an expansion in employment opportunities, albeit often part-time and/or low paid, for women. This in turn has influenced continuing education which has attempted to become increasingly responsive to the perceived vocational needs of women returners or women already in employment.

In addition to the changes associated with the shift to post-industrial society, our continuing education world has also been transformed as a result of the establishment and consolidation of the hegemony of the New Right in the 1980s. We have witnessed the adoption of notions of market-led competition as opposed to centralised planning; (Tett, 1996) and an emphasis on vocationalism and wealth creation as opposed to a targeting of the 'educationally disadvantaged' based on priorities of equal opportunities (Benn and Fieldhouse, 1996). The New Right 'ideology of individualism' was a challenge to collectivist approaches to education, represented a 'conscious rejection of feminine preferences' and questioned the need for a women's education (Coats, 1994, p 4).

Women, in particular, have experienced change in many aspects of their lives: women's presence within the public sphere has increased and there is now the expectation that they will participate in paid employment for a significant part of their adult lives; larger numbers of women are now heading lone parent families; and despite the limitations of the impact of the equal opportunities legislation of the 1970s, a recognition of the importance of anti-discriminatory legislation is beginning to influence the practice of some employers and educational providers.

Adult continuing education traditions

Adult continuing education provision has been informed by two dominant traditions: liberal and radical education. Liberal adult education, as reflected in the university extra-mural departments, aimed to recruit from all sectors of society, offered a range of non-vocational courses and was chiefly concerned with the personal development of the individual. Within this model the experience and knowledge of the student was validated and methods of delivery were informal and student-centred (Benn and Fieldhouse, 1996). The radical tradition was more explicitly committed to the process of social change (Williams, 1989), focused on the working class and other excluded groups and identified with social movements such as the trade union movement (Simon, 1990).

Resulting from the radical tradition in particular, therefore, was an emphasis on the recruitment of excluded groups. In an attempt to achieve this, adult education became increasingly involved with the wider community outside the campus and offered targeted support structures such as creches, guidance and study skills.

Associated with both liberal and radical outlooks, coupled with the non-accredited nature of the provision, were highly innovative approaches to the curriculum (Kennedy and Piette, 1991). These included, for example, interdisciplinary programmes such as Cultural Studies and Women's Studies. Such programmes have challenged traditional knowledge boundaries and fought the traditions which rendered women's experience as invisible. Moreover, as subject boundaries weakened, the possibility emerged for tutors to move from individualised to more collective ways of working (Elliott, 1995).

The continuing education world became distinct from mainstream further and higher education in several ways: there was an emphasis on the targeting of the 'educationally disadvantaged'; most of the provision has remained part-time thus offering opportunities to those groups who are unable to participate in full-time programmes; participants are mature; many programmes are offered on an open entry basis; and there has been an increase in the provision of support services appropriate for adults.

This emphasis was especially beneficial for women and in particular, women returners. There emerged a range of 'second chance' opportunities which either formed part of the traditional liberal adult education programme or, more recently, offered more vocationally relevant courses. An equal opportunities orientation and the resulting provision which attempted to be responsive to women's specific needs enabled many women to return to a supportive educational environment.

Continuing education: far-reaching change

The rapid changes we are witnessing in the world of continuing education must be seen both in the context of the wider societal shifts outlined above and in the systems of further and higher education which have also experienced a rapid transformation. Briefly, further education has traditionally attracted a wide range of participants but university CE and to a lesser extent adult education institutions have excluded a larger section of the community. The role of the university within the wider community is now debated with increasing agreement that the modern university must move away from its exclusive and elitist traditions. Many now accept that education must be more responsive to wider societal and community needs and should be 'in the mainstream rather than at the margins of social change . . .' (Elliott *et al*, 1996: p xiv). The notion of community is contested, however, and with a tradition of vocationalism, within further education and a shift towards vocationalism in higher education, there is an increasing emphasis on the *business* community. Many adult educators welcome this increased responsiveness to community need. However, there is a justified concern that an overemphasis on the needs of the business community could jeopardise the interests of students, and in particular female students. This raises the questions: 'who determines these needs?' and 'how do we ensure that the interests of students and, more specifi- cally, women students remain the main priority?'.

During the 1990s the British further education system expanded by one third and the higher education system has transformed from an elite system recruiting only 15 per cent of school leavers to a mass system recruiting nearly a third of school leavers (Scott, 1995). The education system is now faced with the challenge of a significant increase in student numbers without a pro-rata increase in resources (Elliott *et al*, 1996).

Associated with the increase in student numbers has been a widening of the social base of students with increasing participation from women, mature and working class students (albeit a minority). Responses to these developments remains ambivalent: undoubtedly there is concern about the inadequate funding for a mass education system and the effect of this on non-traditional students, yet adult educators welcome the move away from an elite system and the resultant broadening of the social base of our students.

Many of the recent developments within further and higher education have a direct impact on the work of CE departments. For example, as colleges and universities become fully modularised, and as CE departments become less involved with liberal, non-accredited programmes and increasingly involved with accredited programmes which lead to named awards, what will be the position of the curriculum in CE departments? The flexibility which will result from modularisation may enable mainstream students to follow modules offered by CE departments, and students within CE departments to follow modules offered within the mainstream of the institution. There are several implications for continuing education. An optimistic view would suggest that we might be able to influence the further and higher education agenda. However, it is more likely that there will be pressure on CE departments to offer programmes which are acceptable to the mainstream. There is a need to examine how far we will be able to remain responsive to the particular needs of our women students within this new context.

Undoubtedly the changes outlined above present important challenges to adult educators and we will have to find ways of protecting the best of our traditions and ensuring that we continue to meet the needs of our traditional target groups. We are faced with the challenge that rather than becoming increasingly subservient to the requirements of the academy, we could attempt to find ways of influencing or even subverting the traditional education agenda. There is, however, one constant which remains in our rapidly changing continuing education world and that is the sense that we are educating for change. The context has undoubtedly shifted away from liberal or left-wing notions of change but there remains a reality that the work of adult continuing education is somehow part of a wider process of social, economic and political change. The task for adult educators is to ensure that this process of change does not remain subservient to managerial or other New Right agendas. With the election of a Labour Government in 1997 there is room for some optimism that New Right assumptions can be challenged with the prospect that there should be some channels for more positive changes.

Women and continuing education: reflection in action

This book is divided into four sections. The first section provides the context for the rest of the book. Key themes related to women's experience of continuing education are examined. The emphasis is on the purposes of continuing education in the context of both liberal and radical traditions. The question is raised as to whose purposes? How do we resolve issues of purpose and at the same time recognise both the fragmentation of the concept of 'woman' and the diversity of women's experience: the mediation of women's lives by factors such as class, race and sexuality? These issues are considered in both a historical and a contemporary context.

In the second section, the issue of women studying and studying women is considered. The section focuses primarily on curricula issues both in the narrow sense of what is studied and in the wider sense of women as students and the relationship between the two. Themes discussed in the first section are considered in the context of the teaching of Women's Studies, possibilities for the development of a curriculum for women in the mainstream and the potential for an experiential learning. There is a consideration of areas of disadvantage experienced by women students and the support structures that should be available.

In section three, we explore questions associated with women and research: women researching and researching women. We examine the contribution and nature of women's research in continuing education. There is discussion around the distinctiveness of women's research: what is distinctive about women's research into continuing education? Methodological and ethical issues are considered, particularly in relation to difference.

Section four examines equal opportunities issues in relation to women staff in continuing education. Despite a commitment to equal opportunities, the reality for women staff in continuing education is that structurally their position reflects that of women employed in other institutions in our society: in other words they tend to be clustered in the lower paid, often part-time and temporary posts. Discussion focuses on both full-time staff (academic, administrative and clerical) and part-time tutors. The final section looks to the future and considers the way forward for women in continuing education in the context of some of key issues raised in the rest of the book.

While highlighting some of the problems and concerns, the book ends on a note of optimism and positive anticipation and suggests ways in which we may realise our visions.

References

Bell, D (1976) *The coming of post industrial society,* New York: Basic Books.

Benn, R and Fieldhouse, R (1996) 'Notions of community for university continuing education' in Elliott, J, Francis, H, Humphreys, R and Istance, D (eds) *Communities and their universities: the challenge of lifelong learning,* London: Lawrence and Wishart Ltd.

Coats, M (1994) *Women's education,* Buckingham: Open University Press/SRHE.

Elliott, J (1995) 'Women's Studies and adult education: a shared agenda?' in Bryant, I (ed) *Vision, invention, intervention – celebrating adult education,* Proceedings of the 25th Annual SCUTREA Conference.

Elliott, J, Francis, H, Humphreys, R and Istance, D (eds) (1996) *Communities and their universities: the challenge of lifelong learning,* London: Lawrence and Wishart Ltd.

Kennedy, M and Piette, B (1991) 'From margins to the mainstream: issues around Women's Studies on adult education and access courses' in Aaron, J and Walby, S (eds) *Out of the margins: women's studies in the nineties,* Basingstoke: Falmer Press.

Scott, P (1995) *The meanings of mass higher education,* Buckingham: Open University Press/ SRHE.

Simon, B (1990) 'The struggle for hegemony, 1920–1926' in Simon, B (ed) *The search for enlightenment: the working class and adult education in the twentieth century,* London: Lawrence and Wishart Ltd.

Tett, L (1996) 'Education and the marketplace' in Raggatt, P et al (eds) *The learning society: challenges and trends,* London and New York: Routledge.

Williams, R (1989) 'Adult education and social change' in Williams, R *What I came to say,* Hutchinson: Radius; also in McIlroy, J and Westwood, S (eds) (1993) *Border country: Raymond Williams in adult education,* Leicester: NIACE.

Section One

Contextualising women in continuing education

Chapter Two

Dancing into the future: developments in adult education

Veronica McGivney

In recent years, education for adults in general and for women in particular has resembled a kind of dance – some steps forward, a few back and to the side, some moving up and down on the spot, then a resumption of the original pattern but with significant variations.

From a superficial viewpoint the picture appears largely positive: more education for women and more women in education. Where it still exists, community-based education remains a 'feminised' service attracting more than twice as many women as men. Women also predominate in Access courses and other adult programmes funded by the Further Education Funding Council (FEFC). At the same time they have been entering mainstream further education in increasing numbers (although loss of the Demand Led Element and convergence in further education funding may slow down this trend as well as demolish some of the support structures enabling women to attend). Looking at programmes targeted specifically at women, the situation also looks relatively positive. Charting developments from the 1970s, Maggie Coats (1994) noted a marked increase in the types of education provided for women and a greater aware-ness of the practical difficulties they face on re-entering education. Several years on this is still broadly the case. Although there are significant geographical variations, a range of education and training programmes for women, some with childcare support, are being provided by colleges, universities, local authorities, the WEA, women's training centres and other voluntary organisations, with funding from the European Social Fund, the Further Education Funding Council (FEFC), Training and Enterprise Councils (TECs), local economic development finance, Single Regeneration Budgets and other sources. The overall picture, then, seems promising: but have recent develop-ments in education and training been wholly beneficial for women? A more detailed analysis suggests the situation is more mixed than it first appears.

A question frequently asked these days is why women need special programmes when they are already so well represented in post-school education and training. This can best be answered by considering the impact of recent policy measures on women.

The impact of education and training policies

Since the Further and Higher Education Act (1992), the position of some types of programmes for adults – namely those which meet FEFC Schedule 2 criteria such as Access courses – has been secured through central funding while that of informal, unaccredited courses – the traditional route back into learning for many women – has been weakened as a result of it being left to local authorities to maintain an 'adequate' level of other types of provision. Since the concept of adequacy has, probably deliberately, never been defined, much LEA-funded and community-based provision has been lost. That which survives is often offered at a fee calculated to ensure full-cost recovery. Outreach work with non-traditional learners has become increasingly difficult to fund.

Those most adversely affected by the loss of informal and low-cost re-entry routes are: women who lack the confidence or means to return to formal education; those who left school early with no qualifications; those with little or no post-school learning experience; women with very low incomes; single parents; some groups of ethnic minority women and women living in badly served peripheral estates, rural areas and deprived inner cities (McGivney, 1993).

At the time of writing funding mechanisms operated by the FEFC and TECs favour individuals who have identified specific learning needs and are prepared (both practically and psychologically) to undertake a programme of study over those who need encouragement and support to take the first tentative steps back into learning. It is often pointed out that Access or Return to Learn programmes are more likely to attract people with some previous post-school learning experience than real 'returners'.

Outcome-related funding

As the funding available for the education and training of adults has become increasingly achievement-led, provision has become skewed towards those forms which lead to 'hard' outcomes such as qualifications, educational progression, jobs or placements. This has inevitably led to a growth of instrumental programmes for women and some long-established courses have been reformulated to fit the funding criteria. Although there are still some exploratory Return to Learn and New Opportunities courses, the number of general orientation programmes has dwindled in recent years while vocational, Return to Work and Access courses have burgeoned.

A high proportion of courses specifically for women are now geared to, or incorporate aspects of, training for employment. This is not an unwelcome development. Many women understandably want to return to and gain a more secure foothold in the labour market and it has been found that they are significantly more likely to pay for their own work-related education and training than men 'possibly to compensate for low levels of employer-provided training for them' (Shackleton and Walsh, 1997).

Gender divisions and stereotyping

So far, however, the stress on employment training has not led to any qualitative improvements in women's position in the labour market. Despite a series of European Directives and national legislation, British women still earn less than 80 per cent of men's pay and in some sectors are perceived by employers as low-cost segments of the labour force. The main growth area in women's employment has been in low-paid, part-time jobs, mostly in the service industries. This has accentuated rather than lessened gender stereotyping in the labour market.

As a number of studies (for example, Edwards, 1993) have demonstrated, the private domain of the family and the public domains of employment, education and training remain rigidly determined by gender despite the influx of women into education and employment.

Gender divisions in the labour market are both reflected in and reinforced by current post-compulsory education and training provision. The applications from training providers for the NIACE 1995 awards for Good Practice in Women's Education and Training were:

> heavily skewed towards updating and training in areas that have traditionally and stereotypically been women's work. This may represent an increase in this type of provision particularly in FE colleges (Coats, 1996, p 7).

Theresa Rees (1997) lists a number of ways in which current training arrangements and guidance developments have the effect of consolidating women's position in lower paid, traditionally female occupations:

I.   72 per cent of all sandwich, block and day release students are male.
II. The eligibility criteria laid down by many TECs for employment training programmes have excluded many married women.
III. The Modern Apprenticeship scheme reflects labour market divisions: 'Engineering apprenticeships are the most highly paid (£88 per week on average followed by chemicals and steel). The areas where women [work] are the lowest paid – childcare apprenticeships – £41 per week; business administration [another feminised area] £45 average. The effect of this is to socialise women into expecting low pay even when they have undertaken an apprenticeship'.
IV. Outcome-related funding (ORF) also accentuates sex segregation by encouraging TECs to provide volumes of output at the cheapest cost: 'Training women for non-traditional work and training women returners and other disadvantaged groups may be more expensive. When talking about the process of returning to learning, delivering the desired output within a certain time limit cannot be guaranteed for funding purposes. Hence there is a danger that one of the side effects of ORF formula is to reinforce gender divisions in training.'
V.   The stress on placements in the Careers Service and FE guidance – 'a process not readily metamorphosed into outputs in a specified time' – similarly encourages 'a built-in bias towards steering people into safe, gender-appropriate choices.'

Rees warns that NVQs may have a similar effect: narrow employment training leading to NVQs may not benefit women since it can constrain their choices. It can be very difficult for women emerging from a period of exclusive caring responsibilities to decide on the most appropriate training and employment route.

While accepting that a nationally recognised qualification can be immensely important to those who wish to remain in particular kinds of employment, Coats (1994) argues that training which is narrowly tied to NVQs rather than offering a range of options can result in women's continuing relegation to lower paid jobs, with little prospect of advancement, in traditional female sectors such as office work, personal services and caring.

There is little indication that gender stereotyping and imbalances in the labour market are yet a matter of national concern. On the contrary, the growth in employment for women is frequently cited as evidence of women's achievement of equality in the labour market, irrespective of the part-time and low-paid nature of many of the jobs involved and the limited number of occupational sectors in which women are found. Moreover, as the number of male, full-time jobs has dwindled, resentment against women for actually being in the labour market at all has grown. As observed by Shackleton and Walsh (1997, p 4), any improvement in the position of women

> will probably only be achieved at a cost to male workers (as their relative pay and domination of high status occupations is reduced). There is always likely to be resistance to policies aimed at eliminating disparities in the workforce.

A parallel situation is discernible within post-school education. Despite persisting gender stereotyping and imbalances within subjects and qualification routes, there is a widespread belief that gender equality in education has been achieved – an assumption based purely on the fact that a large proportion of students in further and higher education are now women. During the recent period of cuts, reorganisation and policy shifts, the stress on equal opportunities that gathered momentum during the 1980s was gradually obliterated by emphases of a wholly different nature. As Thompson (1997) put it: 'equal opportunities initiatives became as out of date as popular democracy in quangoland'. Tracing the fortunes of women's education from the 1980s to the mid-1990s, she describes how the aims and passion that inspired earlier developments have been lost and measures initiated wholly in the interests of students transformed into mechanisms to further institutional self-interest:

> The attempts many of us made, and the classes we pioneered in the 80s, in order to make 'really useful knowledge' accessible to 'disadvantaged' groups, especially working class and black women, have now become an industry. No self-respecting FE college is without its Access provision, comprised . . . predominantly of middle class women, No self-seeking university is without its franchise deals and credit transfer schemes, aimed at maximising its quota of 'non traditional' students . . . What counts as the culture and the curriculum of Access, what informs the logic of accreditation, what gets assumed in the promotion of APEL . . . owes less to the arguments about cultural politics and critical intelligence, feminism and empowerment, than to the need to generate 'customers', in line with the ideological and political consequences of applying performance indicators and free market economics to the practices of education.' (Thompson, 1997, pp 116–17)

In such a climate, initiatives to help women learners have been largely confined to recruitment procedures to maintain or improve student numbers. While many formal providers continue to mount some women–only programmes, often because there is European funding available for these, the evidence suggests that these are increasingly viewed as separatist and divisive (Coats, 1994). As in other spheres, women's readiness to grasp available opportunities appears to have fuelled a resistance towards anything that smacks of positive action – something that is now routinely disparaged as 'politically correct', a catch-all term that has become meaningless through overuse. Yet the need for single-sex programmes is still strong, particularly for some groups, such as black women who suffer from more than one dimension of discrimination.

Women-only programmes

According to Rees (1997), women returning to learning need their own:

space to learn that they can learn. What they learn in this context is immaterial. The benefits may be less tangible or measurable than a qualification. It may be loss of isolation, gaining in confidence or direction, enhanced ability to face challenging circumstances or to make important decisions. All this is a good base from which to move on into further education or training.

This is not to say that the same does not apply to men returning to learning, however, the characteristic life patterns of women together with the habitual male dominance of mixed groups combine to make a single-sex group a safe and comfortable place for many women at particular stages of their lives.

In his study of learning in voluntary organisations, Elsdon was struck by the importance women attached to being part of a single-sex group and their perception of its value, especially at times of major role change:

Belonging to something which is especially for them has a particular value . . . Most [interviewees] felt that they are able to be 'more frank' in the absence of men. In women's groups 'women can be in charge', 'they blossom, aren't edged out by men'. This was considered especially important for non-professional women who 'wouldn't rise if men were around'. Women on their own were considered 'more supportive' of each other, 'interested and caring', and observers as well as members noted the freedom from competition in their groups. There was also a distinct absence of any sense of ritualisic structure or behaviour, and of hierarchy, in all-woman groups. On the contrary, responsibility tended to be particularly widely dispersed . . .

Important as they were in general, these characteristics of women-only groups were seen to be most significant at periods of major role change. Some examples of . . . social learning supported by the group at these times drew on the period of isolation experienced by so many women when they have young families. Group support was enabling them to cope, to maintain a sense of identity, proportion and of wider horizons. At the stage of emergence from exclusive domesticity, and suffering from the almost universal loss of confidence in facing the 'outside' world and its tasks, women's groups were reported to be of special value, as they were again when supporting individuals preparing for a new or resumed career and making the requisite changes. (Elsdon et al, 1995, pp 56–57)

These features and processes, as well as the kind of comments made by participants, will be familiar to anyone who has participated as a tutor or student in a women-only education and training programme.

Questions of quality

Among people working at grassroots or community levels, it has long been recognised that women who are under-represented in formal education and training tend to prefer routes back into learning which are informal, women-centred and locally based. It was to meet this need that education schemes and centres specifically for women were established, during the early 1980s, in areas such as Lambeth, Leeds, Liverpool, Nottingham, South Wales and Belfast, with the help of European funding, short-term national and local finance and grants from charities.

There is a wealth of evidence from these initiatives that good quality women's programmes, whatever their focus, enable participants to make positive changes in their lives and progress in a variety of ways. This of course begs the question: what constitutes good quality? A course is not necessarily a good one simply because it is targeted at women, although if there are features that facilitate their participation, especially help with childcare, it will usually attract a good number of participants: 'Women continue to attend provision designed for them, such as ESF-funded programmes, regardless of whether it is in their best interests, purely because they are organised in ways that enable them to attend' (Moss, 1995, p 59).

The features and components that constitute good practice have frequently been listed in the literature on women's education and Jane Thompson in particular has played a key role in defining its essentially political nature and content. To refresh the memory: the characteristics of a women-centred curriculum have been usefully summarised by Maggie Coats (1994) as follows:

[It]

- uses subjective experiences and affective processes (respects individuality, starts from experience, recognises and values subjective experience; acknowledges affective as well as cognitive processes; says it is ok to explore self and feelings and gives space to do this; enhances confidence in knowledge, skills and abilities already possessed);
- locates gendered experience in a wider social context;
- recognises the importance of group support and collective action;
- uses methods and strategies that encourage participation;
- continuously reviews, evaluates and develops;
- removes barriers and improves practicalities;
- provides learners with an opportunity to progress to higher levels. (Coats, 1994, pp 62–63)

Fortunately, provision for women displaying all or many of these characteristics can still be found. Despite all the cuts and changes in funding, many women-only schemes and centres have continued, largely with the help of European finance, to provide a model of positive provision for disadvantaged women returning to education and employment after a period of caring responsibilities. Typically, they offer learning opportunities to women lacking the means, opportunity, qualifications or confidence to consider formal education or training as an option. They reach target groups through localised contacts and outreach activities and support women's participation through provision of guidance and help with finance, travel and childcare. They aim not only to help women learn and progress to higher levels of education, training or employment but also to help them understand their experience in a culture that habitually undervalues women; to recognise their skills and potential, increase their confidence and personal autonomy and raise their aspirations.

For example, key features of education and training centres that have been established specifically for women are:

- awareness of women's diversity;
- recognition of the constraints that operate on women's autonomy and choices;
- programmes that are designed and organised to overcome women's obstacles to access;
- flexibility of programming so as to meet diverse learning and development needs;
- programmes that are based on women's experience and which encourage their full participation.

It is unfortunate that, despite their undisputed value, most women's education and training schemes characteristically lead a precarious existence on short-term funding. Current funding criteria have made it particularly difficult for voluntary groups to provide informal and unaccredited programmes for women:

> The defining characteristics of women's education in the informal and voluntary sector make it highly problematic in relation to FEFC funding methodology, quite apart from the fact that such work is seriously more expensive to do properly than conventional provision.
>
> Informal women's education is probably at least as responsive and wide ranging as any conventional provision but it is extremely difficult to fit into conventional management tools such as target setting, 3-year planning cycles and the like (Scarlett and Winner, 1995, p 61).

Accreditation

One of the most important educational developments for adults in recent years has been the shift towards accreditation. Where women are concerned, this is perceived by some practitioners as a mixed blessing although the benefits to learners can be immense. Many women without qualifications welcome the opportunity to have their learning accredited and gain an important sense of achievement from it.

A number of women's courses are accredited by Open College Networks (OCN). The Open College system is the largest awarding body for adult learners in the further and adult education sectors and provides an accreditation framework that is generally considered to be more inclusive and flexible than other forms:

> The process and the flexibility of that system is least likely to disrupt the essential components of [women-only] provision. Indeed, OCN recognition is essentially recognition of the provision as it exists or as it is planned . . . Another major benefit is that OCN recognition can encompass a very wide range of learning programmes, both formal and informal, with academic, vocational or recreational content (Coats, 1994, pp 10–11).

Open College accreditation allows for recognition of achievements at home, in the community and in voluntary activity. This is especially valuable for women with few formal qualifications but a wealth of life experience.

Some practitioners, however, feel that accreditation is not always appropriate for women. It has been found that it can deter older women and those with little confidence and no post-school educational experience from enrolling in learning programmes. It can also inhibit curriculum development and creative risk-taking by providers and tutors. In several senses too, accreditation seems to run counter to the principles of good women's education as defined earlier: for example, by putting stress on observable and measurable learning outcomes rather than on personal development which, though major in the case of many women learners, can prove difficult to measure:

> The outcomes of a learning process which is deemed to be of high quality by women are defined by them as a growth in confidence and self-esteem, an increase in expectations; greater choice and opportunity on an individual basis; collective empowerment through organising together, decision-making skills, challenging the status quo and gaining access to influence and power . . . Unlike getting a job or enrolling on a college course, these kinds of outcomes may not be easily quantifiable but they are identifiable and describable (Scarlett and Winner, 1995, p 61).

There is also a tension between the stress accreditation places on the individual learning process and the essentially *collective*, group ethos of women's education. One of the main thrusts of recent education and training policy has been to place increasing emphasis on the individual – on individual learning routes and action plans and individual responsibility for planning and financing ones own education and training. This emphasis has figured strongly in both British and European lifelong learning strategies. Some now consider this tendency has gone too far, resulting in the loss of effective and creative adult learning processes:

> *The creation of a Learning Society will require a theory of learning which does not take the individual as the sole unit of analysis and which goes well beyond construing learning as a simple matter of self-direction or of transmission and assimilation. As Lave and Wenger (1991) have argued: 'most accounts of learning have ignored its quintessentially social character. We need a more powerful social theory of learning which will encompass not only the cognitive processes within the heads of individuals but also the social relationships and arrangements which stimulate learning'. In Jerome Bruner's words: 'learning is best when it is participatory, proactive, communal, collaborative and given over to constructing meanings rather than receiving them' (Coffield, 1997 pp 85–86).*

As well as recalling Freirean principles this aptly sums up the best kind of women's education which, it has frequently been claimed, provides a model for all adult education. It is doubtful, however, that there will be a wholesale reversal to earlier principles in a funding climate which has long favoured instrumental, vocational education over community education, and where adult education and training is seen as 'a commodity that can be measured by cost levels and quantitative outcomes alone' (Women's Training Network, 1996, p 19).

Conclusions

The only conclusion to reach from such a brief overview is that, like everything in life, there are both positives and negatives in current developments. About accreditation, for example, one can agree with Coats (1997) whose recent survey of its impact on women led her to the view that 'accreditation is neither good nor bad. The question is whether it's appropriate.'

The same could be said for other developments. Employment-related provision is not good *per se*: it has to be viewed in terms of its appropriateness for those who want or need it. It should not be confined to stereotypically female occupations, should not involve a 'blanket' approach which assumes all women are the same, and should not be prioritised over other forms of provision for women. Exploratory learning routes designed to meet the needs of diverse groups of women are just as important if we are to achieve what has been so frequently urged by policy makers but so rarely encouraged by policy measures – the widening of adult participation and a culture of lifelong learning.

It is heartening, however, that despite all the financial stresses and strains of recent years, good women's education has not totally disappeared. Although a significant proportion of introductory threshold routes have been lost since 1992, some providers such as the WEA still manage to provide women's education that both accords with

the principles of good practice and meets current policy priorities and funding requirements. Thus the applications for the NIACE Good Practice Awards gave cause for
optimism:

> *Despite some worries, diverse good practice, demonstrating innovation and creativity, does
> exist. Adapting to external constraints need not mean compromise (Coats, 1996, p 148).*

It is too early to predict how forthcoming developments will impact on women but
some of the signs are promising: a Green Paper expressing government commitment to
a far wider concept of lifelong learning than the one promulgated in recent years and
recognition of the paramount need to include groups neglected by the formal education and training system; action on some of the recommendations in the Kennedy
Report (1997) on widening participation in further education; a (possibly misnamed)
'University for Industry' designed to create more accessible opportunities in the home,
the community and the workplace; relaxation of the 16-hour study rule for unemployed
people and specific measures to help young unemployed people participate in education or training. So there is some cause for that phrase beloved of politicians – 'cautious
optimism'. There may not immediately be a great leap forward, but those involved in
women's education can at least hope for some new steps in the right direction.

References

Bruner, J (1996) *The culture of education*, Cambridge, MA: Harvard University Press (quoted in
 Coffield, 1996).

Coats, M (1994) *Women's education*, Buckingham: SRHE and Open University Press.

Coats, M (1996) *Recognising good practice in women's education and training*, Leicester: NIACE.

Coats, M (1997) plenary address at the 1997 NIACE International Women's Day Conference,
 Birmingham, 6 March.

Coffield, F. (ed), (1997), 'National Strategy for Lifelong Learning', papers presented at the
 International Conference entitled Research on Lifelong Learning: Implications for Policy
 and Practice, held at the University of Newcastle 25–27 November 1996, Department of
 Education, University of Newcastle

Edwards, R (1993) *Mature women students: separating or connecting family and education*, London and
 Washington DC: Taylor and Francis.

Elsdon, K with Reynolds, J and Stewart, S. (1995) *Voluntary organisations: citizenship, learning and
 change*, Leicester: NIACE.

FEFC (1997) *Learning works – Widening participation in further education* (The Kennedy Report),
 Coventry: FEFC.

Kennedy, H, QC, (1997), Learning Works: Widening participation in further education, Coventry:
 Further Education Funding Council

Lave, J and Wenger E (1991) 'Situated learning: Legitimate peripheral participation', Cambridge:
 Cambridge University Press (quoted in Coffield, 1996).

McGivney, V (1993) *Women in education and training: barriers to access, informal starting points and
 progression routes*, Leicester: NIACE.

Moss, C (1995) 'Women, quality and further education', *Adults Learning*, 7 (3) November,
 pp 58–59.

Rees, T (1997) *How women's training has evolved*, keynote address to the NIACE 1997 International
 Women's Day Conference, 6 March.

Scarlett, C and Winner, A (1995) 'Quality issues in informal women's education in the voluntary
 sector', *Adults Learning*, 7 (3) November, pp 60–62.

Shackleton, L and Walsh, S (1997) 'Gender inequality in education and training', *Return*, Women
 Returners Network, March.

Thompson, J (1997) *Words in edgeways: radical learning for social change*, Leicester: NIACE.

The Women's Training Network (1996) 'The way to work for women', *Women's Training Network
 Review*, Sheffield, Women's Training Network.

Chapter Three

Continuing education in the universities: the old, the new and the future

Viv Anderson and Jean Gardiner

This chapter explores the different traditions in university continuing education that were brought together by the creation of the Higher Education Funding Councils in 1993 and the Review of Continuing Education which followed the integration of the polytechnics and old universities into a unitary higher education (HE) system. We start with an overview of the development of continuing education (CE) from the different perspectives of the old and new university sectors. The institutional context meant that gender divisions were more apparent in the way continuing education evolved in the old universities than is the case in the new universities. The chapter argues that the restructuring of university continuing education in the 1990s offers an opportunity and impetus to re-examine and reshape the concept and culture of continuing education. It suggests a rethinking and integration of the traditional divisions within continuing education. This is necessary both to support student-centred lifelong learning and to sustain a space for radical thought and action.

In the old university sector, prior to 1993, a strict division was maintained between liberal and vocational courses because of distinct funding mechanisms (Duke and Taylor, 1994). These funding mechanisms were not available for those working in the polytechnic sector and the distinctions always appeared somewhat artificial. Wagner (1995) proposed the adoption of the National Advisory Board's definition of continuing education as 'any form of education undertaken after an interval following an end of initial education' (NAB, 1984). Using this definition, it can be argued that all mature students within the new university sector, and indeed the old university sector, are engaged in continuing education.

Continuing education in the old university sector

Two separate traditions of CE evolved in the old university sector, both separate from mainstream HE and, to a significant degree, separate from each other. The liberal and the vocational strands both had a marginal existence in the old university sector but also the benefits of a high degree of autonomy by comparison with the polytechnics, in which CE was always more integrated into the mainstream. The focus within liberal adult education (LAE) was on individual enlightenment and social and community emancipation through the construction of radical alternatives. There were different strands of radicalism within this tradition (Westwood and Thomas, 1991). Sometimes radicalism related to what was seen to be the purpose of adult education, with the emphasis being on social justice and changing society, rather than solely individual development. Sometimes it related to what was studied and what voices were represented (for example, as with trade union studies or women's studies). Sometimes radicalism focused on methodologies of teaching and learning (as with notions of reflective practice and active and experiential learning). Often the three aspects of radicalism were interconnected. Liberal adult education was developed by at least two dozen universities, designated by the Department of Education and Science as 'Responsible Bodies', who were in receipt of core funding for this area of work.

Within continuing vocational education (CVE), the focus was on economic improvement and accountability to the organisations that funded programmes. CVE never received core funding, only development funding, hence CVE programmes had developed as a separate self-financing system. The requirement to self-finance, superimposed on a labour market in which employees below the higher echelons were traditionally regarded as disposable labour, meant that CVE programmes inevitably focused on the more highly educated and normally graduate and professional occupational groups. The traditional division in university CE in the old university sector between liberal adult education and vocational education inevitably had a gender dimension. Male students generally predominated in CVE programmes and female students formed the majority of liberal and access programmes (UCACE, 1993, p 8). Sitting somewhat uneasily between liberal and vocational education was the radical tradition that located itself primarily in trade union and community-based adult education but also in access and women's education, as well as black studies and initiatives with students with disabilities.

The faultlines between liberalism and instrumentalism were fuzzier organisationally and ideologically than they sometimes appear in retrospect. For example, the radical credentials of adult educationists were sometimes equated with willingness and ability to teach shop stewards and other trade unionists. Yet the trade unions and Trades Union Congress which sponsored trade union education programmes generally did so with the aim of training their members to carry out their union roles more effectively, not for self-development or social change. The most influential strand in the development of liberal adult education provision itself was radical in reformist rather than revolutionary terms (Fieldhouse, 1985).

For those feminists who sought a radical and creative space in adult education from the 1970s onwards, the notions of individual enlightenment, social empowerment and economic improvement seemed inextricably connected and mutually supportive. The personal was political and feminism enabled women to make links between individual lived experience and socio-economic structures. Yet within the small world of a university adult education department, battle lines could be drawn on the basis of whether individual, social or economic purpose was given priority in the education of adults. The internal tensions and conflicting ideological agendas of university adult education seemed perplexing and irrelevant to feminists, often also coping with being among the first women to be employed as full-time academic staff in these departments. Adult education was both a welcoming space and a contradictory place for a feminist to be (O'Rourke and Gardiner, 1996 and Chapter 15 of this book).

Intellectual certainties were promulgated which our own understandings of feminism required us to question. In retrospect this strange encounter between radical liberal adult education and socialist feminism appears just one example of the fragmentation of intellectual radicalism which gained momentum in the 1980s under the influence of post-modernism on the one hand and neo-liberal market ideology on the other. There was a growing tension within the radical tradition from the mid-1970s onwards around the relationship between social movements and individual self-development. These tensions in the radical tradition also had a gender dimension. In the male-dominated trade union tradition individual self-improvement was often seen as a threat to the social movement, a route out of the class struggle.

On the other hand in community education, where women predominated, involvement in a social movement was often experienced as, and predicated on, explicit self-development because of women's need to assert themselves in the context of patriarchal household relations and economic dependence on men. What was often ignored was that men generally had more opportunity than women to achieve personal development through skilled manual work and trade union activity and education. For men self-development and economic survival could be achieved alongside a commitment to a social cause. These routes to personal development were less available to women who more often sought it through liberal adult education or professional training as teachers and nurses. Up to the 1970s, apprenticeship into a skilled manual occupation was a route to self-development and economic improvement, not available to women from working class backgrounds, many of whom went instead into teaching and other non-manual occupations and/or formed the backbone of many adult education classes (O'Rourke and Gardiner, 1996). By the 1990s, of course, there have been significant shifts in these relationships between gender, work, trade union participation and opportunities for personal development which have affected the pattern of adult and continuing education provision.

Another aspect of the tension between the liberal and the radical traditions was the interpretation of objectivity. Within the radical tradition there was an unease with academic objectivity and a recognition that it might muffle experience and mask understanding. And yet the traditional notions of coherent argument, proper conceptual underpinning, hierarchical progressive notions of learning, alongside the three-year tutorial class, were also paramount. These tensions have a parallel in more recent feminist debates about knowledge and research (Harding, 1992). Such complex issues were rarely explored in depth. In practice, it was often easier and more pressing to discuss recruitment and organisational issues, not pedagogy and the purpose of educating adults. From the late 1970s, funding began to be restricted, initially with the tightening of local education authority budgets and subsequently with cuts in Universities Grants Council (UGC) grants to universities and DES grants for adult education (Forster, 1990). Survival began to emerge as the overriding concern and ideological disputes gave way to pragmatism, target-setting and the pursuit of funding. Centralised control of adult education was increased through the mechanism of outcome-related funding. Ideological agendas remained but became tacit, theoretical and less self-confident in place of the transparent, explicit and unquestioning positions promulgated in the 1970s.

In 1992 the 'binary line' separating universities and polytechnics was abolished and a unitary university system was established in 1993. The separate funding councils (Polytechnics and Colleges Funding Council – PCFC and Universities Funding Council – UFC) were replaced by the Higher Education Funding Council for England (HEFCE) and parallel bodies for Scotland and Wales. HEFCE set up a CE Review Group to make recommendations on continuing education policies and funding. The review resulted in HEFCE Circular 18/93 which announced that the bulk of future funding for LAE would go to accredited programmes and this funding would remain with the old universities. There was also to be some funding for non-award-bearing work and this would be available across the unitary HE system. Separate CVE development funds would also continue to be available. However, the traditional divide between liberal and vocational programmes was to be bridged by the impetus for nearly all programmes to be accredited and for CE programme funding to be mainstreamed in a way that paralleled provision in the new university sector.

University continuing education was being redefined for the old universities as part-time university education, a definition which was closer to that of the new universities, in which CE was generally seen as a more integral aspect of the whole institution and where the proportion of non-standard students, studying both full- and part-time was much more significant (see below). With the accreditation of CE, and associated changes in funding in the mid-1990s, the division between liberal and vocational education has become increasingly fuzzy. At the same time mainstreaming means that adult and continuing education is becoming more integrated and less marginal but also less autonomous and less able to offer radical alternative programmes. Many question whether there is a future for radicalism in continuing education.

Continuing education in the new university sector

Continuing education in the new university sector has a very different history. The old polytechnics developed out of the vocational further education system and were rooted in professional and vocational learning. In Leeds, for example, there were several monotechnics encompassing engineering, building, art and design, whose higher level courses were creamed off in order to create one polytechnic. Along with many other polytechnics, courses were rapidly developed in subject areas which were missing from the portfolio but units or departments solely catering for mature students were not generally considered necessary or appropriate. The distinctions which existed within continuing education in the older university sector did not apply and the definition of continuing education in the former polytechnics was always a much broader one. The Advisory Council for Adult and Continuing Education (ACACE), which was established by the Secretary of State for Education and Science to advise generally on matters relevant to the provision of education for adults in England and Wales, was very clear on this point:

> We do not think that it is useful to draw artificial boundaries between education and training, between vocational and general education, or between formal and informal systems of provision. We include systematic learning wherever it takes place: in libraries, in the work place, at home, in community groups and in educational institutions. (ACACE, 1982, p 2)

ACACE argued for a comprehensive and systematic provision for continuing education. By comprehensive was meant general educational opportunities as well as vocational ones, since each would contribute in different ways to the greater adaptability of the whole adult population. Systematic provision would be based on an analysis of the needs of different sections of the population in the light of economic and social priorities. There was perceived to be a need to co-ordinate the activities which are carried out in different sectors – industry, the public education sector, the voluntary sector and statutory bodies. The aim would be to equip adults to play an active and constructive part in the process of economic and social change.

Unlike the old universities, polytechnics did not include a strong liberal educational tradition grounded in personal development and learning for the sake of it. Also, perhaps surprisingly, they did not enjoy the same substantive links with trade unions and community agendas as the old universities. They were perhaps closer to and more knowledgeable about shifts and changes in the labour market, in industry and in commerce. Continuing education in this context had more to do with returning to learning and reskilling. Although many students came directly from school, there was always a high proportion of adult returners and retraining activity.

The former polytechnic sector was governed by the regulations of the Council for National Academic Awards (CNAA) and Stoddart was concerned that 'The course planning system and the previous administrative and academic approvals mechanism . . . reinforced rigidities in the system, making it difficult to accommodate the needs of *individual* students'. (Stoddart, 1990, p 8).

However, there were advantages to the CNAA system. As a controlling body it had a number of positive effects. The result of its control was that the polytechnics were able to act in a corporate, rational manner. The CNAA was bureaucratic, but it was also forward-thinking and this resulted in creative and innovative approaches to course development. The system of peer validation and review meant that good practice was able to expand rapidly throughout the sector. Subject group networks were well established. Innovation was encouraged and easily promoted and colleagues were able to debate issues and test out ideas in the forum of a validation or review event. Nevertheless, the programmes of study were very definitely developed and delivered as accredited courses which meant that students had little choice about their programmes. Potentially, therefore, the old universities were more geared up for the facility for students to follow individual and personal interests within a continuing education programme. Also missing was the concept of non-accredited 'education for pleasure and leisure' which the liberal adult education of the older universities was able to provide.

The old university sector as a whole tended to be socially exclusive in the sense that it catered for traditional school-leaver students and only for the highest status professions like law and medicine. Within this sector, it was the small CVE units that were responsive to the training needs of a wider range of professions while the extramural and adult education departments were concerned with social inclusion through, for example, community and trade union studies. The new university sector was generally more responsive to demands for accredited training in the workplace and to managerial and technological changes taking place in the public and private sector, for example the development of multiskilling. The new universities actively sought out and recruited traditionally excluded groups and took more initiatives than the old universities in developing positive action programmes. For example, they pioneered access courses for women into engineering and IT, through partnership arrangements with further education colleges, and set out to overcome some of the barriers to HE faced by women, people from minority ethnic communities and mature students. The widening of access was one of the more radicalising aspects of the new universities.

Scott (1996) points out that according to one view of continuing education, a primary responsibility of CE is to widen access, through the development of systems for Accreditation of Prior Learning (APL), Accreditation of Prior Experiential Learning (APEL) and Credit Accumulation and Transfer Schemes (CATS). These are areas in which the new universities have certainly taken a lead. Many have systems for awarding credit for prior experiential learning, recognising that learning does not only take place in classrooms, but also from experience generally. In many institutions students are able to gain credit for their experience, not only from the work-place, but also from voluntary work, and indeed work in the home. In general these systems are based on learning outcomes, and many will allow substantial claims for credit for students with wide experience in the area of their choice of study.

Many of the new universities also have very well-developed CAT schemes which vary considerably from institution to institution. Some restrict the choice of programme to subjects and modules available within individual departments; some merely offer students the opportunity to follow a Combined Studies route; others have more sophisticated models whereby students can theoretically choose from any of the modules on offer in the institution. This is normally controlled by the requirement on the student to plan and agree a coherent programme of study, to ensure that flexibility does not result in superficiality and a lack of coherence. Inter-institutional CATS arrangements are undergoing continuing development and there is not yet a nationally agreed credit framework. Some institutions operate on a 'learning outcomes for credit' basis, others on the basis of notional hours of study.

The development of provision which is responsive on an individual basis may have costs as well as benefits for students. The mature student, often female, and often with little previous experience of formal education beyond 16 or perhaps 18, may find it difficult to benefit from the important social and peer group aspects of university education. Therefore, although CAT systems allow for great flexibility, there is always the potential problem of isolation of students if they do not form part of a general cohort. The new universities continue to offer flexibility of provision. Although their programmes of study are almost invariably accredited, there have been attempts to create structures whereby students are not required to study for the standard three or four years (or six years part-time) in order to receive an award. Not only is there the possibility of gaining a university certificate or diploma as well as a certificate or diploma of higher education, attempts are also being made to 'package' short courses to enable students to study for relatively short periods of time, and still gain an award. These approaches to flexibility are now being adopted and adapted in institutions which were formerly part of the old university sector.

Into the future

The separate histories of old and new universities in relation to CE have increasingly come together since the early 1990s. However, the nature of those histories means that the restructuring of CE in the 1990s has been experienced in very different ways in the old and new university sectors. For many in the old universities there is a strong sense of loss of flexibility and of opportunity to work with groups traditionally excluded from the parent institutions. On the other hand, new universities have experienced enhanced flexibility in their widening access work. The accreditation of continuing education is not an issue here, where accreditation has always been in place.

Looking to the future, it appears that the new institutional framework for continuing education established in the mid 1990s may make a student-centred approach to programme development more feasible in both sectors. Student-centredness means engaging with the complexities and shifting nature of motivation for study. Within this approach the different strands of CE are unlikely to have the resonance they had formerly in the old university sector. There are several reasons why it is helpful to move on from the traditional divisions that characterised continuing education in the old universities, while we attempt to sustain an identity and a mission as educators of adults. This latter is not an easy task, either in the new university context, or in many of the old universities where separate continuing education departments are becoming less and less common.

First, the traditional divisions have little meaning even for many continuing education practitioners themselves, especially those working in the new university sector. Even within the old universities, the distinction between liberalism and instrumentalism was never as clear in practice as in theory and was also gendered. In the context of women's education the distinction was sometimes perceived to be unhelpful. It is now generally accepted, across the old binary divide, that the vocational/non-vocational division represents a false dichotomy (UACE, 1996).

Second, we believe it is in the interests of adult learners that higher education offers people a holistic educational service. Students have a multiplicity of purposes for study, the significance of which may vary over the life cycle, and as a result of the educational experience itself, and motivation is likely to be highly individual. For some, higher education will be seen as the only way they are likely to achieve promotion, or to get back into employment after redundancy, or to enter the labour market for the first time. For others personal development, the wish 'to get my brain going again' or simply to gain a qualification, is the primary motivation. For many, motivation will be based on a combination of factors. Most research on motivation in continuing education suggests that there are three main, overlapping, motives for engaging in learning – vocational, academic and personal interest and development (McNair 1996). West (1995) has criticised the way in which many of these studies are conducted, pointing out that researchers tend to frame questions regarding motivation in such a way as to require a choice to be made, for example between personal or vocational motives:

> *Not surprisingly, if asked to make a choice between vocational or personal motives, most people will tend to give vocational justifications rather than anything more 'personal'. (West, 1995, p 35)*

This leads researchers to conclude that adults look to higher education for applied work-related studies rather than to meet liberal aspirations. High unemployment and job insecurity, of course may encourage adults to perceive higher education in this way. However, as McNair (1996) points out, it is not easy to separate vocational reasons from interest in the subject or in personal development. Adult students all have complex identities. They have to earn a living and/or cope with financial problems; they have families and other personal or voluntary commitments, religious, ethical or political affiliations; they have leisure interests; they are members of communities, regions and nations. Should we not encourage students to perceive the benefits to be derived from education in relation to all the different aspects of their identities?

The expansion in HE, coupled with new funding arrangements, should facilitate widened access for previously under-represented groups: women, people from working class backgrounds and from ethnic minority groups. It is crucial that HE responds to such groups in positive ways, recognising that they 'do not just bring their experience with them, they *are* their experience' (Edwards, 1993, p 10). This experience needs to be engaged with, not negated, in order that diverse student groups achieve their potential and higher education as a whole becomes more responsive to real life concerns.

Third, the future of continuing education needs to be discussed in the context of major changes in employment, mass higher education and the restructuring of the labour market as outlined in the introduction to this book. Clearly there is not enough space to explore the implications of these changes in depth here. But a number of issues are relevant to this discussion. There has been a large expansion in the supply of qualified labour with the development of mass higher education and at the same time the pattern of labour demand has produced a growth in part-time, temporary and other types of 'flexible' labour contract. Whereas, in the past, most graduates (male at least) would have gone into full-time permanent employment, this is now the experience of a shrinking proportion of graduates. While employability becomes increasingly important in this competitive and unstable environment, specific job-related training is of less value to the individual, especially where there may be little hope of a permanent job at the end (UACE, 1996). Moreover, employers are becoming less interested in employees with narrow vocational skills or purely knowledge based academic ability. They want a work force with general, transferable skills and an educational system capable of responding rapidly and effectively as new skill and management requirements present themselves in business and the economy at large. Lives of qualified people are structured less by the particular job and more by the portfolio of work and the patchwork of experience. Of course, this is a pattern that, although new for middle class men, has been familiar to women and to many men in working class occupations for a much longer period. The general skills and capabilities sought by employers in their skilled work force, such as communication, team work and problem solving, overlap increasingly with those required by individuals for their own personal development, for their care responsibilities and as active citizens.

The challenge for continuing education practitioners, working across the old binary divide, is to reconcile student-centredness with both the shifting labour market context and the radical intellectual heritage, to be responsive to very different constituencies, under-represented groups on the one hand and employers on the other. This is an ambitious project. And within this framework, gender awareness, alongside awareness of other aspects of social exclusion, remains an important radicalising and mobilising force within continuing education. Gender is one of a matrix of elements which constrain access to individual and social empowerment for different groups of women in different ways.

An important issue in women's education is access to time for learning. Analysis of trends in the labour market indicates that the female labour force is becoming, like the male labour force, increasingly polarised and differentiated. On the one hand there is an expanding sector of educated professional and managerial women, mostly tied to full-time employment, and increasingly to care responsibilities as well, with very small amounts of leisure time. On the other hand there has been a large growth in the numbers of women in low-paid part-time service jobs where training and formal skill opportunities are low but where informal skills may be significant and undervalued.

Many of these women combine employment with major care and household responsibilities. Higher education should engage with this reality and diversity.

With the disappearance in the traditional overall underachievement of girls in schools and the trend towards equalisation of participation rates in higher education, educational underachievement and access to higher education among women has become a less visible issue and access initiatives have increasingly focused on aspects of educational inequality other than gender. Yet women continue to be significantly under-represented in certain subjects and in full-time study (Rivis, 1995). Moreover, when gender is placed alongside social class, disability, ethnicity and care responsibilities, it is apparent that gender remains a strong dimension of educational exclusion.

Continuing education has played a significant part in the transformation of some women's lives and must in turn adapt in order to sustain its radicalising and transformative potential. Women's and men's working lives have been restructured over the last 20 years and more research is needed on how these changes have impacted on continuing education. For example, is it possible that for women the radical edge of CE may be shifting from the community where it was most strongly experienced in the 1970s and 1980s to the workplace where, even in lower paid and part-time employ-ment, women often find more space for social and intellectual engagement and personal development than elsewhere, just as men have done in the past. This possibility suggests that the feminist project needs to explore and engage further with work-based learning developments. There may be an opportunity here to bridge the traditional divisions in CE in the interests of sustaining its radical heritage. Many institutions have already begun to adapt and respond to the changing needs of the labour market, and have had to take into account new systems of government funding. It may be harder for institu-tions to respond to the needs of the expanding numbers of CE students arriving at universities as a result of these changes.

In this context an important role for continuing education staff in new and old universities will be to develop and embed new and responsive infrastructures of support for mature and, especially, non-traditional students, which facilitate student-centredness and take account of the social and economic context in which university learning takes place. A support framework which addresses (on an institution–wide basis) the issues of pastoral and tutorial support for mature students, which provides personal and study skills development as well as specific responses to the needs of traditionally excluded groups, will provide a challenging agenda for all universities and for radical and com-mitted CE practitioners within them, especially in a context in which institutions are having to adapt to new financial and policy constraints.

What is certain is that such support systems must be recognised as essential founda-tion stones in the new structures of continuing higher education. Increasingly the focus of continuing education will be to seek to ensure not just the presence of diverse groups of mature students in higher education, but that these students' university learning experience makes them critical thinkers and practitioners who can move at ease between the university and the learning society outside.

References

Advisory Council for Adult and Continuing Education (1982) *Continuing education: from policies to practice*, Leicester, Advisory Council for Adult and Continuing Education.

Duke, C and Taylor R (1994) 'The HEFCE review and the funding of continuing education', *Studies in the Education of Adults*, 26(1), pp 86–94.

Edwards, R (1993) *Mature women students: separating or connecting family and education*, London: Taylor and Francis.

Fieldhouse, R (1985) 'Conformity and contradiction in English Responsible Body adult education, 1925–1950', *Studies in the Education of Adults*, 17(2), pp 121–134.

Forster, W (1990) 'Comment', *Studies in the Education of Adults*, 22(1), pp 107–112.

Harding, S (1992) 'The instability of the analytical categories of feminist theory', in Crowley, H and Himmelweit, S (eds), *Knowing women*, Cambridge: Polity Press.

McNair, S (1996) *An adult higher education: a vision*, Leicester: National Institute of Adult Continuing Education.

National Advisory Body for Local Authority Higher Education (1984) *A strategy for higher education in the late 1980's and beyond.* London: NAB.

O'Rourke, R and Gardiner, J (1996) 'Heroic student – souls': attitudes to women in the department, in Taylor, R (ed), *Beyond the walls: fifty years of adult and continuing education at the University of Leeds 1946–1996*, Leeds: University of Leeds, Leeds Studies in Continuing Education, pp 283–295.

Rivis, V (1995) 'Maintaining and monitoring quality for women learners in higher education', *Adults Learning*, 7(3), pp 54–57.

Scott, P (1996) *The future of continuing education*, paper delivered at the UACE Annual Conference, University of Leeds.

Stoddart, J (1990) *Developments in continuing education – the next ten years in higher education*, London: PACE.

Universities Association for Continuing Education (UACE) (1996) Evidence to the National Committee of Enquiry into Higher Education.

Universities Council for Adult and Continuing Education (UCACE) Women and gender issues working party (1993) Report on women and gender issues in continuing education, UCACE Annual Conference.

Wagner, L (1995) *The new agenda for continuing education*, occasional paper No. 1, Forum for the Advancement of Continuing Education.

West, L (1995) 'Beyond fragments: adults, motivation and higher education', *Studies in the Education of Adults*, 27(2), pp 133–156.

Westwood, S and Thomas, J E (eds) (1991) *Radical agendas? The politics of adult education*, Leicester: National Institute of Adult Continuing Education.

Chapter Four

Locating women, theorising women[1]

Miriam Zukas

Introduction

This book is a testament to the fact that women are considered to be a special group within continuing education, that they are worthy of study in their own right – that they are, collectively, more than the sum of their parts. And this implies that, as a group, they have special features in common. The definitions of and reasons for these common features are determined by different feminist positions taken by those making the argument – but the mere recognition of women as a group raises a number of often unspoken (if somewhat familiar) questions. Within a continuing education context, what features link women together as a group? Why are they different from men (or even, are they different from men)? How and why does this influence them as learners? What does it mean to be a woman and how does this intersect with the membership of other social categories like class, race and sexuality? Do women learn in a different way to men? If so, why and what should we do about it? In what ways do the different structures of men and women's working lives impact on continuing education, as Viv Anderson and Jean Gardiner ask in this volume? What impact does gender have on the curriculum? And what is our vision of continuing education if we do take account of women? Indeed, do we have a vision of a continuing education that takes account of women?

Many of these questions are considered elsewhere in this book (and, of course, have been discussed by many others), but they all hinge on the underlying idea of women as a group: as a gender defined in opposition to men and with common threads linking all women together. What are our theories about why this should be so? How do we account for gender in continuing education? How do we deal with the many complex levels at which gender might work (for example the psychical, the social, the structural) and the place of continuing education in constructing, replicating or changing gender relations? The answers affect the practices of continuing education – if one takes a feminist stance, the curriculum, process and delivery of continuing education are all potentially imbued with possibilities for change and challenge.

Underlying these perspectives and, indeed, within most feminisms, lies a view that there is something that binds women together, as Liz Stanley and Sue Wise put it:

> the viewpoint that, although the specifics of subjugation will certainly differ in particular times, places and circumstances, nevertheless the result is always to position women in relationships of subordination to men. (Stanley and Wise, 1993, p 210)

Sometimes this perspective is criticised for its tendency to 'essentialise' the experience of women, and to privilege that experience over and above other experiences such as class, race and so on. In many ways, gender is assumed to precede everything else. As Diana Fuss argues:

Essentialism emerges perhaps most strongly within the very discourse of feminism, a discourse which presumes upon the unity of its object of inquiry [women] even when it is at pains to demonstrate differences within this admittedly generalizing and imprecise category. (Fuss, 1989, p 2)

If feminism's premise is that women are oppressed, there is no logical necessity for this essentialism. Nevertheless, within educational discourses, feminists may find themselves repeatedly arguing that women share common psychological characteristics without regard for the problems that this position generates.

Even the simplest argument, that women are under-represented in the educational system (the so-called liberal perspective), carries potentially essentialising theories of gender. Thus the reasons given for women's under-representation might range from a socialisation account (women were not raised to expect to achieve educationally or otherwise; there were few role models; etc) to a deficit account (women lack confidence; perhaps they have learned to be helpless[2] and need special care and attention to ensure that they are ready for education). Sometimes the reasons for women's under-representation will be more focused on structural explanations (women face barriers in their education which need removal – see for example the approach taken on many courses in Coats, 1996), but even these seem to essentialise women's experience as unitary, coherent and fixed.

This chapter reflects my dissatisfaction with my own unspoken explanations of gender and highlights my search for some understanding of gender at a theoretical, political and educational level (and of course, the three are linked) – a search which is clearly ongoing.

I began my academic career as a feminist psychologist, appointed to teach in university continuing education. Over the last 16 years, I have been involved in many feminist initiatives with both adult students and undergraduates: women-only courses, Women's Studies courses, special initiatives for women including a programme to educate women about new technology and so on. I have also retained a foot in the psychology department teaching a course about women and psychology[3]. Over the last few years, I have taught on the Masters programme for continuing educators, initially on a course entitled *Women and continuing education* but more recently, together with Janice Malcolm, on *Gender and post-compulsory education and training*. This is not merely a change of title – instead, it signals my (perhaps our) changing theoretical understanding of what it means to be a woman. I want to explore some of the themes and conflicts that are emerging in this part of my intellectual journey.

Until recently, most of my theoretical discussions about gender took place within a critical psychological framework. The recent Masters courses forced me to consider, somewhat more reflexively than I had done, my own stance on gender within continuing education. I also had to think about the implications of disciplines for such teaching and elsewhere I have written about the impact of feminism on the study of the education of adults (Zukas, 1997). But together with Janice Malcolm, the experience of inventing a curriculum, of trying to determine what went into such a course and how to teach it, was exhilarating, if unnerving. We tried to relate theoretical perspectives to practices, to reconcile structural, individualistic and other accounts of gender. We tried to consider the many interfaces between gender and race, class and sexuality as well as the challenge of thinking about men and masculinity. And this process broadened my necessarily partial and all-embracing view of the relationship between feminism and continuing education.

Taking women for granted

Like many other feminists within continuing education, I took gender for granted. In the early 1980s, it was easy to make the case for women to be treated as a separate group because continuing education had always been concerned with social groups. There have long been liberal, radical and socialist traditions (regardless of gender) that have made it possible to conceptualise the 'disadvantaged', the 'under-privileged', the 'under-represented' (each term reflecting different political perspectives) as audiences for continuing education.

Of course, depending on one's political perspective, the outcomes of such education might be very different: from individual enlightenment and change through to social revolution. Perhaps this link between ideological beliefs and the practices of continuing education is most clearly seen in relation to working–class men in the late nineteenth and early twentieth century (although Julia Swindells, 1995, argues that the role of women's organisations in these debates is very much underplayed). With the second wave of feminism, the suggestion in the 1970s and 1980s that women might also qualify as a disadvantaged or even oppressed group was much easier for continuing educators to consider (Thompson, 1980, 1983) than it would have been in many disciplines, particularly when statistics on female academic participation were garnered for evidence. And the resulting classroom practices which emerged for women drew heavily on the ideologies of feminism (consciousness raising groups, 'the personal is the political' rhetoric and later assertiveness training).

Psychological theories of gender

Despite the radical and socialist feminist traditions which influenced continuing education's project, the dominant discourse for many feminist educators within the classroom was psychology because it held out the illusory promise of explanatory and predictive power. It was certainly my starting point because of my disciplinary background but it also reflected feminist educators' concerns with the learning process. Within both scientific and humanistic traditions, psychology's focus on the individual (or subject) and the ways in which the individual might apparently be more effectively educated offered the educator the promise of applying theoretical principles to educational practice (Tennant, 1988). But many educators found the knowledge generated by psychology unhelpful – it seemed too narrow, and 'removed from the concerns of everyday life' (Usher and Edwards, 1994, p 47).

The reasons for psychology's empty promises have been discussed within the discipline by both feminist and postmodern critics, and, of course, outside it by dissatisfied continuing educators (for example, Usher et al, 1997). Postmodern criticisms focus principally on psychology's scientism (Hollway, 1989) and its object of study, the subject (Henriques et al, 1984). Within psychology, history and culture are removed from the scientific equation – they are 'controlled' in an attempt to discover universal truths that apply to all individuals (in imitation of the natural sciences). But what makes us human is our very situatedness: our history and culture which precedes and constructs our own self-understandings, self-consciousness. These are ever-present and cannot be eliminated by control. Furthermore, psychology treats individuals as if they were rational, autonomous, unified, consistent beings – a much criticised perspective.

So, not only is psychology's notion of the 'subject' in question, the discipline itself does not exist outside particular social and historical moments. It serves both to explore and to justify particular ideological practices such as racism (for example, Wetherell and Potter, 1992), heterosexism (for example, Kitzinger and Perkins, 1993) and sexism (for example, Bem, 1993). These practices, justified by psychology, exist in the real world and continuing education is not immune from them. Indeed, continuing education often uses such justifications to support its own pedagogies.

I now explore this latter criticism, that psychology serves to justify sexism, more thoroughly and demonstrate why it has implications for those in continuing education. For some feminists, the problem is not the nature of psychology itself, but the 'unscientific' approach to problems involving gender. For example, in debates about intelligence and gender, it has been argued that women appear to have less mathematical ability than men, not because they actually do, but because the conduct of tests and the statistical analysis and publication of results may be biased against women (for example, see Hyde, 1994). Instead, it is recommended that feminists beat the male establishment at their own game by conducting 'better' science. Thus, the continuing educator, convinced by this argument, might set out to rebut the common belief that women are biologically less able to do mathematics by setting up special classes for women (see Coats, 1996, for examples of such projects).

Fundamental to the argument that psychology has been 'biased' against women is the belief that there is nothing wrong with psychology *per se* that cannot be corrected through the scientific method. This ideology lies closest to the heart of the movement to make education more accessible for women. Although I am oversimplifying, there is a belief that all women, regardless of race, class and sexuality, could benefit from education provided the barriers facing them (structural, institutional, inter- and intrapersonal) could be overcome. In other words, feminist educators and psychologists need to challenge the *status quo* using a range of strategies in order to enable women to gain their rightful (and *equal*) place.

But other feminist psychologists argue that there is a profound misogyny buried within psychology that raises doubts about its theories, methods and even its content. They claim that women have a special psychology that is unrecognised, uncelebrated and untheorised. This particular perspective is perhaps most closely related to the Women's Studies movement which was built on the notion that traditional disciplines had ignored women's history and experience; a new perspective was required which would fundamentally change the androcentricity of traditional disciplines to one in which women's ideas, experiences and interests were central (Bowles and Duelli Klein, 1983).

Within psychology, Carol Gilligan (1982) became the most influential representative of this new movement. Drawing on Nancy Chodorow's (1978) feminist interpretation of British object relations, she argued that our ideas about developmental progress – what it means to grow up and be a healthy adult – were profoundly androcentric. Psychology's developmental model of the individual who is increasingly individuated and separate from others implied that the centrality of relationships for women was childish, even pathological. Using the study of morality to develop her ideas, together with a very different method from those usually applied in psychology in which she talked to women about real-life moral decisions, she argued that women and men follow different pathways of moral development which had not, until then, been detected because so much psychological theory was based on male samples, male points of view. For women, she argued, their identity is defined in the context of relationships and is judged by the level and standard of responsibility and care. For men (the more usual model), identity is defined as separation. Both models of identity come about because of early parenting experiences (see Chodorow) and, as a result, Gilligan claimed, men's morality is dictated by an ethics of 'rights' while women's morality is influenced by an ethics of 'care':

> *Thus in the transition from adolescence to adulthood, the dilemma itself is the same for both sexes, a conflict between integrity and care. But approached from different perspectives, this dilemma generates the recognition of opposite truths. These different perspectives are reflected in two different moral ideologies, since separation is justified by an ethic of rights while attachment is supported by an ethic of care. (Gilligan, 1982, p 164)*

This argument proved to be intuitively appealing to many feminists within psychology and education. It was suddenly possible to provide a theoretical justification for a different pedagogical model for women – to argue that women needed to learn in a relational context rather than as individuals (see Belenky *et al*, 1986, and a critique, Zukas, 1992), and to argue that women's qualities should be celebrated and developed.

But there are many dangers in such a position. Apart from the dangers of over-generalisation, of ignoring class, race and sexuality, in short – of essentialising and privileging women – there remains an attachment to a dichotomous approach: men are to be replaced by women as the basis for theory. This dualistic reversal, often associated with the celebration of female nature and qualities such as caring and community, does little to recognise the oppressive nature that such dualisms can lead to for women: the celebration of female qualities may ensure the continuing employment of women in the so-called 'caring' professions, or women's continuing involvement in childcare, but it does little to change women's relationships with men or indeed, their employment opportunities. And in my view, many continuing education classrooms included unquestioning 'celebration' of these attributes.

Other feminist psychologists have been very critical of this woman–centred approach. For example, Sandra Bem (1993) believes that, despite years of feminist interventions, biological sex differences continue to be the focus for most discussions of sexual inequality. She asserts instead that we should be fighting for a world in which gender polarisation (the organising of social life around the male–female distinction) no longer exists at cultural or psychical levels, although she recognises that it would continue to be significant in 'narrowly biological contexts like reproduction':

> *The absence of gender-based scripts should not be taken to mean that males and females would merely be freer to be masculine, feminine, or androgynous, heterosexual, homosexual, or bisexual, than they are now. Rather, the distinction between male and female would no longer be the dimension around which the culture is organised which means, in turn, that the very concepts of masculinity, femininity, and androgyny, heterosexuality, homosexuality, and*

bisexuality, would be as absent from the cultural consciousness as the concepts of 'hetero-eye-coloured' eroticism, a 'homo-eye-coloured' eroticism, and a 'bi-eye-coloured' eroticism are now. (Bem, 1993, pp 192–93)

She lays out her grounds for such an argument by claiming that gender 'difference' and inequality exist because of three gender 'lenses' through which all (North American) cultural discourses, social institutions and individual psyches operate: androcentrism (male-centredness), gender polarisation and biological essentialism. These three lenses operate at two levels: first in discourses and social institutions by channelling females and males into different and unequal life situations, and second, within the individual by the gradual internalisation of these cultural lenses and the resulting self-construction of an identity that fits within them.

Her argument, that gender should become irrelevant, is utopian. It also fails to deal once more with other differences – of class and race. Presumably, the 'lenses' of race and class could also be identified – and thus alerted, we could inoculate ourselves and our children against them. In many ways, these arguments are familiar to continuing educators in the shape of the critical thinking debate.

But such conclusions may ultimately be uncomfortable for feminists, or black people, or working-class individuals because this strategy seems to rely very heavily on the idea that these 'lenses' can be uncovered for what they are without action being taken. Power is asymmetrical – why would those who benefit from gender polarisation wish to sacrifice those benefits? Why would those who enjoy middle-class security and self-confidence wish to sacrifice their advantages? And, does an understanding of a situation change it?

Thus far, I have been trying to show how feminists have used the discipline of psychology, despite its problems, to offer explanations of gender, and to demonstrate how these could and have been used within continuing education. It is important to challenge these ideas because psychology is not an innocuous subject. Despite its narrowness and abstraction, psychology is deeply implicated in modern forms of disciplinary power (Rose, 1990). In other words, we discipline ourselves through both our own self-scrutiny and the scrutiny of 'experts'. Psychology has a lot to answer for.

Outside the discipline itself, psychoanalytic accounts of gender have become increasingly popular, particularly for those influenced by Lacanian postmodernism; those within both continuing education and psychology remain suspicious of these developments (although Usher and Edwards (1994) had some fun trying to link the two together, particularly in discussion of the teacher role).

Emerging ideas of 'difference'

So, in my search for theoretical understanding of the impact of gender on continuing education, if psychology had little to offer me, perhaps recent feminist discussions about the importance of 'difference' would be more fruitful. Such discussions of 'difference' emerged from black feminists' criticisms of (white) feminist thinking which were two-fold: first, many white feminist theories were essentialist (as mentioned earlier), and second, they ignored diversity among women (for example, Amos and Parmar, 1984; hooks, 1984). In some parts of continuing education, as elsewhere, this rallying cry of diversity led to an emphasis on 'difference' as a new way forward. A few brave souls ventured to say how this affects political and pedagogical practice (for example, O'Rourke, 1995; Stuart and Thomson, 1996) but discussions so far have been limited.

There is a problem – it is almost easier to ignore the complex and sometimes contradictory impact 'differences' make within education. The impact of difference for, say, a white working-class woman returning to education who faces not only economic and social disadvantage but the 'shame' of her class (see Steedman, 1986; Reay, 1996; Walkerdine, 1990) will be quite distinct from the experience of a middle-class woman who might perceive her lack of education as her own problem (a source of a rather different kind of 'shame'). Ironically, despite its historical importance in the development of radical adult education in Britain, class is rarely a matter for investigation for those studying women's education (see Julia Swindell's work mentioned earlier). It is often a term reserved to pit work with working-class men against lower-middle-class or professional women (O'Rourke and Gardiner, 1996). And, while the 'difference' of sexuality is named in lists of diversities, it is even less overtly examined for its relevance to continuing education[4].

So the concept of 'difference' has been most extensively developed in relation to 'race'. In her discussion of 'race', gender and difference in feminist thought, Mary Maynard (1994) outlines two ways in which the differences between women have been conceptualised, one focusing on diversity of experience and the other informed by postmodernist thinking. The 'diversity' approach, with its roots in both feminism and radical education traditions, focuses on difference in experiential terms. It recognises that within the label 'black', there can be many differences of culture, class, religion and so on.

But the emphasis on 'experience' may hide assumptions about its taken-for-granted authority:

> *Exactly what counts as 'experience' and should we defer to it in pedagogical situations? Does experience of oppression confer special jurisdiction over the right to speak about that oppression? Can we only speak, ultimately, from the so-called "truth" of our experiences, or are all empirical ways of knowing analytically suspect?' (Fuss, 1989, p 113).*

Others have been similarly critical about experience's cornerstone in feminist education because it is never as unified, as stable, as universal as it is presumed to be within the classroom. Its special place within continuing education, dressed up as 'experiential learning' has also been challenged on similar grounds: Usher and Edwards try to 'get away from an educational discourse which constructs experiential learning in logocentric terms as a "natural" characteristic of the individual learner' (1995, p 205).

Postmodern versions of difference avoid the appeal to 'truth' of experiential accounts, and the grand narratives of race, class and so on. Instead, postmodernism

> *challenges the perceived essentialism of modernist thinking by positing difference as being at the centre of the postmodern world and by championing deconstruction as the method through which this is to be analysed. (Maynard, 1994, p 6)*

But many feminists, including Maynard, argue against such ways of dealing with difference. Maynard is critical of both approaches: the 'us' and 'them' connotations of difference as experience; the endless possibilities for diversity within both and the slide towards relative pluralism; the belief that postmodernism's concern with discourses and its exploration of multiple modes and forms of identities leads to inactivity: 'Paradoxically, although everything is about the subject, no one in postmodern analyses actually appears to *do* anything'. (1994, p 19)

Similarly, Jane Thompson is impatient with postmodern ideas:

> *The concerns of postmodernism – to do with linguistics, culture and identity – are far from accessible to the general feminist reader. And in their most extreme expression come with a denial of any form of material reality. (Thompson, 1995, p 131)*

She argues that we cannot ignore 'big' questions about gender, class and race – we cannot deny the material impact of the 'structures in the background' (p 132) if we are to advance the possibility of women's independence.

But I still have questions about how we do that in practice. I am no clearer about the ways in which our focus on the 'big' questions actually helps us achieve political change. Despite my long history of feminism, in working on the gender module I was confronted with the realisation that I had never really considered the ways in which men and masculinity are intrinsically related to theories about women: how it is impossible to talk about women without reference to the shadow of men. So, to move from 'women' to gender was not a political cop-out as might be seen by some. It was an attempt to move away from a necessarily essentialist perspective to try and take account of some of the other issues confronting continuing educators. It enabled me to think more systematically about 'big' issues without being forced into naming hierarchies of oppression.

There is another way in which postmodern ideas are quite comforting, despite criticisms of postmodernism's relativism, even nihilism. The ideas of partiality, of resistance, are more appealing than grand schemes of emancipation if I am to explore the difficult present. I am confronted with the rather bitter realisation that the success we have had in opening the academy up for women has not resulted in the mysterious structural changes we expected to emerge. Instead, the academy had already undergone its own dramatic conversion: the fragmentation and segmentation of education, the increasingly scrutinised and narrow educational experience complete with overassessment at every turn, together with hugely increased students numbers. This does not provide our students with the same opportunities for challenge, for intellectual engagement, for debate as we might once have liked to think they had. I cannot escape the realisation that I (like many continuing educators) actively participated in the demise of our corner of resistance – in my case, through my belief in feminism.

I have not lost my fundamental belief in feminism. Instead, I need to look for more complex ways of understanding what it means to be a feminist trying to work as an educator – ways to comprehend what I am part of as well as what I am not.

Notes

1. My thanks to Janice Malcolm for all the stimulating and challenging theoretical discussions on this issue over the last five years.
2. See for example Gerry Holloway and Mary Stuart's account of a Women's Studies Access course, 'Mothers and sisters: power and empowerment in Women's Studies' in Mary Stuart and Alistair Thomson, *Engaging with difference: the 'other' in adult education*, NIACE, 1995.

3. The use of 'and' rather than 'of' serves a political purpose: it does not imply that there is a special psychology pertaining to women; rather, that women have a particular perspective on psychology. Thus a course might include issues that were of special interest to women (for example, menstruation, motherhood) but would be more concerned overall with the development of psychologies that took gender into account.

4. A number of publications outside continuing education have considered the issue from a lesbian perspective but heterosexuality, like whiteness and middle-classness, remains strangely absent as a matter for consideration. This is well demonstrated in Sue Wilkinson and Celia Kitzinger (1993) which attempts to explore heterosexual 'identities'.

References

Amos, V and Parmar, P (1984) 'Challenging imperial feminism', *Feminist Review*, 17, pp 3–19.

Belenky, M F, Clinchy, B M, Goldberger, N R and Tarule, J M (1986) *Women's ways of knowing*, New York: Basic Books.

Bem, S (1993) *The lenses of gender: transforming the debate on sexual inequality*, London: Yale University.

Bowles, G and Duelli Klein R (eds) (1983) *Theories of Women's Studies*, London: Routledge and Kegan Paul.

Burr, V (1995) *An introduction to social constructionism*, London: Routledge.

Chodorow, N (1978) *The reproduction of mothering*, Berkeley: University of California.

Coats, M (1996) *Recognising good practice in women's education and training*, Leicester: National Institute of Adult Continuing Education.

Davis, K (1997) 'Ambivalences of professional feminism' in Stanley, L (ed), *Knowing feminisms*, London: Sage.

Fuss, D (1989) *Essentially speaking: feminism, nature and difference,* London: Routledge.

Gilligan, C (1982) *In a different voice: psychological theory and women's development*, Cambridge, MA, Harvard University.

Henriques, J, Hollway, W, Urwin, C, Venn, C and Walkerdine, V (eds) (1984) *Changing the subject: psychology, social regulation and subjectivity*, London: Methuen.

Hollway, W (1989) *Subjectivity and method in psychology*, London: Sage.

hooks, b (1984) *Feminist theory: from margins to centre*, Boston: South End Press.

Hyde, J S (1994) 'Should psychologists study sex differences? Yes, with some guidelines', *Feminism and Psychology*, 4(4), pp 507–12.

Kitzinger, C and Perkins, R (1993) *Changing our minds*, London: Onlywomen Press.

Maynard, M (1994) 'The dynamics of "race" and gender' in Afshar, H. and Maynard, M (eds), *The dynamics of 'race' and gender: some feminist interventions*, London: Taylor and Francis.

O'Rourke, R (1995) 'All equal now?' in Mayo, M and Thompson, J (eds), *Adult learning, critical intelligence and social change*, Leicester: National Institute of Adult Continuing Education.

O'Rourke, R and Gardiner, J (1996) ' "Heroic student souls": attitudes to women in the Department', in Taylor, R (ed), *Beyond the walls: fifty years of adult and continuing education at the University of Leeds*, Leeds: Leeds Studies in Continuing Education, University of Leeds.

Reay, D (1996) 'Dealing with difficult differences: reflexivity and social class in feminist research', *Feminism and psychology*, 6, pp 443–456.

Rose, N (1990) 'Psychology as a "social" science', in Parker, I and Shotter, J (eds), *Deconstructing social psychology*, London: Routledge.

Stanley, L and Wise, S (1993) *Breaking out again*, London: Routledge.

Steedman, C (1986) *Landscape for a good woman*, London: Virago.

Stuart, M and Thomson, A (eds) (1995) *Engaging with difference: the 'Other' in adult education*, Leicester: National Institute of Adult Continuing Education.

Swindells, J (1995) 'Are we not more than half the nation? Women and "the radical tradition" of adult education 1867–1919', in Mayo, M and Thompson, J (eds), *Adult learning, critical intelligence and social change*, Leicester: National Institute of Adult Continuing Education.

Tennant, M (1988) *Psychology and adult learning*, London: Routledge.

Thompson, J (ed) (1980) *Adult education for a change*, London: Hutchinson.

Thompson, J (1983) *Learning liberation: women's response to men's education*, London: Croom Helm.

Thompson, J (1995) 'Feminism and women's education', in Mayo, M and Thompson, J (eds), *Adult learning, critical intelligence and social change*, Leicester: National Institute of Adult Continuing Education.

Usher, R, Bryant, I and Johnston, R (1997) *Adult education and the postmodern challenge*, London: Routledge.

Usher, R and Edwards, R (1994) *Postmodernism and education: different voices, different worlds*, London: Routledge.

Walkerdine, V (1990) *Schoolgirl fictions*, London: Verso.

Wetherell, M and Potter, J (1992) *Mapping the language of racism: discourse and the legitimation of expolitation*, London: Harvester.

Wilkinson, S and Kitzinger, C (eds) (1993) *Heterosexuality: a feminism and psychology reader*, London: Sage.

Zukas, M (1992) 'Feminist issues in adult education research: links and conflicts', in Miller, N and Jones, D J (eds), *Research: reflecting practice. Papers from the 1993 SCUTREA conference*, Boston: Standing Conference on University Teaching and Research in the Education of Adults.

Zukas, M (1997) 'Disciplining gender: the impact of feminism and women's studies on the study of adult education', in Armstrong, P, Miller, N and Zukas, M (eds), *Crossing borders, breaking boundaries*, Leeds: Standing Conference on University Teaching and Research in the Education of Adults.

Chapter Five

Still struggling

Roseanne Benn

We have so far examined the purposes and rationale for continuing education, exploring contexts, concepts and traditions. We have also discussed the very nature of the concept of 'woman' with its fragmentation and lack of homogeneity. This chapter develops these themes further, establishing them within the historical context of the last two centuries. Here we concentrate on provision for women as students. The story of women as tutors and organisers is examined in Section Four, *Engaged to the institution*.

The history of educational provision for women is like a plait interwoven with the political and economic history of Britain in the nineteenth and twentieth centuries and the evolving position of women in society. As we might expect, the strands are class as well as gender constructs, consisting of middle class liberal provision of education for its own members, especially women denied conventional openings; middle class provision for the working class; and working class for working class (Coats, 1994). Strands could alternatively be categorised as relativist, where women are only seen in relation to others, particularly their husbands and children; compensatory, where it is assumed that women's disadvantage can be overcome by incorporating them into existing structures and norms; liberal, with its emphasis on individual development and limited social reform; and radical, where education is seen as a site for collective action and social change. The form and content of adult education provision for women has varied over time, place, class and in relation to women's position in society. What has not varied is women's hunger for learning which survived even when the ethos and structures were against them.

Most nineteenth-century adult education was developed primarily for men but there were notable exceptions, and increasingly women found ways of accessing it and adapting it to their needs. However, to do so they needed to overcome both structural and cultural barriers. They had to struggle for adult education. Patriarchy was predominant, with women allocated the private sphere of the home and men the public sphere of work. This domestic ideology dominated bourgeois society for the whole century and the working classes more as the century progressed. It resulted in formal and informal barriers to access to education, a curriculum linked to domestic and child-rearing roles and basic literacy, and hence a reinforcement of the restriction on women's life chances (Purvis, 1980). Early provision for women was for salvation and domestic vocation, and was frequently a process of normalisation and socialisation to male norms. The higher illiteracy rate for women restricted access to much adult education until the advent of compulsory state schooling (Hamilton, 1996).

All adult education at this time was through voluntary rather than state provision and attendance was also voluntary. Religious salvation was often a triggering force. The very first Sunday school exclusively for adults was a school established for young working class women in the lace and hosiery factories in Nottingham in 1798 teaching bible reading, writing and arithmetic. This movement developed from middle class initiatives with the involvement of non-conformist religious groups, especially the Quakers. There was normally separate provision for men and women with equal access for both, and a narrow curriculum with emphasis on literacy and religious reading. The number of such schools expanded over the years with more women participating than men. This was probably because of their openness to women, the higher illiteracy rate among women and the attraction that their children were also being taught to read. The non-conformist churches were unusual in arguing for full education opportunity for girls and women which derived from their belief that the intellectual capacity of women was equal to that of males. However, with the development of other forms of adult education such as the Mechanics Institutes, the Sunday schools began to decline (Fieldhouse, 1996a, Purvis 1980, Watts 1980).

The Mechanics Institutes, which began in the 1820s and are regarded as the major adult education movement of the nineteenth century, were founded to provide useful knowledge for working class men. Women had to struggle to be admitted and were allowed in reluctantly. When enrolled, they did not enjoy equality of membership or equality of treatment, typically not being allowed to vote or hold office. The curriculum for women, when offered, was located in a domestic ideology enabling women to become good wives and mothers and to run a household and ignored the fact that large numbers of working class women were also wage earners. The story was similar in the Lyceums and the literary, philosophical, scientific and mutual improvement societies. Education for females was summed up at the time as

> a mere blank, or worse, a tissue of laboured frivolities under a solemn name; a patchwork begun without aim, fashioned without method, and flung aside, when half finished, as carelessly as it was begun (Grey and Sherreff, 1856)

During the first part of the century, pressure was building up for a change in women's roles. Economic pressures were acting on women, both pushing them into the labour market and depriving them of a satisfactory economic function in their own homes. The 1851 census showed that not only were there more women than men but also that many men either did not marry or emigrated (Watts, 1980). So there was a need for women, even middle class women, to be able to earn a living since marriage was not a possibility for all of them in a society which proclaimed this as their only role. At the same time women shared the same ethos as men that happiness was to be found in work and that idleness was intolerable (Bryant, 1979). Add to this the romantic idealisation of womanhood and the Victorian conception of the family and home and it can be seen that many women experienced tensions and frustrations and looked partly to education for an acceptable way out. Educators such as Emily Davies (1866) and philosophers such as John Stuart Mill (1869) were arguing for women to be seen as human beings first and foremost.

The women's movement of the nineteenth century neither attempted nor wished to alter the framework of society, nor its system of shared values, but did want women to be educated and to participate in the advantages of better schooling and higher education. Women started to campaign for particular reforms, not because they saw themselves as 'feminist', but because of the circumstances and restrictions of their lives (Rowbotham, 1973). Even those who campaigned for more radical reform were caught in the dilemma of both wishing for education on equal terms but not wishing to appear unfeminine (see Delamont, 1978 for an interesting discussion of this bind of 'double conformity'). By 1870 women were still not citizens with educational rights, voting rights, property rights or union rights.

This history of either exclusion or a differentiated, more limited curriculum was reflected in the Working Men's Colleges and the burgeoning elementary day school provision. The foundation of the separate women's-only College for Working Women formed in 1874 in Fitzroy Street, London raised the issue that women–only provision could be tailored to women's circumstances and needs, moving away from the 'deficit' model but could also lead to marginalisation. The double bind that women were invisible in the mainstream and underfunded in their own separate provision continues today (Fieldhouse, 1996, Purvis, 1980).

The founding of the Women's Co-operative Guild in 1883 was a move of fundamental importance for liberating provision for women. Though at first much of the curriculum was located in domesticity and women defined primarily as customers, nevertheless the Guild was organised by the women themselves. Gradually the Guild expanded its activities into campaigns for social reform against the desperate condition of life of many of its members. It was also instrumental in training women to fill leading roles in the Co-operative Society and other social and political organisations (education for participation) through training in public speaking, committee work and publicity formation. This fulfilled the Co-operative Society's aim to allow men and women to take part in industrial and social reforms and municipal life generally (Fieldhouse, 1996a, Purvis, 1980).

By the 1850s and 1860s, the universities of Oxford and Cambridge were looking for ways of meeting the educational needs in the wider world but needed local organisational help. At the same time ladies' educational associations in the large provincial cities of the North were looking for lecturers. This led in 1873 to the birth of university extension in Cambridge, London and Oxford. The aims of this movement, although directed primarily at the education of all who had not had access to university scholarship but especially working class men, included the provision of courses to satisfy the growing demand for better education for women. Probably two thirds of the participants were women. However, few were working class. This was not a result of any formal restriction but probably caused by the curriculum offered, the level of literacy demanded, the middle class ethos, fear of the male middle class academics, domestic responsibilities and the cost of attendance. It is also probable that the patriarchal structure of working class society permitted attendance at adult schools and Mechanics Institutes but drew the line at university education. The attitude of higher education to women can be summed up in this quote from the July 1887 edition of the *Durham University Journal* during the debate in Durham about the education of the 'gentle sex': 'The intellectual inferiority of women as a class to man seems clear. It is also probable that this inferiority is inherent, and cannot altogether be eliminated'. (Fieldhouse, 1996a, Purvis, 1980, Watts, 1980).

By 1901, there were over a million more women than men in England and Wales. Opportunities for employment needed to grow for women but these were hindered by poor education. The educational process was still made difficult for women by their domestic circumstances, the lack of attention paid to their needs and current ideology. Motherhood was reconstructed at the turn of the century as a result of concern over the falling birth-rate, a high infant mortality rate, the growth in importance of the Empire and a perceived lack of morality. 'Schools for Mothers' were established by middle class women to give advice and guidance on maternal and domestic skills to working class women. Adult education began to develop the 'women's interest' curriculum which was to encompass an aesthetic focus as well as practical skills, centring women's development in the cultural as well as manual skills of the home (Coats, 1994, Davin, 1978, Westwood, 1988, Hughes, 1992).

But still, in much provision, women's voices were not heard. This invisibility of women occurred in the early days of the newly-formed Workers' Educational Association (WEA) (1903). Mansbridge's vision of education for the betterment of the working class did not exclude women but did not recognise women as workers in their own right. The overwhelming majority of participants in the early days was male but in 1909 the organisation decided to move into education for women by setting up a Women's Department whose role was to make 'a special effort' on behalf of women (WEA, 1995, p 16). By 1916, this initiative for women-only classes had lapsed due to the non-replacement of the National Women's Officer and the collapse of the Women's Advisory Committee (Jones, 1985). Westwood (1988) suggests that women were integrated into the WEA not as equal workers with men, but as people whose lives were located in domestic circumstances and hence as a case of special need. Mrs Bridge Adams clashed with Mansbridge over this and the issue of working women and their role in relation to knowledge and power (Mansbridge, 1944, Stocks, 1953). She also tried unsuccessfully between 1909 and 1912 to establish a Women's Labour College. The Women's Labour League had been calling on women since 1906 to 'educate themselves on political and social questions, work in social work, promote full citizenship rights of men and women' (Rendell, 1977) but the Women's League of the Central Labour College, when founded, was seen as subordinate and ancillary. Only about five per cent of those who attended classes were women but women answered the call (as they always seem to do) to support the social and domestic side of the College (McIlroy, 1996; Westwood, 1988).

New voluntary bodies for women called Women's Institutes were established in 1913 and their numbers grew rapidly to 1,405 centres by 1919. Though the curriculum was heavily concentrated on domestic issues, as with the Women's Co-operative Guild, involvement in the organisation of the local and national group gave some women members a practical training in participation, democracy, committee work and public speaking (Baynes and Marks, 1996).

In 1918, women over thirty, married women and graduates were given the parliamentary vote. In 1919 the Sex Disqualification (Removal) Act admitted women to the legal profession, higher grades of the Civil Service and the magistrature and women were admitted to Oxford as full members in 1920. Women had been given full degrees at London University from 1878 and from the beginning in the new city redbricks. Women had to wait until 1948 to receive the same privilege at Cambridge.

In 1919, the Adult Education Committee of the Ministry of Reconstruction surveyed provision for women (Ministry of Reconstruction, 1919). The Committee's Final Report (the '1919 Report') provided a vision for the role of adult education in British post-war reconstruction which imaginatively included women. It noted that adult education classes had often been the only means of humane education open to women and occasionally classes had adapted to the special needs of women, perhaps by providing a nursery or by making women-only classes available as 'the men were so much more advanced' (p 256). The Report identified the Women's Co-operative Guild with its emphasis on public questions, as being one of the most important movements for women's education of the day (p 258).

The Report clearly noted the needs of women for more knowledge in their new roles as citizens and condemned the constraints of poor housing which demanded all their time (p 255). It avoided the trap of assuming equality of availability meant equality of opportunity and noted that men formed the great majority of students in classes as 'women have far less opportunity than men for continuing their education, owing to an unceasing round of household duties and care of children' (p 255). The Report fragmented the concept of 'woman' and validated an emancipatory form of adult education for women as well as the domesticatory version which was so frequently provided. Its call for classes to have a large measure of self-government and to be relevant to women's experiences foretold the developments in women's education later on in the century (p 261). The Report was liberal rather than radical and did not attempt to upset the *status quo* or separate women from their domestic sphere but it did recognise the hardships of women's lives and the need for adult education to see women's special circumstances and not subsume them in the category of men. Unfortunately these particular recommendations did not have a major impact on subsequent adult education provision in the inter-war years nor in the immediate post-second world war years.

The end of the first world war, combined with the 1919 Report, had created a need for new approaches to adult education for demobilised ex-service-men and -women and women wartime workers displaced by men. Women's training was promoted for industrial and domestic work. This was organised from 1920 to 1939 by the Central Committee on Women's Training and Employment who had the limited vision of training women as homemakers or domestic servants and instructing women in 'the duties of a capable housewife or servant' (Field, 1996).

The Townswomen's Guild was established in 1928, the year that women were given the vote on the same terms as men. This Guild, which grew out of the suffrage movement, was centred in urban areas. It was led by well-to-do academic women who aimed to improve the status of women through education in handicraft, music, drama and social studies. The Guild continued to grow through the middle of the twentieth century campaigning for women's legal and economic rights. Meanwhile, the Women's Co-operative Guild membership peaked in 1939 and in response to changes in retail societies gradually became a less active force in women's adult education (Baynes and Marks, 1996).

By 1936/7, one-third of all LEA enrolments were in women's subjects and recreational activities and 56 per cent of students were women (NIAE, 1951, pp 7, 9).

The rhetoric of the 1944 Act was that of equality of access. However, this concentration on access rather than equality of outcome allowed women's secondary status and subordination to still remain invisible, and women were silenced by the ideology of equal opportunities (Wilson, 1980). Certainly the concept of education for domesticity continued to be hugely influential. The Norwood Report in 1943 stressed the importance of relating boys' education to the labour market, but emphasised that girls' schooling must relate to their eventual place in the family. The pamphlet *Further Education: The Scope and Content of its Opportunities under the Education Act 1944*, sometimes referred to as the post-war 'bible', took its tone from current social policy which continued to emphasise the importance of motherhood and the family (Ministry of Education, 1947).

At this time, more married women were entering the world of work but in low-paid unskilled jobs. However, by the 1950s, upskilling meant that more jobs required educational qualifications and technical skills. This, together with better contraception and the need for a larger labour force, meant that improved education was needed for the middle class girls to cope with their dual role. However, working class girls were still educated for domesticity (Deem, 1981).

In 1951, the NIAE statistical survey showed that enrolments of women in evening classes in evening institutes and major establishments between 1930 to 1950 had risen to 60 per cent of all students (NIAE, 1951).

In the 1950s and early 1960s, an increasing number of women entered the labour market encouraged by the economic growth, an increase in educational opportunities for girls and women, contraception and the consequent reduction in family size, and the growth of the welfare state which released women from some of their obligations (Deem, 1981). Nevertheless, the notion that women's place was in the home was still strong. The emphasis in educational change and development of this period, from primary through to adult, concentrated on class rather than gender but there were improved educational opportunities for women in the establishment of the Open University (see Chapter Eleven) and the provision of special training or refresher courses for married women taking up or returning to teaching. Work-place training was developing during this period but women were receiving considerably less training opportunities than men (Field, 1996).

The proportion of women in the student body continued to grow. The expansion of LEA adult education in the 1960s meant that by 1968/9 there were 1,701,070 students of whom 69 per cent were women. The background of students was changing as well. For example, by the 1950s, WEA students included fewer manual workers and more technical and supervisory workers as well as more housewives. Many of the WEA's married women students were from higher social categories (Fieldhouse, 1996b).

As recently as the Plowden Report of 1967, official ideology for girls' education assumed a homogeneity of female interests, notably with regard to domestic interests. Women were ignored in the political arithmetic. However, during the 1960s, the tensions between women's position in the home and the demands of the labour market surfaced in the second wave of women's liberation. Demands began to be made over such issues as the sexual division of labour, the unequal power balance between the sexes, the construction of knowledge and women-centred learning. So women's educational studies evolved, focusing initially on making women's education visible and hunting out obstacles to the development of their full potential. These challenges to women's role in the family and the labour market were linked to other social liberation movements, the literacy and community education developments as well as to the passage of the Equal Pay Act in 1970 (Arnot, 1995).

The 1944 Education Act and the expansion of the universities in the 1960s led to a growing discontent among women about their lack of career opportunities, their exclusion from institutions and skills at all levels and the nature of knowledge. The Women's Liberation Movement grew through consciousness-raising groups, a very powerful example of informal adult education, where women-only groups shared their experiences and began to understand that 'the personal is political'. The Movement was a real focus of adult learning in the 1970s but its supporters, being suspicious of experts, generated their own counter-knowledge and spread this mainly through non-formal self-directed learning, campaigning groups and the agency of adult education. The WEA and university extra-mural/continuing education departments responded/led the way, followed by the Inner London Education Authority (Thompson, 1983; Taking Liberties Collective, 1989; Hughes and Kennedy, 1985). The Sex Discrimination Act was passed in 1975 but without resources and real political commitment, its impact was questionable.

However, a reaction was building up against the continued emphasis on education for women consisting of parenting and domestic skills. 1981 saw the opening of the first feminist-influenced Women's Education Centre in Southampton with funding and provision shared by the University, the LEA, the WEA and the Equal Opportunities Commission. This was part of a growing movement in the 1970s and 1980s for a widening of the curriculum as well as the development of women–only provision influenced by feminism and economic changes. Coats (1994, p 17) identified five major strands in this provision. First, there were the re-orientation courses for women returning to study or work after a period of domestic responsibility to compensate for initial under-achievement or to allow for a change in direction, updating and prepara-tion. These were centred round a curriculum of confidence building, counselling, self-defence, study skills and academic content. An early example was the New Opportunities for Women Course at Hatfield Polytechnic in 1971. The Manpower Services Commission and LEAs offered Wider Opportunities for Women courses from 1978. Second, there were courses, usually taught by women, in areas where women were traditionally under-represented such as manual trades, electronics, computing, etc. An example of this was the Women's Technology Scheme in Liverpool which was set up in 1983 to offer vocational and educational training for women in areas such as micro-electronics. Third, there were the positive action courses such Women into Management. Fourth, courses such as Professional Updating for Women provided updating courses for professional or qualified women for return to their career. Last, there were the feminist Women's Studies courses with their radical questioning of what is 'really useful knowledge' for women.

This provision of women–only courses in adult education has been challenged on the grounds that if institutions were constantly reminded that women were different from ordinary students, then they might reasonably assume that ordinary students were not women. It was also open to the accusation of marginalising women's issues with the consequent lack of impact on mainstream provision (Malcolm, 1992). However, the history of women's education shows continuous marginalisation, lack of resources and little policy support. Within this context, women–only provision represented a real advance.

The influence of feminism and Women's Studies from the mid–1970s helped to broaden out women's education and the curriculum because of the inter-disciplinary approach, the concern to change the way knowledge is constructed and the emphasis on student-centred, participatory learning. These issues will be explored in greater detail in the next section.

One of the major initiatives of this period was the provision of Access to Higher Education courses. From the start, these courses attracted mainly women and approximately two thirds of the 30,000 students on over 1,000 courses in 1995 were women (Benn and Burton, 1995). These courses were often timetabled in school hours and school terms with creche facilities and sometimes supported by discretionary grants in order to attract women who had missed out on higher education the first time around.

The Women's Institute's residential college, Denman (founded in 1948), continued to attract large numbers of participants and by 1995 over 215,000 members had attended its courses. Meanwhile, alternative national women's bodies emerged in the 1970s and 1980s. One of the most significant bodies in self-education and personal fulfilment was the National Housewives Register, later changed to the National Women's Register (Baynes and Marks, 1996).

In the 1990s, worrying indications occurred in adult education's provision for women. The Government continually emphasised the importance of the family and that a woman's place was in the home. Social policy supported these sentiments and welfare support was gradually eroded. The period of rapid growth of interest in education for women coincided with severe funding cuts and many women's courses were developed with short-term funding which remained marginal to institutional provision and were the first to disappear in the various round of cuts of the late 1980s and 1990s (Malcolm, 1992). This was reflected in developments in the WEA. In the later 1980s, the WEA had employed a full-time woman National Officer to develop women's education and published an excellent range of materials to support women's education. However, when in 1993, the Women's Education Committee analysed the state of women's education in the WEA it revealed that the early 1990s had seen a significant decline in provision for women and such provision that there was focused on individual development (Women Returner courses) rather than collective issues (Women's Studies provision). The Committee has developed a strategic plan to mainstream women's education in WEA provision to counteract these tendencies (WEA, 1995).

Even in the early- and mid-1990s, women experienced constraints in adult education whether these were from earlier experiences in school and work, lack of confidence, inappropriate provision or were cultural in origin. Much provision tailored to women's needs was threatened by student and institutional funding problems, inadequate child care facilities and a lack of political support for women's education and training (McGivney, 1994). Most of the advances achieved by women have occurred in periods of full employment and in the context of social democratic policies and ideologies (Deem, 1981). Women's education can be seen as cyclic. Periods of raised awareness, action and some gains are followed by periods of reaction, backlash and lost ground (WEA, 1995). The early 1990s saw a backlash against equal opportunities and were dominated by an ideology premised on individualism, the free market and the sanctity of the family. The Thatcher years permeated this period with an anti-feminist return to Victorian family ideology, yet at the same time the functionalist approach of the Conservatives acknowledged the need for a well-educated workforce. This formed a complex framework within which education for women operated. The reduction in the Welfare State re-imposed domestic burdens on women. The employment situation with the massive increase in part-time women's work increased the need for education and training for women while lack of financial subsidies put it out of the reach of more and more (Coats, 1993). The increased emphasis on continuing education and training may ironically have excluded from social participation as many women as it included.

This brief overview has shown that women were present in the nineteenth and early twentieth centuries but not treated equally, with a curriculum restricted to the division of labour in the home and the demands for a cheap workforce. Independence, where it existed, was located in the separatist bodies such as the Women's Co-operative Guild and the Suffrage Movement. In the middle- and late-twentieth century, women were in the majority in much adult education, and gradually at least some provision was developed to meet their particular requirements. By the mid-1990s, the situation appeared to be reverting. Women are still struggling for accessible 'really useful' adult education provision.

This chapter is a shortened version of the chapter 'Women and Adult Education' in Roger Fieldhouse, *A History of Modern British Adult Education,* 1996.

References

Arnot, M (1995) 'Feminism, Education and the New Right', in Dawtrey, L et al (eds), *Equality and inequality in educational policy,* Clevedon, Multilingual Matters Ltd and Open University Press.

Baynes, P and Marks H. (1996) 'Adult Education Auxiliaries and Informal learning', in Fieldhouse, R (1996), pp 308–32.

Benn, R and Burton, R (1995) 'Targeting: is Access hitting the bull's-eye?', *Journal of Access Studies,* 10(1), pp 7–19.

Bryant, M (1979) *The unexpected revolution,* London: Institute of Education, University of London.

Coats, M (1993) 'Women's education: a cause for concern?', *Adults Learning,* 5(3), pp 60–63.

Coats, M (1994) *Women's education,* Buckingham: SRHE and Open University Press.

Davies, E (1866) *Higher education for women,* London. Publisher not known.

Davies, M (1904) *The Women's Co-operative Guild 1883–1904.* Publisher not known.

Davin, A (1978) 'Imperialism and motherhood', *History Workshop Journal,* 5 Spring, pp 9–65.

Deem, R (1981) 'State Policy and Ideology in the education of Women, 1944–1980', *British Journal of Sociology of Education,* 2(2), pp 31–143.

Delamont, S (1978) 'The contradictions in ladies' education', in Delamont, S. and Duffin, L. *The nineteenth century woman: her cultural and physical world,* London: Croom Helm.

Field, J (1996) 'Learning for Work', in Fieldhouse, R. (1996), pp 333–75.

Fieldhouse, R (ed) (1996) *A History of Modern British Adult Education,* Leicester: NIACE.

Fieldhouse, R (1996a) 'The nineteenth century', in Fieldhouse, R (1996) pp 10–45.

Fieldhouse, R (1996b) 'An overview of British adult education in the twentieth century', in Fieldhouse, R (1996) pp 46–76.

Grey, M and Sherreff, E (1856) *Thoughts on self-culture,* London. Publisher not known.

Hamilton, M (1996) 'Literacy and adult basic education', in Fieldhouse, R (1996) pp 142–65.

Hughes, M (1992) 'London took the lead', *Studies in the Education of Adults,* 24(1), pp 41–55.

Hughes, M and Kennedy, M (1985) *New futures: changing women's education,* London: Routledge.

Jones, A (1985) 'The WEA and women's education', in Hughes, M and Kennedy, M (1985). pp 113–117.

Malcolm, J (1992) 'The culture of difference: women's education re-examined', in Miller, N and West, L (eds), *Changing culture and adult learning,* Boston: SCUTREA, pp 52–55.

Mansbridge, A (1944) *The kingdom of the mind,* Dent.

McGivney, V (1994) 'Women, education and training: a research report', *Adults Learning,* 5(5), pp 118–120.

McIlroy, J 'Independent working class education and trade union education and training', in Fieldhouse, R (1996), pp 264–89.

Mill, J Stuart (1869) *The subjection of women,* London. Publisher not known.

Ministry of Education (1947) *Pamphlet number 8, further education: the scope and content of its opportunities under the Education Act of 1944,* London: HMSO.

Ministry of Reconstruction (1919) *Final report of the adult education committee, Cmd.321,* London: HMSO.

NIAE Executive Committee (26 June 1951) Appendix 111, *Relations between adult education and other forms of further education.*

Norwood Report (1943) *Curriculum and examinations in secondary schools: a report of the secondary schools examination council*, London: HMSO.

Purvis, J (1980) 'Working class women and adult education in nineteenth-century Britain', *History of Education*, 9(3), pp 193–212.

Rendell, M (1977) 'The contribution of the Women's Labour Movement to the winning of the franchise', in Middleton, I (ed), *Women in the Labour Movement*, London: Croom Helm

Rowbotham, S (1973) *Hidden from history: three hundred years of women's oppression and the fight against it*, London: Pluto Press.

Stocks, M (1953) *The Workers' Educational Association: the first fifty years*, London: Allen and Unwin.

Taking Liberties Collective (1989) *Learning the hard way*, Southampton: The Southampton Women's Education Centre.

Thompson, J (1983) *Learning liberation: women's response to men's education*, Croom Helm.

Watts, R (1980) 'The Unitarian contribution to the development of female education, 1790–1850', *History of Education*, 9(4), pp 273–86.

WEA (1995) *Annual report 1995*, WEA.

Westwood, S (1988) 'Domesticity and its discontents: feminism and adult education in past times (1870–1920)', in Lovett, T *Radical approaches to adult education: a reader*, London and New York: Routledge.

Wilson, E (1980) *Only half way to Paradise*, London: Tavistock.

Section Two

Women studying and studying women

Chapter Six

Locating women: theorising the curriculum

Jane Elliott

Introduction

The liberal and radical traditions of continuing education (CE) have facilitated the emergence of a range of provision for women. These have included non-vocational programmes offering many opportunities for personal and intellectual development and, more recently, vocational programmes targeted at women returners. We have also witnessed the emergence of a more radical curriculum that poses far-reaching questions about the nature of our society and aims to be an integral part of the process of social change. This radical agenda has been reflected in curriculum initiatives such as Women's Studies. Questions that are raised include 'what constitutes an appropriate curriculum for women?', 'who determines what is an appropriate curriculum?' and 'how do we reflect the diversity of women's experience?'.

It is not my intention here to offer a prescription or prescriptions for the ideal curriculum for women. Instead this chapter examines curriculum issues in the context of current feminist and liberatory debates which explore and challenge traditional assumptions about what constitutes knowledge.

It has been suggested that all research is based on the epistemological assumptions of the researcher and 'research communities' and is therefore partial as opposed to value free (Usher and Edwards, 1994). This is also true of the curriculum which emerges from the epistemological positioning of those who determine curriculum content. Thus, the content of what is taught must be seen in the context of a wider set of values. Hence, the curriculum we propose for women will be located in a specific theoretical framework. Liberal feminists, for example, would be likely to propose a curriculum which is rooted in 'rational', 'objective' and 'impartial' notions of knowledge, while standpoint feminists epistemologies would challenge the validity of such notions of knowledge.

My aim in this chapter is to consider the relationship between particular feminist and liberatory perspectives and curricula decisions. First, I look briefly at the implications of the traditional liberal feminist perspective in order to establish the theoretical context in which much of the CE provision for women has been established. I then consider the more radical standpoint and Freirean approaches. While Paulo Freire's work is based upon his experience of Brazil and Chile, his transformative vision is, arguably, of relevance for adult educators elsewhere. Finally, I explore a curriculum approach which aims to reflect these debates: Women's Studies.

Liberal feminism

The feminist approach that was initially influential in terms of women's education was liberal feminism which maintained that equal access to educational provision was central if women were to be emancipated. The position was put forward by early feminists such as Mary Wollstonecraft in the late eighteenth century and by John Stuart Mill in the latter part of the nineteenth century (Wollstonecraft, 1792; Mill, 1861). Liberal feminists such as Wollstonecraft did not challenge the notions of the Enlightenment which promoted scientific knowledge and a privileging of 'rational' thought; what they did do was challenge the exclusion of women from the Enlightenment project. Their primary objective was to ensure that women gained access to scientific and 'rational' forms of knowledge on an equal basis to men. The feminist epistemology which is most closely related to liberal feminism is 'feminist empiricism' in which it is argued that sexist assumptions and biases should be eliminated from scientific methodologies, thus producing a 'better' science (Harding, 1991).

However, liberal feminism does not aim to transform the society in which we live and has not addressed the underlying causes of women's subordination, its primary aims being to achieve 'equality' and 'justice' for women within the system.

In Chapter Five of this book, Roseanne Benn refers to Maggie Coats' five key strands of continuing education provision for women which emerged in the 1970s and 1980s. Coats also identifies those categories of curricula initiatives which emerge from a specifically liberalist or contemporary liberal feminist perspective: courses which are compensatory in the light of early academic failure such as 'return to learn' and 'access into higher education' programmes; courses for 'women returners', often aiming to facilitate re-entry into employment such as 'New Opportunities for Women'; and positive action programmes which seek to challenge gender divisions within employment such as 'Women into Management' programmes (Coats, 1994, p 21.). Such programmes reflect the liberal feminist concern that women's education should enable them to compete in the labour market on an equal basis with men. These programmes are frequently women-only and have often been funded by the European Social Fund. In addition, liberal feminism has worked to ensure that women are included in the academic curriculum where their achievements or experiences have been excluded. So, for example, as Blundell points out, they will ensure that a session on the 'role of women' is included in a history course (Blundell, 1992). Finally, in line with the liberal respect for scientific knowledge, liberal feminist initiatives have sought to encourage women to study more scientific programmes, such as 'Girls into Science and Technology' provision.

Liberal feminism has clearly played a progressive role in that it has challenged the exclusion of women from the academic curriculum and the public sphere and has enabled women to claim educational opportunities on the same basis as men. Liberal perspectives have been influential in our systems of adult continuing education and have informed policies which have had considerable impact on the participation of women in post-compulsory education.

Nevertheless, while there have been important liberal feminism achievements within adult education, it does not pose the more far-reaching questions regarding the validity of the traditional academic curriculum and its claims to a value-free knowledge. It questions neither the legitimacy of our education system nor of the wider society in which we live. Finally, it does not address the wider structural and economic power relations which act as constraints on women's ability to compete on an equal basis with men. The discussion that follows focuses on perspectives that do raise these questions – standpoint feminism and liberatory perspectives.

Standpoint feminism and liberatory perspectives

I discuss standpoint feminism and liberatory perspectives together as I will argue that a liberatory view of education can emerge from a standpoint perspective. Standpoint theorists argue that knowledge is not partial but is 'socially situated' (Harding, 1991). All knowledge therefore flows from the class, gender and race of the knower. It is argued that all knowledge is distorted but that the knowledge emerging from women's experience, ie the experience of the oppressed, is less distorted than knowledge which emerged from the oppressor.

Sandra Harding addresses the question as to why a feminist's or woman's standpoint is less distorted than the standpoint of the oppressor. This assertion is justified in several ways. For example, it is suggested that 'Women's oppression gives them fewer interests in ignorance' (p 125). Thus it is in the interest of oppressed groups such as women to demystify myths about the social order, while it may be in the interest of the oppressor to perpetuate such myths. Similarly it is suggested that . . . 'trying to construct the story from the perspectives of the lives of those who resist oppression generates less partial and distorted accounts of nature and social relations' (p 126).

Harding continues to argue that knowledge is produced as a result of the struggle of the oppressed against the oppressor and provides, as an example, the struggles for formal equality for women within the sciences. It is through the success of these struggles, she argues, that we learned that women need more than formal equality. In addition, it is claimed that 'Women's perspective is from everyday life' (p 128). Thus we can increase our understanding about the world through understanding women's lives from a woman's standpoint.

The notion that a knowledge that emerges from the standpoint of the oppressed is more impartial than the knowledge of the oppressor is also supported by Alison Jaggar who argues that such knowledge:

> . . . is more impartial because it comes close to representing the interests of society as a whole; whereas the standpoint of the ruling class reflects the interests only of one section of the population, the standpoint of the oppressed represents the the interests in totality in that historical period. (Jaggar, 1983, p 371)

In relation to feminist theory this would suggest that knowledge from the standpoint of women is superior to knowledge which emerges from the standpoint of men. Thus standpoint theory would suggest that the traditional knowledge of the academy emerges from the standpoint of men and is therefore more partial than is the knowledge emerging from the feminist challenge.

This perspective clearly relates to liberatory notions of education. Both Harding and Jaggar draw parallels between standpoint and Marxist perspectives which prioritise the knowledge of the proletariat. Educators working from a liberatory position, such as Freire, have always prioritised the knowledge of the oppressed. Hence a curriculum for women emerging from this perspective would need to recognise and validate women's experience and should offer challenges to traditional epistemologies. Programmes such as Women's Studies and Black Studies are examples of such a curriculum. However, while we may not wish to construct hierarchies of oppression, we must also recognise that some women experience oppression more than others (see Miriam Zukas' chapter in this book for her discussion of diversity among women). Thus, for example, a curriculum that reflects standpoint assumptions should draw on the experience of black women who may experience multiple oppressions in our society: oppression resulting from, for example, race, class and gender. A problem with much of the early 'second wave' feminist work of the 1970s was that often the specific oppression of black women was denied by subsuming their experience into that of more privileged white women Bulkin, 1980). There has always been the possibility that the curriculum in continuing education will reflect this denial of a specific black experience. Part of the problem is that too often in adult education classrooms it is white academics who are attempting to represent the range of black women's experience, often inadequately. Clearly, it is likely or possible that black women's lives will be misrepresented by white women and hence a partial knowledge will be produced. However, if issues of relevance to black women are ignored by white women, the resulting knowledge is even more partial. While we need to ensure that there are more black women teaching in adult continuing education, it is also important from a standpoint perspective that *all* teachers are sensitised to the experiences and needs of black women when considering a curriculum for women. I discuss these issues in more detail elsewhere (Elliott, 1996).

As I have already suggested, a standpoint perspective can be related to the practices of radical educators such as Freire whose transformative visions have inspired many radical educators (Freire, 1972). Freire argues that education is never neutral, a view which can be seen as parallel to the standpoint notion that all knowledge is partial. Whereas standpoint theory argues that the knowledge of the oppressed or marginalised groups produces a 'better' knowledge than the knowledge of the oppressor, Freire aims for an 'education for freedom' in which the oppressed become aware of the nature of the world and act to transform it. It needs to be noted, however, that developing an education with and for the oppressed is a complex and contradictory process. For example we need to agree the nature of oppression or, as Kathleen Weiler points out, individuals may experience oppression in one sphere while becoming the oppressor in another. An example of this would be the man who is oppressed by his boss in the workplace and who oppresses his wife in the home. In response to Freire's proposal that we should aim for an 'education for freedom' which seeks to facilitate a collective knowledge and action, Weiler asks, 'But what if that experience is divided? What if different truths are discovered?' (Weiler, 1991, p 453). An added hurdle is that during the 1980s and 1990s the climate in which we have been working has not encouraged notions of 'education for freedom'. As a consequence of New Right ideology, during this period there was a shift in emphasis away from 'social collective subsets' such as the working class or women towards imperatives of economic regeneration (Benn and Fieldhouse, 1996).

The feminist educator working from a standpoint perspective, and within Freirean principles can, nevertheless, aim to develop a curriculum that emerges from the multiple experiences of women, the obvious examples being Women's Studies. However, while this discussion focuses on Women's Studies, it is important that this perspective should inform the whole curriculum.

Both standpoint and Freirean perspectives imply more than curriculum content. It is also important to consider how we design our programmes: a programme designed by female academics in a university or college will not necessarily constitute a programme for the oppressed. Consultation with those whose lives we are attempting to represent becomes crucial to the process. The liberal, non–award–bearing, tradition in continuing education offered possibilities for a curriculum that was negotiated with students and communities. While these consultation processes may still be available to some extent, the increased emphasis on mainstreaming and accreditation act as a serious limitation as course proposals must now conform to the requirements of the academy (Elliott, 1995).

Moreover, both perspectives suggest that central to a liberatory notion of education is the transformation of the teacher/student relationship with the teacher becoming learner and *vice versa*. The teacher and student therefore 'become jointly responsible for a process in which all grow' (Freire, 1972, p 53). The logical conclusion is that the role of the teacher as sole definer of the learning process is challenged.

However, the reality of a mainstreamed CE is that tutors become increasingly involved with determining issues such as the appropriateness of the curriculum for the level of programme, standards and grading criteria. (See Chapter Seven in this book for a discussion of the problems associated with accreditation.) This clearly contradicts the tutor/student relationship of equality as proposed by Freire. There is also a conflict with the Freirean notion that 'the educator no longer has the right to establish the curriculum–content of education' (pp 20–21).

Nevertheless, while appreciating the many constraints that limit the ability of the adult educator to operate within genuine liberatory frameworks, it is important that radical adult educators do not lose sight of these visions. These very contradictions can, in themselves, provide a learning experience for both tutor and student.

Women's Studies as liberatory knowledge

Women's Studies is an example of a liberatory approach aiming to constitute a 'knowledge of the oppressed', its early roots being not in the academy but in a major twentieth century social movement: the women's movement. There are several ways in which Women's Studies shares with adult continuing education a challenge to traditional notions of knowledge (Elliott, 1995). It is my intention here to look at two important challenges: the emphasis on experiential learning and interdisciplinarity.

Central to Women's Studies is the understanding of the need to challenge the absence of women's experience from traditional academic knowledge and to encourage the theorisation of that experience. This recognition of the value of experiential learning has implications for the nature of the tutor/student relationship as knowledge emerging from the student experience is valued as highly as the more abstract academic knowledge. The experiential nature of Women's Studies relates closely to the recognition among many adult educators that a good adult education curriculum should draw upon student experience and not abstract theory (see Steele, 1994). This is not to suggest that Women's Studies or adult education generally should not engage with theoretical issues, it is simply recognised that any theoretical explorations should emerge from life experience.

However, this emphasis on experiential learning is not unproblematic. As I have pointed out earlier in this chapter, the experience which forms the basis of learning may not necessarily be unified (Weiler, 1991). Zukas addresses this point in Chapter Four and suggests, for example, that a focus on experience may mask all kinds of assumptions about its commonly accepted authority. Moreover, is there a danger that experiential knowledge will produce its own partial knowledge which does not necessarily reflect the knowledge of the oppressed?

On a more pragmatic level, there is a conflict between the experiential nature of Women's Studies and traditional academic approaches which tend to be non-experiential. While we may wish to validate a woman's experience, it is not possible to generalise from that experience: feminist theory must be grounded in the plurality of women's experience. Moreover, in higher level courses the use of personal experience is only acceptable if couched within an academic discourse. There is also the possibility that some students may assume that the validation of personal experience implies an approach which is purely anecdotal and does not move beyond the personal. Finally, there is a danger that students will receive contradictory messages in terms of the validity of their experience: personal experience is both central and lacking in validity! There is no simple resolution to these tensions. Nevertheless there are positive ways of dealing with many of the problems. For example, the tutor can discuss with students ways in which the use of personal experience is helpful and ways in which its use may not necessarily encourage the development of an understanding of issues within a wider context. The very process of discussing the role of personal experience in an academic programme can help to facilitate this wider understanding. It is thus possible to develop a feminist and Freirean notion of 'education for freedom' through tutors and students engaging in a joint analysis of the tensions between these radical challenges and incorporation into the academic mainstream. Moreover, in raising the issues within the academy, there is at least a challenge presented to traditional epistemological assumptions that deny any validity in experiential knowledge.

Having looked at some of the issues in connection with the notion of experiential learning, I now look at interdisciplinarity and its challenge to conventional notions of what constitutes academic knowledge and the validity of widely accepted disciplinary boundaries. By interdisciplinarity I refer to programmes in which separate subject disciplines become closely integrated, thus breaking down traditional subject barriers. The approach emerged in the 1950s when adult educators such as Raymond Williams combined Marxist sociology, social history, textual analysis and literary criticism into what is termed Cultural Studies (Steele, 1994). Similarly, in the 1970s Women's Studies courses were developed through a merging of academic disciplines such as sociology, anthropology, literary theory and philosophy. This approach reflected a recognition amongst feminist educators that traditional disciplinary boundaries could not always offer an adequate vehicle for the development of an understanding of women's position in different societies. As Cathy Lubelska puts it: 'Lived realities do not fall into neat disciplinary categories, nor do the ideas and sources through which we attempt to make sense of them' (Lubelska, 1991, p 43).

Thus, through the integration of several disciplines, the problem–centred approach of interdisciplinary programmes such as Women's Studies can enable learners to gain a deeper understanding of women's lives. So, for example, if we are attempting to understand young women's experience of formal schooling, we may draw on historical studies in order to understand, within an historical context, the ways in which their experience of formal schooling has differed from that of men; psychological studies can enable us to explore theories of gender difference and learning theories; while sociological theories can help us to understand ways in which the processes of schooling may or may not facilitate the reproduction of patriarchal gender relations. By drawing upon and integrating several disciplines, our understanding of a particular problem is, therefore, deepened.

The teaching of interdisciplinary programmes can have an important effect on the thinking of both tutors and students. Early supporters of interdisciplinarity such as Basil Bernstein have suggested that new ways of working among teachers who move from individualistic working practices to more collective approaches may result from the breaking down of subject barriers (Bernstein, 1975). Moreover, teachers, many of whom may have themselves been educated within traditional disciplinary boundaries, find that their own academic assumptions are challenged: they now have to take into account other approaches when considering a particular problem. Often this will entail an attempt to understand the place of several disciplines within Women's Studies, disciplines which do not necessarily form part of the tutor's original area of expertise. This is of particular relevance, bearing in mind my earlier observations regarding the Freirean challenge to the authority of the teacher and his recognition that the teacher is both learner and teacher.

It is important to note, however, that while an interdisciplinary programme such as Women's Studies can offer radical learning possibilities and can challenge traditional notions of what constitutes academic knowledge, it does not *necessarily* constitute liberatory learning. It is possible to think of interdisciplinary programmes that are not intended to be liberatory. For example at an international conference on 'Project Work in University Studies' in Roskilde University in 1997, it became clear that some contributors supported interdisciplinarity in scientific and technological fields because it encouraged students to develop the flexibility required in the labour market. While this may be a realistic vocational aim, it is not in any sense liberatory.

Thus, interdisciplinarity is not intrinsically radical but it does offer possibilities for a radical curriculum and, as with experiential learning, can broaden our definitions of what constitutes academic knowledge. It is, however, the democratic learning processes as noted earlier that ultimately determine whether or not our adult education classrooms are liberatory.

Conclusions

In this chapter, I have looked at liberal feminist, Freirean and standpoint perspectives and show how they relate to particular curriculum initiatives. With regard to liberal feminism, I suggest that there have been important achievements in terms of enabling women to gain access to provision. However, I argue that their vision is limited in that they do not question traditional assumptions regarding the nature of academic knowledge and do not address the wider questions relating to the nature of the society in which we live. In exploring liberatory and standpoint perspectives, I suggest that Women's Studies is an example of a curriculum incorporating such perspectives. While noting that there are important constraints in terms of achieving a genuine 'education for freedom', I do suggest that there are radical possibilities in the teaching of programmes such as Women's Studies. In particular, I look at the traditions of experiential learning and interdisciplinarity within Women's Studies. Again, while there are limitations in terms of the liberatory potential, both experiential learning and interdisciplinarity do offer possibilities for a Women's Studies curriculum which challenges traditional epistemological assumptions within the academy and enables learners to explore women's position in different societies.

This chapter incorporates discussion included in 'Women's Studies and education: a shared agenda? in Bryant, I (ed), *Vision, invention, intervention – celebrating adult education,* Proceedings of the 25th Annual SCUTREA Conference.

References

Benn, R and Fieldhouse, R (1996) 'Notions of community for university continuing education' in Elliott, J, Francis, H, Humphreys, R, and Istance, D (eds) *Communities and their universities: the challenge of lifelong learning,* London: Lawrence and Wishart.

Bernstein, B (1975) *Class codes and control: volume 3 Towards a theory of educational transmissions,* London: Routledge and Kegan Paul.

Blundell, S (1992) 'Gender and the curriculum of adult education', *International Journal of Lifelong Learning,* 11(3), pp 199–216.

Bulkin, E (1980) Racism and Writing: Some Implications for White Lesbian Critics, *Sinister Wisdom,* 13, 3:22.

Coats, M (1994) *Women's education,* Buckingham: SRHE and Open University Press.

Elliott, J (1995) 'Women's Studies and adult education: a shared agenda?', in Bryant, I (ed), *Vision, invention, intervention – celebrating adult education,* Proceedings of the 25th Annual SCUTREA Conference, pp 57–62.

Elliott, J (1996) 'Teaching Women's Studies: whose experience?' unpublished paper presented at *Teaching cultures and the cultures of teaching,* conference held at University of Sussex.

Freire, P (1972) *Pedagogy of the oppressed,* Harmondsworth: Penguin.

Harding, S (1991) *Whose science? Whose knowledge? Thinking from women's lives,* Milton Keynes: Open University Press.

Jaggar, A (1983) *Feminist politics and human nature,* Sussex: Harvester Press.

Lubelska, C (1991) 'Teaching methods in Women's Studies: challenging the mainstream', in Aaron, J and Walby, S (eds), *Out of the margins: Women's Studies in the nineties,* Sussex: Falmer Press.

Mill, J S, (1861) *The subjection of women,* New York: Prometheus Books (Reprinted, 1986).

Steele, T (1994) 'Representing the people: university adult education and the origins of "Cultural Studies" ', *Studies in the Education of Adults,* 26(2), pp 180–200.

Usher, R and Edwards, R (1994) *Postmodernism and education,* London: Routledge.

Weiler, K, (1991) 'Freire and a feminist pedagogy of difference', *Harvard Educational Review,* 61(4), pp 449–474.

Wollstonecraft, M, (1792) *Vindication of the rights of woman,* Harmondsworth, Penguin (Reprinted, 1982).

Chapter Seven

Accrediting women, normalising women

Cheryl Law

> Would a large gift of cash from a porn baron
> who wanted to endow a chair of feminist literature
> be graciously accepted by a British university? (Kingston, 1996)

Recently one of my research students came to her tutorial with a blinding revelation. She had spent some weeks trying to pin down the concepts of identity and place, 'I finally realised – it's all chaos, life is just chaos!' She was disappointed and relieved that she had discovered that the intellectual certainties she sought don't seem to exist. My jumping-off point for this chapter bears similarities to that of my student's: identity and place within a context of uncertainty and confusion.

The transcendence of the new orthodoxy of marketplace economics and monetary pragmatism which have engulfed the academy have been so successfully implanted that to raise an objection or question their validity marks one out as a dangerous, obstructive anachronism. Previous feminist discomforts about the advisability of Women's Studies within the academy have been supplanted by more fundamental threats to the integrity of the principles and practices of the discipline. This chapter will explore the nature of these threats as they exist within the continuing education sector and how they operate to undermine the values which are integral to Women's Studies. In laying out the territory within which this new confrontation is being waged, the implications for Women's Studies students will be considered with regard to commonalities and questions of diversity. This line of investigation will raise questions relating to student need and the objectives and outcomes of the discipline. Questions relating to academic freedom and the nature of the required accommodations to be made will be set against what are perceived as potential benefits.

Continuing Education (CE) has always been distinguished by and infused with a value system bearing something of the evangelical within it. The spirit of access, acceptance, participation, shared pleasure and approval within a practice of co-operation have signified to CE practitioners values to be cherished and protected. It is precisely these values and aspirations which are no longer under threat because I fear we have passed that marker, they are disappearing. In educational provision, education itself is becoming another quaint concept. Training, vocationalism, the course as commodity culture – pass one and get one free, are replacing the development and nourishment of the intellect, the cultural and moral being. It is evidently a post-educational world just as it is a post-feminist one!

Set against the traditional CE background, what has Women's Studies been engaged in, what have been its objectives and what have been its students' expectations? It is undoubtedly a distinguishing feature of the discipline that it presents an exciting intellectual challenge and part of that challenge lies in its ability to keep moving and engage in a transformative process. Its most crucial recent development has been its expansion in terms of revealing the complexity of the category 'woman':

> *Women's Studies has learnt to recognise and examine differences between women, to stress the fluidity of female identity and to reject the idea that all women are essentially the same. (Cosslett et al, 1996, p 4)*

The heterogeneity of the manifold needs and priorities of women as learners with regard to race, sexual orientation, class and, increasingly, able-bodiedness, has been recognised more fully within this discipline as part of its own self-exploration and development. The diversity of women's experience and the acknowledgement of so many different voices is reflected in the variance of courses on offer in Women's Studies programmes. Provision has been driven by the range of expectations with which women enrol on such courses. Women attend for self-development; to gain a qualification; to have an educational experience; to nurture study skills prior to more advanced study; for employment enhancement; to gain a new perspective on their professional/employment activity; for human contact; to meet like-minded people; and for their own personal pleasure and space. Under the catch-all of self-development, autobiographical understanding contextualises the adoption of new skills, be they academic ones, for personal interaction, confidence-building or, in the case of refugee women, improving their English. Many women want to understand the construction of gender in society, how it impacts on their life and how they might explore a gender-free identity or investigate their sexuality; women who have suffered deep emotional trauma want to confront this and start the healing process; there are women learning to live autonomous lives who need support and encouragement. Other women want to explore their individuality once their children have left home or examine the results of divorce. All these women come to engage intellectually within an accepting, affirming and safe space.

From a lesbian perspective, Graham suggests that:

> *For groups which experience discrimination and cultural exclusion that education should enhance career opportunities, and provide individuals with qualifications information and skills to combat discrimination. Also that cultural perspectives and achievements of the group are recognized, validated and disseminated. (Graham, 1994)*

She also delineates the heterogeneity within the lesbian experience where:

> *Black lesbians experience additional negative stereotyping and discouragement with the particular difficulties of integrating gender, sexuality and race perspectives in their work. (Graham, 1994)*

The demands which lesbians may also make of Women's Studies mirror the 'imperative for lesbians to support themselves independently of men' (Graham, 1994) and may necessitate an emphasis on courses which facilitate career progression.

The citing of lesbian studies within a Women's Studies framework rather than Gender Studies or Cultural Studies is significant because the latter often still display a dominance of male-dominated 'queer' theory which precludes the concerns of lesbians being adequately addressed in the curriculum. There is a tendency 'to exclude those areas of lesbian thought most inimical to men – particularly radical lesbian feminism' (Graham, 1994). Similarly, for women wishing to employ academic tools to understand their sexuality and emerging lesbianism, a safe women-only space is an essential starting point.

There is a similar motivation at work for black women to challenge discrimination and prejudice by finding a space in order 'to reveal the myths about black women's underachievement' (Mirza, 1995, p 145). At Birkbeck, motivations for black women additional to those that prompt all women to take up Women's Studies courses have related to a desire to explore issues of identity through black women's history and writing courses. These are courses which are integrated within the general Women's Studies programme. The self-defined educational needs which provided the basis for a Certificate in Black Women's Studies at the University of Leeds Continuing Education Department responded to issues such as those of race and identity, citizenship and migration, the changing expectations of different generations of black women, black women's history, gender relations in the black community and educational access for black women as a tool for self-expression (Virk, 1994).

Although these have been courses specifically designed to provide black women with their own space, there are inevitable tensions and seeming contradictions for such students in claiming a space which is nevertheless provided for and within the confines of a dominantly white institution. However empathetically originated, being designed and taught by black women tutors, these courses are still constructed within a cultural framework which symbolises and carries within it the myths which the courses seek to dispel. This is an issue about the redistribution of resources within communities which is outside the remit of this chapter but which is crucial to the provision of continuing education which truly seeks to empower its students.

Previously, no other site in the education field has been as well-suited in terms of ethos, institutional structures, pedagogical methodologies, geographical locations, personnel and commitment to embrace the objectives of Women's Studies and help to fulfil the needs of its students as that of CE. There was an empathetic engagement between the discipline and the provider. This partnership between CE and Women's Studies has witnessed innovative projects such as 'the evolution of women's centres from political action to education' in Banwen as part of the Community University of the Valleys in South Wales. A project which has enabled women 'to define and express their own and community needs' as part of the process and the product of courses in Women's Studies (See Chapter Ten.) However, the flexibility and imagination which characterises Women's Studies methodology as being an integral analytical tool in the transformation of students' lives is one which is now directly threatened by the mainstreaming of CE provision and the new funding requirement of compulsory assessment in line with a market economy ideology.

What are the problems which accompany such compulsory assessment and what are the options for limiting the damage? The imposition of compulsory assessment as a measure for grant delivery is a system fuelled by a particular ideological engine involved in a 'transition from welfare to market values' where 'the methods of managerial capitalism are entering and reshaping the academy' and 'oppressive patterns from the private sphere have been reproduced in the public services' (Morley and Walsh, 1995, pp 1–2). We are not merely being asked to integrate assessment into our courses, we are being told to embrace an ideology which is totally at odds with the ethos which underpins both Women's Studies and CE. The antipathy of assessment to the nature and delivery of much of expressed student need in this discipline is an obvious and damaging outcome, but more insidious and potentially damaging on a broader scale is the accommodation of a value system which is a direct attack on the work we are engaged in – the application of equality.

As Women's Studies practitioners we are being trapped, in marketplace jargon as 'deliverers' between those who dictate our conditions of operation, the 'providers' (the funders, representing the *status quo*) and those whose needs we seek to satisfy, 'the purchasers' (our students). In marketplace economics, standardisation is what pays dividends, the mainstreaming of provision through the control of assessment is one way to standardise need, even to dictate it. Diversity as a concept cannot be matched to this model. 'We will no longer be able to cater for minority needs' and 'Our provision is too diverse to make economic sense' are two chilling statements I have heard recently in this context which indicate a threat to the continuation of the discipline. Generating excess income on the basis of Women's Studies student intake is unlikely to be a feasible objective while provision which caters for diverse needs is problematic to standardise and, therefore, more costly to deliver. These are all factors which mitigate against our continuance in such a fiscally determined climate.

There are a number of significant and damaging implications to this new funding situation which impact on Women's Studies in CE. The new funding orthodoxy obdurately constructs a chain of reaction which begins with minimum enrolment targets; travels through course completion; and comes to rest with compulsory assessment. All three parts of this chain discriminate against our provision and negate the enshrinement of equal opportunities. Minimum enrolment figures without the benefit of a dispensation which takes regard of the special nature of provision involved with lesbian or black women's studies immediately prevents significant numbers of women from ever getting off first base. The gender dimension of the barriers to women's regular and complete course attendance are not even entertained in this model. The phrase, compulsory assessment, carries within it the implicit denial and rejection of many of the expressed needs of women students which we examined earlier in the chapter. The irony which has manifested itself since the introduction of this new funding system lies in decreasing enrolment from students on previous courses who, much as they wish to continue or enter this pattern of study, have no desire to enter assessment. Gaining an award was never part of their motivation for study. Rejection also comes from those women who having enrolled and discovered the obligation of compulsory assessment, then drop-out. Women find it difficult to sustain their refusal to enter assessment when others in their group are submitting work, making them feel as if they are disloyal, lazy or uncooperative. They do not come to a Women's Studies class to have such negative experiences; they cope with them by leaving. Significantly, both for students and tutors, needs are not being met because the intervention of assessment necessarily alters the priorities, pace and tenor of the syllabus, as well as classroom practice.

Reducing academic criteria to a numbers game can only restrict and smother the hitherto creative curriculum development which has characterised so many CE Women's Studies programmes. Attracting large numbers of students to cushion drop-out incises experimentation; the emphasis on funding criteria dictates uniformity and prohibits risk-taking. All such inhibitions result in an intellectual straitjacket and a failure to reach out and embrace those people and ideas who stand on the periphery. The standardisation of which I wrote earlier entrenches the marginalisation of those most in need of a place to express and explore their experience of discrimination. We are headed towards academic homogeneity, intellectual sterility and the domination of popular culture in the academy.

The economic straitjacket necessitates new working practices which we have recently been experiencing as 'increasingly coercive working environments . . . together with increased surveillance and control' (Morley and Walsh, 1995, p 2). Self-policing takes over and the loss of our value-system becomes the norm, we are no longer aware of the compromises we make. What are the ramifications for academic freedom when our core decisions are so prescribed? How can we evaluate our work when in order to judge the value of this work we need to express it in the terms of the known, and the terms of the known present us with a contradiction? We are trying to deliver Women's Studies in a format and within structures and strictures which deny our objectives with regard to equality and autonomy.

Some readers will find this an extreme representation of the current scenario; that accommodations can be made, new formulae devised, strategies adopted to preserve much of what we wish to claim and defend. I have already put forward how significant the siting of Women's Studies in CE has been in the past to the successful delivery of its objectives. Equally critical is the appreciation of whether a subject is susceptible to the concept of assessment and what the nature of that assessment would need to be in order to accommodate the discipline's distinguishing features. Assessment needs to consider the nature of the knowledge involved. In Women's Studies, this must include its multi- and inter-disciplinary profile, the nature of the students and their needs, as well as the teaching and learning methodologies employed. The content of Women's Studies melds intellectual analysis with personal experience; teaching methodologies are experiential, process-orientated, based on democratic teaching and learning models. These features all combine to set Women's Studies apart from traditional, mainstream disciplines. Women's Studies shares a commonality and a common heritage with Peace Studies, Human Rights Education and Development Studies, all disciplines where study is directed towards political activism. What forms of assessment mirror the objectives of political activism? What evaluation criteria can be placed on a presentation by a woman on the global nature of violence against women when that woman has experienced years of domestic violence, left her home, has no post-16 education and is taking her first adult education class? Good pass? Merit? Distinction?

Are any modes of assessment currently available which are acceptable in CE institutions and are receptive to the positive models which Women's Studies brings to the academy? However flexible and well-intentioned the operation of such procedures is, they do, if they are to be invested with credibility, embody certain bureaucratic regimes which are intrusive to the teaching and learning process. That is to say nothing of the psychological and emotional impact such procedures make on a client group with needs (see earlier) hardly in keeping with appraisal, no matter how empathetically applied. What choices are left to us when working in the public sector (a political choice) is now dictated and defined by market values and managerial capitalism? When does a new realism become capitulation? What room is there for adjustment within parameters which largely fail to take on board a gendered perspective of the CE academic landscape?

There are those students who push themselves through the process and come out triumphant, glad to have achieved, ready for bigger challenges. Graham has concluded that 'In order for lesbian studies to gain recognition as a "serious" subject of study, it needs to seek accreditation' (Graham, 1994). Also her point about lesbians' need for economic independence entails that there is a 'greater emphasis on career enhancement and qualifications by lesbians than heterosexual women' (Graham, 1994). Indeed, this also embraces other students for she understands that this 'is often the case with students who experience class or race discrimination' (Graham, 1994). While accepting that Women's Studies within a CE framework can provide a valuable and attainable preliminary route for those previously denied the opportunity of qualifications, there are also others who feel confirmed in their life experience of failure. Their quest for a more positive, nourishing and empowering educational experience (which may then furnish them with the self-esteem to pursue qualifications) has been hijacked by management consultants whose vision is of students as funding units, colleges with virtual reality libraries and a negative deficit nirvana. Some educationalists have been persuaded to believe that measurement now represents the ultimate value. It is not a twenty-first century vision I want to embrace, but then, I'm not a post-feminist either . . .

References

Cosslett, T *et al* (eds) (1996) Women, power and resistance: an introduction to Women's Studies, Buckingham: Open University Press.

Graham, P (1994) The impact of accreditation on lesbian studies, unpublished paper, UACE Women and Continuing Education Professional Network seminar, 24 November.

Kingston, P (1996) 'Temptations of filthy lucre', Guardian Education Supplement, 23 April 1996, p 3.

Mirza, H S (1995) 'Black women in higher education: defining a space/finding a place', in Morley, L and Walsh, V Feminist academics: creative agents for change, London: Taylor & Francis.

Morley, L and Walsh, V (1995) 'Introduction', in Feminist academics: creative agents for change, Taylor & Francis, 1995.

Virk, L (1994) A pilot course in black women's studies, unpublished paper, UACE Women and Continuing Education Professional Network seminar, 24 November.

Chapter Eight

Recentring quality: assessing the feminist classroom

Sue Webb

Women's Studies is now well established in the UK and courses can be found within most education institutions (Aaron and Walby, 1991). Feminist scholarship has also grown and is a significant influence across the humanities and social sciences (Kramarae and Spender, 1993). More specifically, women's education has frequently been seen as synonymous with liberatory models of adult education (Elliott, 1995). In this chapter I will argue that examination of the participation of women as part-time adult students and their experience of the so called 'feminist' classroom provides a critical moment to explore how continuing education is responding to changes in funding and quality control. In other words, this focus will enable study of the question of whether the continued and increasing presence of these courses and students in continuing education will be a stimulus for change as education institutions begin to engage with the idea of lifelong learning, or whether 'mainstreaming' of this provision will mean incorporation of the margins.

The discussion in this chapter is premised on an interest in feminist pedagogy. It arises from a concern to implement Women's Studies (following Lather, 1991) as a counter-hegemonic practice designed to create and sustain opposition to social inequalities. In attempting to do this, I will suggest that there are a number of issues that need to be addressed when assessing what is going on in feminist classrooms. For example, what, if any, are the relationships between quality mechanisms and feminist articulations of good practice in teaching and learning now that women's education within continuing education is subject to external quality assessment? Is the teaching and learning similar or different from that of other classrooms and how appropriate are the criteria developed by the funding and quality agencies for measuring the fitness for purpose and standards of these continuing education courses? More specifically, if women's education purports to be progressive and critical in that it is different and more centred on girls and women, to what extent do the evaluative criteria of teaching quality assessment take account of the possible differences in pedagogic focus?

Some writers, such as Shrewsbury (1987), have looked to a Freirean agenda to measure the success of the Women's Studies classroom. She suggests that 'evaluative criteria [should] include the extent to which a community of learners is empowered to act responsibly toward one another and the subject matter to apply learning to social action' (p 6). Weiler (1991) takes these ideas further in a language that echoes the feminist discourse on research, and argues that feminist pedagogy should focus on three areas: the power dimension of teaching, including the role and authority of the teacher; the epistemological dimension, including the way knowledge claims relate to personal experience and feeling; and the challenge to essentialist thinking from new feminisms around the issue of difference. These writings endorse the view that feminist pedagogy has the goal of emancipatory learning that will continue beyond the classroom door, in a similar way to how the writings on feminist research argue for praxis oriented work that should be participatory and lead to change (Lather, 1991; Stanley, 1990). With the mainstreaming of some women's education provision in continuing education departments in the 1990s, the question arises about the extent to which these goals can be sustained and measured using the instruments which are prevalent in teaching quality assessment.

These issues will be explored in this chapter through discussion of a case study of the quality assurance processes associated with accredited work in a continuing education department of a pre-1992 university, and the courses that will be discussed are those associated with a modular degree programme in Women's Studies delivered in that institution. The chapter will discuss the implications of current arrangements for quality control and assessment of teaching quality within the programme and suggest some tensions that have arisen in relation to assessing a women-centred curriculum that has a liberatory orientation.

Frequently women's education and adult education have been characterised as sites of liberatory practice which can provide springboards for movements for social justice and equity or individual change and mobility (see for example, Steele, 1995; Coats, 1994). As a result their location in formal education has been contested not only by the gatekeepers of the academy but also by those groups and social movements who identify their learning objectives in social change, and so, they consider, beyond the walls of academe. Continuing education departments in universities have been the sites where traditionally these struggles have been played out, and where different forms of university teaching and learning such as the tutorial class have been actively promoted by working class interest groups and social movements. But over the last fifteen or so years structural changes have undermined these groupings and organisations, and they have been accompanied by the move to more accountable education systems disembedded from local interests and influence.

For example, in the case study, new course proposals from the continuing education department are subject to the same procedure for approval as is found in the rest of the university. As a consequence when the women's education programme developed a degree proposal there was an attempt to identify generic threshold standards for each level of study, and course aims and assessments that were comparable to those of similar interdisciplinary degrees, yet at the same time acknowledged the critical nature of Women's Studies as an educational practice which values women's experiences. In many respects this proposal was regarded as exemplary within the institution, it received peer approval, and the threshold standards were adopted by the appropriate faculty as guidelines for good practice in course development, and subsequently appeared in the tutors' handbook.

In due course though, as further modules were developed, which were part of other explicitly standpoint-knowledge based programmes (such as those associated with the African Centred research group), module validation was more difficult, and some warning bells were sounded about the 'fitness *of* purpose' of educational outcomes which valued experiences and social change. I perceived that these validation discussions involved an alignment of the criteria for quality with a focus on the purposes of education, and that by doing this a particular external reference system was being invoked, and this was one which privileged so-called objective knowledge over subjective experience. More explicit assessment criteria were required by the faculty to justify the use of what were regarded as 'non-traditional' assessment methods such as learning diaries and group project assessments. These were provided, and in the internal quality assessment review the Women's Studies programme was regarded as meeting well the requirements of 'fitness for purpose'. Through validation and the subsequent teaching assessment review the discussion about quality had shifted away from external considerations about what education should be provided, and it had become more focused on internal consistencies and relationships between aims, objectives, assessment methods and learning outcomes, in other words, fitness *for* purpose, rather than *of* purpose. By providing answers which only addressed these internal concerns quality could be demonstrated without the need to make explicit the differences between the discourses of equity and social change and that of quality. Nevertheless, this example serves to illustrate the tension in the quality discussions between models premised on fitness *for* purpose and those premised on fitness *of* purpose. In this chapter I will argue that as the 'standards' debate comes to the fore these questions about the purposes of higher education are more central to the notion of quality, and the place of an empowerment curriculum, such as Women's Studies, within the mainstream is increasingly contested.

Such contestation was found in the case study, when in response to student demand modules were developed in 'Black Women's Studies', and difficulties were experienced during the course approval process. The example illustrates the different ways in which people's experiences are regarded as a basis for the development of knowledge and shows how particular experiences may become the legitimated area of academic study, perhaps to the exclusion of others. Fellow professionals involved in the process of peer scrutiny suggested that the course aims showed a 'lack of objectivity' in the way women's experiences would be considered, and these had to be amended before approval was given. In contrast, the module proposers, writing from their own experience as women of African descent who had felt marginalised within academic discourses suggested that the modules would examine a number of factors which they said 'had conspired' to render invisible black women's experiences of life in contemporary Britain. This perception that invisibility was a social construction actively promoted and sustained by particular institutional and academic gatekeepers was also widely accepted by the students, who had requested that the degree programme take more account of the contributions of Black feminists to the development of feminist theory. For example, one woman, who defined herself as African-Caribbean, spoke of her isolation on the course and indicated that she would have 'appreciated more black women to talk to' and to 'learn of theories [that] Black women had developed'. The quality process though ensured that the particular conspiracy theory proposed by the black tutors and students, and derived from their experiences, could only be a legitimate area of academic study if its validity was questioned. To begin to understand the issues that arose within quality assurance practice, I would like to discuss further the tensions and ambiguities within the quality debates. I suggest that such contestation about quality has opened up a discursive space about the purposes of higher education and in part this is why the experience of the mainstreaming of the continuing education curriculum, and in particular women's education, needs to be documented and reflected on. My concern is that on the one hand, the location of women's education in higher education may be under continuous scrutiny if it retains a critical engagement with feminism outside of the academy, and yet on the other hand if this link is severed the courses may no longer meet the interests of potential women learners. A quote from one of the students on the programme summarises this dilemma: she said in a presentation to the 1997 Women's Studies Conference: 'I had expected the course to be a medium for feminist activism, but given the constraints of academia and the need to set work specifically for the qualification meant this was only possible on a limited basis'.

Throughout the 1980s and early 1990s successive Conservative governments sought to exert more and more control over the size and shape of the higher education system, albeit indirectly through the funding agencies (Duke, 1997). Underpinning this strategy has been a concern with accountability, and so intrinsic to the funding mechanisms, formulae and criteria, are arrangements for quality audit, teaching quality assessment, performance indicators, and research assessment. However, the system to which these arrangements have been applied is far from homogeneous. Others for example, have argued that old diversities and sectoral interests are leading to a re-stratified system within unified funding arrangements as universities seek to re-position themselves in the 1990s (Duke, 1997; Scott, 1995), and examination of one of these mechanisms, that for teaching quality assessment may begin to through light on how such diversity is maintained.

Teaching Quality Assessment (TQA) may be characterised as an ideal type expert system which on the one hand is embedded in the connoiseurship model (Wright, 1996), and on the other is looking to more explicitness about educational outcomes (Middlehurst, 1997). Yet, I would suggest that these two apparently opposing models can be reconciled because TQA is premised on external peer scrutiny and institutional reflexivity, and so discursive space is created for diversity in the institutional measures used.

These two aspects of quality, the implicit 'standards' of the academy, and the increasing concern for explicitness about outcomes coupled with a process based on peer review and reflexivity, have had a particular impact on women's education and feminism (Duke, 1997). In the early 1980s resistance to the feminist curriculum was frequently presented within the discourse of standards (Kramarae and Spender, 1993; Schuster, 1994). By the 1990s, while modules in feminist issues and aspects of women's lives had become a major feature of many programmes in higher education, the feminist curriculum and Women's Studies had come under increased pressure from academic peers to redefine the subject in terms of Gender, and Cultural Identity Studies, and in some locations the standards debate returned with a vengeance. It is not surprising therefore, to see echoes of these quality debates articulated within Women's Studies.

For example, a central thrust of Women's Studies has been about challenging the implicitness that has surrounded the locations and political positions of those who have constructed the theories and bodies of knowledge that have dominated many curriculum areas. This challenge has involved questioning the relationship between the knowledge makers, who have been white, middle class men, in the main, and the knowledge produced, which has frequently neglected or rendered invisible many women's experiences and contributions to ideas. Yet through this practice of making explicit the process and products of learning increasingly some have argued that Women's Studies has set up its own academy or connoiseurship which needs to be challenged (see for example, Hill Collins, 1990; Lennon and Whitford, 1994). The feminist view that 'better' knowledge is defined in terms of the extent to which previously invisible women are rendered visible, and the expectation that this will follow from processes that prioritise women's experiences, and encourage reflexivity has resulted on the one hand, in some women continuing to feel excluded from the academy, and on the other hand, in discussions of experiences that frequently become a reified and formulaic activity in the higher education classroom (Morley, 1997; Middleton, 1993). In other words, in striving to meet the quality criteria of higher education some of the evaluative criteria set out by feminist writers such as Shrewsbury (1987) and Weiler (1991), which privilege the use of women's experiences and feelings, and encourage the application of learning to social action and individual empowerment, may have become marginalised. Analysis of the discourse and practice of TQA may begin to provide some understanding of how this might occur.

TQA has become a condensation symbol for standards, objectivity and accountability and what can be measured has been central. As a consequence, there has been a tendency for the focus to be on inputs and outputs because these appear to be more easily measured, and a neglect of process and the student experience (Barnett, 1992) even though the discourse of quality has been predicated on a consumer model and customer satisfaction (Dearing, 1997, p 9). More recently, in the late 1990s, the terms quality and standards have been disassembled, and debate is centring on defining the threshold standards or learning outcomes of the higher education experience rather than simply measuring the relationship between inputs and outputs (see HEQC, 1997; Watson, 1997). Similarly, my experience of undertaking a self-critical review of the Women's Studies programme (an internal institutional requirement) has suggested that quality assessment systems can become more than ways of measuring inputs and outputs. I would suggest that the process can provide a lever for institutional change, and that empowerment based curricula can find a space within the mainstream of higher education by manipulating the ambiguities within the discourse of quality. Reflexivity and collaboration which are central elements of the evaluation criteria of feminist pedagogy chime with the self-reflective process of TQA, and its emphasis on the use of external peer scrutiny to ensure comparability and maintain standards.

Preparation for the production of the self-critical review began almost one year before the report was to be scrutinised by a process of external peer review, which in this context was a process managed by the institution. It was distinct from the funding and quality agencies' external audits and teaching assessments, although the documentation of this institutional process was considered a central part of its quality system which could be externally evaluated. As course director I raised the issue of how the review should be conducted at a meeting in the summer of 1995 of the Board of Examiners for Women's Studies: this comprised the course team, ie myself, the course director, several part-time staff, the external examiner, and three other full-time staff from a relevant subject department who sit on a cross-departmental Advisory Board for Women's Studies, and so provide a professional linkage between continuing education and another cognate department. In view of the limited contractual responsibilities of the majority of those involved in teaching the programme, it was agreed that I would produce a draft document which would be discussed with the course team and the student representative, and the agreed version would be sent to the faculty for the peer review in May 1996. In other words, collaboration and reflexivity, and triangulation of the course director's and tutors' perceptions with those of students, and the external examiner were key features of the process adopted.

The institution provides considerable documentation to support course directors in producing these self critical reviews and the guidelines drew heavily on the funding councils' teaching quality assessors' handbook. As a consequence I felt well informed about the process of review and the expectations about the type of documentation I would need to produce to support the course teams' reflections on the teaching and learning over the previous four years, for this was the period under review. This included producing a self critical review which mirrored the funding councils' TQA areas of interest such as curriculum design, content and organisation; teaching, learning and assessment; student progression and achievement; student support and guidance; learning resources; quality assurance and enhancement; and finally identifying areas of good practice, and an action plan that focused on areas for immediate and future attention. However, the more that I and my colleagues considered the detail of TQA, the more convinced we were that the distinctiveness of continuing education needed to be made explicit in the account. This was because during this review period continuing education experienced a major change in the funding of the liberal adult education and the move to mainstream all part-time study. It was with this in mind that the self-critical review noted that:

> During this period participation across the whole programme has increased from 69 individual students to 93, and the proportion achieving credits has grown. Measurement of this is complex and will be discussed more fully [a later section] but here it may be useful to note that whilst only 6% of the Certificate intake in 1991–92 completed the qualification, in 1994–5, 75% of the intake obtained credits. (Quadrennial Review, 1996, p 1)

Analysis of this text shows just how aware we were at the time of the need to construct the 'story' of Women's Studies within the parameters of input and output measures detailed in the TQA guidelines, although the complexity and perhaps inappropriateness of these measures was also being signalled. Further on in the account an analysis of entry qualifications was provided which showed that:

> students accepted have a wide variety of qualifications . . . [and that] trends within these entry qualifications are difficult to establish from only two cohorts but this analysis would seem to confirm the view that at level one the programme is recruiting students from a wide variety of backgrounds including those who may not have had access to higher education when younger, and at level two the programme is providing access to lifelong learning for those who wish to change direction or build on previous higher level qualifications (p 10)

To support this narrative an expectation that statistical indicators should be provided was perceived, and this was duly done. However, analysis of these data suggested that the output measures such as completion rates, credits and awards achieved, and first destinations were inappropriate ways of describing the variety of student experiences, and the complexity of their perceptions of achievement and success. For example, analysis of non-completion year on year suggested that the courses were becoming more successful because more students were gaining credits. Yet, our concern as tutors was that there was no simple relationship between achievement rates in credits and the continuous satisfaction expressed on the student evaluation forms and by the external examiner over these four years. Also, the apparent non-completion by 25 per cent of the group in 1994–95 did not imply persistent dissatisfaction or poor quality teaching.

I began to develop an argument that in the case of continuing education and Women's Studies within this, there was a need to develop statistical measures that accorded with the complexity of the learning process and product. For example, measures were needed that took account of the range of reasons different students might have for taking part-time Women's Studies courses, and that looked more at the relationship between process, the student experience and outcomes which may be skills or practice based rather than pure knowledge acquisition. My contention was that unless space is negotiated within teaching quality assessment for these issues, the Women's Studies move into the mainstream may be at the expense of feminist pedagogy or such pedagogic claims to be relating learning to social action, will become empty rhetoric.

It was encouraging then to find support for these perceptions of quality when the self critical review document was discussed by the external peer group within the faculty, and that the faculty board became a lever for raising the issue more widely within the institution. The faculty board agreed the following:

The Committee is generally satisfied that quadrennial course reviews and Departmental self assessment statements have made appropriate use of supporting statistical data but it acknowledges the need to review the guidance it issues to course teams undertaking quadrennial course reviews, both in general terms and in respect of statistical indicators. Previously the Faculty has refrained from defining what statistics should serve as indicators, whilst acknowledging that HEFCE guidance is not appropriate in respect of continuing education or postgraduate education. To date, the Faculty has advised that Departments should discuss the issue of appropriate statistical indicators at staff meetings and define the statistics which are most meaningful to the Department. (Annual Faculty Report, 1996–97, p 4)

The report went on to suggest the following:

in the absence of meaningful data on first destinations of students in continuing education, other indicators may be appropriate. A question in the student evaluation survey on the relevance of courses to career aims might be useful as an alternative. (p 4)

In other words through this process of teaching assessment some tensions and ambiguities in the discourse of quality became transparent. Peer support was gained for the view that quality measures were frequently predicated on a model of learning associated with full-time first degree studies, and that these may be inappropriate for measuring achievement of education and programmes such as Women's Studies based on a lifelong learning model.

In addition, at the time of the review the significant emphases that I perceived to be underpinning the areas of the TQA outlined in the assessor's handbook included the following: a need to demonstrate fitness for purpose which included showing how the programme fitted within the institutional mission and was capable of achieving this; that the providers had regard for the student experience, and in particular were aware of the programme's strengths and weaknesses, were responsive to critical comments and were able to show how they had responded to these to improve the quality of the provision; and finally that they could provide evidence of appropriate standards of student achievement.

As I have already suggested, the construction of a reflective, collaborative and triangulated review was considered to be the 'best' strategy for demonstrating quality and so, in relation to the institutional mission a rational story was presented. The account invoked the notion of institutional planning so that departmental and course strategies could be mapped onto the wider institutional policy. Policy and practice chimed, and where tensions were alluded to, such as what place there would be for the student groups who had attended previously the non accredited liberal adult education, these illustrated that the providers were self critical:

> *The most significant of the changes . . . have been changes in the funding of Liberal Adult Education and the move to 'mainstream' all part-time study. At one level, the development of Women's Studies in the CE department during this review period illustrates the Department's response to these changes. . . . More specifically, in the Annual Planning documents and in its Self-Assessment Statement, the Division of Adult Continuing Education has acknowledged a commitment to the provision of university level education on a part-time basis to adult learners. It offers modular courses within an academic framework of credit (CATS) and it is concerned to fulfil the university's strategic mission 'to expand provision of courses of relevance to the community within the context of lifelong learning involving maximum flexibility for accumulating the necessary life skills to provide the potential to fulfil their role in society.' (Quadrennial Review, 1996, pp 1–2)*

In other words, the teaching quality review provided a place to legitimately document an interpretation of lifelong learning within the practice of an institution. In addition the process involved the faculty in identifying examples of good practice and issues for further attention at the level of departments, faculty or the university as a whole. This may have helped to inscribe distinctive Continuing Education practices within the mainstream of that institution.

Returning to the specific experience of Women's Studies a number of examples of good practice were also acknowledged in this process and these included the following:

> *the TQAC identified good practice in respect of Women's Studies whereby students are subject to the same assessment and examination board regardless of the end award they are aiming for. (Annual Faculty Report, 1996–97, p 8)*

and,

> *the attention of the committee is drawn to the way in which the course team has acted appropriately on student evaluation comments. (p 6)*

What is interesting about this last comment is the way in which the TQA process supported the re-inscribing of a women-centred curriculum by noting that:

> *students had not found the modules [shared with another programme] stimulated women-centred studies and, as an interim measure, separate tutorials for students on shared modules had been established to help students on the Women's Studies course to overcome some of the shortcomings of the teaching materials in promoting women-centred studies. (p 6)*

Similarly, encouragement was given for the course team to explore 'the need for the development of differential assessment [and] exploration which would take account of the abandonment of the 16 point marking scale in relation to learning diary–based assessment' (p 10).

These last two examples are interesting because they begin to make normal some of the main features of the feminist curriculum, that is women–centredness and the use of personal experience. In authorising the course team and department to explore these assessments and grading issues, some legitimacy has been conferred on feminist educational practices which, first, begin to redefine the power relation between tutor and student in the assessment process and, second, begin to acknowledge the importance of personal experience and feeling in learning and knowledge construction. In this way the experience of quality assessment of the Women's Studies curriculum may be beginning to make a difference to higher education and may in part enable practical teaching and learning detail to be mapped on to the notion of the lifelong curriculum.

In conclusion this case study has shown that while at first sight the discourses of teaching quality and feminist pedagogy, equity and social change seem far apart, the practice of the former may not always be at odds with the latter. Quality is a contested concept fraught with tensions and ambiguities and so, a discursive space is available for new definitions and redefinitions of the purposes and standards of higher education to be negotiated. Moreover, quality assurance is a process that operates at many levels within the institution and is practised by players who may align themselves with a variety of debates and positions. As a consequence the ambiguities within quality assessment enabled practitioners and peer scrutineers in continuing education to claim a normalcy for some features of the feminist classroom. These include, for example, the focus on the power dimension of teaching; the affirming of the epistemological approaches which base knowledge in women's experiences and feelings; and to redefine what counts as achievement acknowledging the appropriateness of personal fulfilment and empowerment. It is too early to assert that the mainstreaming of Women's Studies and other similar continuing education programmes will construct a new learning society premised on relating learning and social action but nor should one conclude that mainstreaming will simply lead to incorporation of the margins.

References

Aaron, J and Walby, S (1991) (eds) *Out of the margins,* London: Falmer Press.

Annual Faculty Report (1996–97) *Report of the Faculty of Educational Studies to the university teaching committee,* Faculty of Educational Studies, Sheffield: University of Sheffield.

Barnett, R (1992) *Improving higher education: total quality care,* Buckingham: SRHE/Open University Press.

Coats, M (1994) *Women's education,* Buckingham: SRHE/Open University Press.

Dearing, R (1997) 'A view from the National Committee', in Aylett, R P T and Gregory, K J (eds), *The single quality agency: the future quality agenda and its implications,* London: University of London, Goldsmiths College.

Duke, C (1997) 'Towards a lifelong curriculum', in Coffield, F and Williamson, B (eds), *Repositioning higher education,* Buckingham: SRHE/Open University Press.

Elliott, J (1995) 'Teaching Women's Studies in adult education', in *Adults Learning,* June pp 295–297.

HEQC (1997) *Graduate standards programme final report Vol 1,* London: HEQC.

Hill Collins, P (1990) *Black feminist thought: knowledge, consciousness and the politics of empowerment,* Boston: Unwin Hyman.

Kramarae, C and Spender, D (eds) (1993) *The knowledge explosion,* London: Harvester Wheatsheaf.

Lather, P (1991) *Getting smart: feminist research and pedagogy with/in the postmodern,* London: Routledge.

Lennon, K and Whitford, M (eds) (1994) *Knowing the difference: feminist perspectives in epistemology,* London: Routledge.

Middlehurst, R (1997) 'Enhancing quality', in Coffield, F and Williamson, B (eds), *Repositioning higher education,* Buckingham: SRHE/Open University Press.

Middleton, S (1993) 'A post-modern pedagogy for the sociology of women's education', in Arnot, M and Weiner, G. (eds), *Feminism and social justice,* London: Falmer.

Morley, L (1997) 'All you need is love: feminist pedagogy for empowerment and emotional labour in the academy', in *Transitions in gender and education* (Conference Proceedings) Warwick: University of Warwick.

Quadrennial Review for Women's Studies (1996) *Report to the Faculty of Educational Studies by the course director for Women's Studies,* Faculty of Educational Studies, Sheffield: University of Sheffield.

Schuster, M R (1994) 'Transforming the curriculum', in Davies, S, Lubelska, C and Quinn, J (eds), *Changing the subject,* London: Taylor and Francis.

Scott, P (1995) *The meanings of mass higher education,* Buckingham: SRHE/Open University Press.

Shrewsbury, C M (1987) 'What is feminist pedagogy?', in *Women's Studies Quarterly,* 15 (Fall/Winter).

Stanley, L (1990) (ed) *Feminist praxis,* London: Routledge.

Steele, T (1995) 'Mainstreaming, critical histories and cultural identities', in Hamilton, M and Withnall, A (eds), *Innovations in continuing education provision, teaching and learning: research perspectives,* Lancaster: University of Lancaster.

Watson, D (1997) 'Who is responsible for standards?', in Aylett, R P T and Gregory, K J (eds), *The single quality agency: the future quality agenda and its implications,* London: University of London, Goldsmiths College.

Weiler, K (1991) 'Freire and feminist pedagogy of difference', *Harvard Educational Review,* 61(4), pp 449–74.

Wright, P (1996) 'Mass higher education and the search for standards: reflections on some issues emerging from the graduate standards programmes', *Higher Education Quarterly,* 50(1), pp 71–85.

Chapter Nine

Learners, experiences and lives in the curriculum

Sue Shuttleworth

This account is based on reflections on my own experience as a working class returner to education and draws on the experiences of a group of working class students currently studying on a social science degree programme. The students are low-paid workers with few formal educational qualifications. They have all progressed into continuing education from programmes such as Return to Learn courses sponsored by trade unions, and Paid Educational Leave schemes sponsored by more enlightened employers. I have been involved with this group of students for a number of years, initially, as a tutor on their returner courses and now, as tutor on their part-time degree course. During this time we have experienced a shared learning process. Reflections on that process will in part form the focus of what follows here.

In thinking about the experiential dimension of my own work as a tutor, I began to examine more directly how life outside the 'classroom' informs approaches adopted inside. When I asked students about their experiences of learning, their observations suggested similar interconnections between real life and subjects studied – ie between curriculum and learner, lives lived and lessons learned, between individual needs and educational provision. There is nothing new in this. Along with other readings here however, this chapter is an attempt to build on such a realisation, and to move towards what Freire (1985) terms 'maximally systematised' knowledge – in this case a more thought out, conscious understanding of how lives and the curriculum interconnect. In particular, how women's and men's lives can become the curriculum, or the 'learning exemplars', Negt (1975) has drawn to our attention, heightening the active process of learning, to engage the student in a conscious, reflexive process which sets learning in a social and historical context.

Issues addressed here touch particularly on the experience of women's education, specifically from a social class perspective, and relate to a theoretical concern with dimensions such as self, identity, social capital and the negotiation of self-imposed and institutionalised barriers. The engagement with experiential frameworks can be seen as a methodological device in this process of negotiation, particularly relevant in counteracting the feelings of 'personal erasure' which students from non-traditional backgrounds seem to encounter in trying to make sense of academic culture. Within experiential frameworks the tutor, and other members of the learning group, become an important resource, facilitating learning. This facilitative process has itself become a specific focus, in particular in the work of what might generally be termed collaborative researchers (Elden and Chisholm 1993; Forrester and Thorne, 1993; Shuttleworth *et al*, 1994; 1995). In current work this focus is taking shape in the notion *process as outcome*, and is something I will explore in discussion here.

Alongside all this, issues addressed also touch on the role of Women's Studies and

Gender Studies as a transformational dynamic in the curriculum as the subject has moved from margins to mainstream, becoming a discipline to engage both women and men. What follows then is something of my own story, and something of the interconnecting stories of students and situations encountered in learning experientially.

Gathering experiential exemplars: the beginning . . .

I am a lecturer in Continuing Education. Among other things I teach, assess work, set exams, attend meetings and make decisions about the educational futures of other people. I came in by the back door. No one else in my family has ever done this kind of thing. My parents think me an oddity and wonder where I came from, which means I tend not to talk about work and close off from the people I am supposed to know well, a major part of my life. Both my parents were low-paid factory workers. Except for my dad's failed venture into self-employment, and my mum's temporary upward mobility as a school caretaker, they spent their working lives in jobs with low satisfaction and little money. I left school too early ('girls don't need education, they only get married', was something actually said to me by my mother) and took a series of low-paid jobs myself.

Then . . .

It is September 1974. After six years at work I am returning to education. By registering unemployed, I get my fees paid while doing A levels part-time – English, History and something called Sociology. Tutors in the traditional subjects are both men with traditional views and traditional approaches to teaching. This means that although the student body in each class is mainly female, they manage to concentrate on the more worthwhile males. In sociology I encounter a feminist. At this point I need to remind you that I am working class, to tell you I was once heard at a party shouting: 'what's wrong with a bit of sexism anyway?', and see feminism as middle class claptrap. I begin my real education, confronted by argument and evidence about women's lives and power relationships which brings on a culture shock that never goes away again. For the first time there is mention that I might be able to do a degree. Thanks to the encouragement of my sociology tutor, I manage this, and later a PhD, and begin teaching adults, mainly women, in Sociology and Women's Studies.

For a number of years I work part-time in several colleges, and sometimes in the homes of the students I teach. Rehana is an Asian woman keen to learn English. I go to her twice a week to talk and set exercises which are supposed to help her. On each visit I am given strong Indian tea with a plate of something tasty like samosas. I take this treat alone while Rehana and the female members of her family watch and wait for an appreciative response. Sometimes her children are in the room as we try to speak English together. Her small son plays a vigorous game of football across the room – we seem to be sitting in the goal area – as I ask her, from exercise four in the book, to describe the directions to the town bus station. This, after weeks of visits, is where I discover she is rarely allowed out of the house and has no idea of buses, streets or anything locally that is not within five minutes walk of where she lives.

In a Women's Studies class at the Adult Education College I mention Rehana to introduce the topic of women cross-culturally. We discuss as a group our experiences, realising common reality of restrictions on our freedom to move around – as children told to stay near to the house while our brothers were allowed to roam; as adolescents living out the obsessions of 'the fan' in the smallness of our bedrooms; as women taking up less and less space in public settings, avoiding dark carparks and unlit walkways. From the experiential and particular we identify wider structural issues of social control through physical and emotional social exclusion and differential access to space.

Later . . .

It is March 1993. The Return to Learn class meets every two weeks at 7:30 pm on Mondays. We meet in a semi-detached house, just off campus, as part of the Department of Adult Education. The students are mostly over 40 years old, low paid County Council workers, mainly women. Margaret, Elsie, Lillian, Liz and Janet are home helps, bringing to the tutorial meetings a wealth of funny anecdotes about their work; Hazel is a night sitter for Social Services; Betty is a cook in a residential home for adults with learning difficulties; Bill is a building maintenance worker and Andrew is a store keeper. They are a lively group and together we make it through the first year of my involvement in worker education.

In a typical session completed work is handed in and work to be tackled in the two weeks until we meet again is discussed. Assignments range from writing about education experiences to investigating the community. Throughout the course discussion is varied and we all come to expect any topic to develop. For example, one student tells us about a local character who dresses as Wild Bill Hickock in the winter and Jeronimo in the summer. He is fond of eccentric clothes, but when sunbathing, no clothes at all. We use this to consider whether there is such a thing as normality, and how behaviour can lead to labelling. Others talk about their experiences of hormone replacement therapy and feelings of losing control because they can't concentrate. This leads us on to a discussion about health, social expectations and the differential treatment of social groups. Out of the discussion that night Margaret, a home help, produces a short story based on her work experiences. The story introduces Miss Armstrong:

> a six foot two giant with a week's growth of whiskers. She wore a brown tweed skirt and a green twin-set. The single row of pearls was just the finishing touch. Her big feet were escaping from a pair of fluffy pink boudoir slippers, and her hands, as large as shovels, had bright red finger nails. Miss Armstrong started life as Gerald Armstrong, but after years of misery, his GP finally sent him to see a consultant who agreed to operate and remove his male sex organs.

The story goes on to describe Margaret's reaction to her work experiences which every day bring her into contact with the unexpected. Read out loud in a class some weeks later, we use it as an experiential vehicle to raise structural questions about marginal workers who are paid little, in jobs which demand a lot. The common bond or experiential framework for this learning group is the shared reality of low status work and low pay in a society which needs home helps, cooks, night sitters, building maintenance workers and store keepers but behaves as though it doesn't and tells them they are not worth a great deal. We use this joint experience as a way into discussion about structural issues relating to class and gender at work, looking at the County Council's equal opportunities statistics on gender distribution in employment. The students engage in an assimilation of the experiential and personal with the more factual, and supposedly objective, statistical evidence and recognise a structural reality in the trends which tell them their employer concentrates women at the bottom of the jobs hierarchy and men at the top in all departments. In some departments there are no women at all.

Later still . . .

It is 1994, 9:00 on Tuesday morning. I enter a seminar room in the main campus building carrying a bag full of books and readings which might be picked up in the session. This is a sharp group and I have to work hard to keep up. In another bag is a kettle, coffee, biscuits and mugs. The first task is to put the kettle on and to rearrange the room from traditional rows into a discussion circle. Some students in the group have progressed from the Return to Learn course to do this two year Paid Educational Leave (PEL) course organised by the university. Now, few such courses offering two years day release from work, with job cover and with employer-paid fees, can be found. By the time I am writing this (1997) the PEL course is no longer viable. Local employers have withdrawn sponsorship. It is another sign of financial closure. Without employer help for students such as this, confidence building, foundation continuing education is a luxury they cannot afford either in terms of fees or time out of their already work-heavy week.

In one of the early sessions we explore experiences of being a woman and being a man. I ask students how they feel they have to behave because of their gender, and what they feel would be possible if they were the opposite gender. The outcome of such an exercise is always interesting. This time Bill produces a poem which in later sessions is the key to deep discussion and analysis.

> Because I am a man I must, be one of the boys, revel in lust, know about cars, engines and rust, enjoy sports say tits and fart, get pissed out your head, pick up a tart. Tough guys don't dance, tattoos are neat, compare your manhood to the size of your feet, be racist and sexist in front of your mate, mix curry and lager love and hate. Man the exploiter I know how to use, seldom the victim, I rape and abuse. Domination and power the name of the game, the old boys' network, man untamed. If I was a woman, I WOULD BE ANGRY.

Creative writing such as this often springs from group discussion. This piece became in future work a supportive illustration of a dimension of women's education which comes particularly out of an examination of gender in context. The deeper structures of dominance and subordination inherent in long term, persistent power relationships, became the focus of discussion for this group of students. The sharpness of focus was helped along by Bill's willingness to examine his own experience in a mixed group. It is probably significant that the group was an established one with friendships and trust which went beyond the formal learning context. Again, the experiential and particular provided a way towards a conscious reflection on wider structural issues.

And now . . .

It is the first Sunday in July 1996. I'm sitting in a corrugated tin shed known as a Shebeen – a traditional African gathering place for drinking beer. I'm in the Masiphumulele squatter community on the Cape Flats in Cape Town, South Africa. Miriam, an African woman is serving a group of us a lunch of chicken, bread and salad. This is her way of paying her university fees, selling beer to township locals, and lunches to visitors of Cape Town University doing the 'township tour'.

I have been attending a conference on Experiential Learning. Now, my last day in South Africa, I'm 'really' experiencing life in an informal settlement – township, shanty town – the terminology changes with the politics. Local people sit around and we try to talk, but many of them seem to be drunk and the whole place is filled with smoke from a burning pile of rubbish. Apparently white people come down to the squatter communities to dump their rubbish. The communities themselves have no facilities, this includes no refuse collection. The only way they can deal with the growing mess is to burn rubbish in big skips, with the result that they live in a constantly smoke-filled atmosphere.

We leave after a while and drive along a dirt track lined with crowds of leaning wooden and corrugated tin shacks stretching for miles across flat, unproductive sandy land. We pass children playing in raw sewage and dogs scavenging around bags of rotting food which are everywhere. Here and there though in the middle of all this are occasional, incongruous looking shacks which squatter families have decorated by painting them pink and yellow. They have staked out a plot of earth outside with makeshift trellis which they use to tie up the washing line and to support a few flowers. Its all hard to describe and experience. I cannot put the impressions out of my mind.

Can Miriam's life as an African woman living in absolute poverty inform the curriculum in the classroom where students like Margaret, Ann, Brenda and Joyce are studying for their degrees? Miriam is a part-time student, working to put herself through a university degree. She is the first in her family to take a place at university, but is forced, as a working class woman, to make her own living along the way. In a socio-economic context of poverty and deprivation she manages her life by taking low paid, low status employment which, predictably, is also temporary and precarious. Her experi-ence, like that of other women in the developing world, serves as an experiential exemplar to extend the local context into a context emphasising global interconnec-tions. In this way a visibility is given to lives which have parallels in a shared experience of struggle – in work, education and home life, and in experiencing marginality. Across the world women like Miriam, Margaret, Ann, Brenda and Joyce have a common bond embedded in the objective reality of oppression. They force us to recognise the determination of their spirit in struggle.

Links between local and global contexts, explored to explain social divisions and to consider their production and reproduction, appear in the work of Reagon (1985) which maps out an illustrative journey of economic, social and historical interconnec-tions. Setting out relationships between workers, Reagon tells us a story about the making of a blouse which is 'touched by hands from all over the world'. Made from cotton and polyester, the blouse starts out in the cotton fields of El Salvador, a place 'soaked in blood' where 'pesticide-sprayed workers toil in the boiling sun pulling cotton for two dollars a day'. In Venezuela, oil workers 'bring up oil from the earth for six dollars a day', while in Trinidad and Tobago Exxon Oil workers upgrade the product to produce strands of polyester filament for the Petro-Chemical Mills of Dupont. The raw materials are transported by Cargill, a large trading conglomerate, through the Panama Canal and into the USA, to South Carolina and the Burlington factories which 'hum with the business of weaving oil and cotton into miles of fabric for Sears'. The fabric goes to Haiti where women 'toil doing piece work to Sears specifications for three dollars a day'. As the journey ends, Reagon says, the blouse made by her sisters, is sealed in plastic and sold in the Sears department store where she can buy it on sale for twenty per cent discount. 'Are my hands clean?' she asks.

Used in group work this story is an effective facilitator of discussion, showing that experience can be contradictory when global economic structures seem to make oppressed into oppressors. A transformational dynamic that changes the learning group may be set in motion when students are confronted with experiential exemplars such as this, linking their own experience to the heightened inequalities experienced by women in other cultures. There is a health warning though, in what might be seen as a central contradiction – what happens when we find cross cultural experiences too unbearable to confront? Others have asked the same question (Brown, 1994). I am still looking for an answer to this.

Theoretical frameworks

So, what does it mean to engage with experiential frameworks? Engagement can be explained as a *process* linking the practical and theoretical; moving from particular to general and generalisable; legitimating particular and normalising. What is happening to the learner engaged with experiential frameworks? Learning theorists have argued that subjective, concrete experiences of participants are connected to a wider structural view, promoting a heightened understanding of *processes* which in turn empowers the learner as insights become more systematised. In this part of the chapter I will attempt to explain further, by relating to theoretical frameworks, some of the issues embedded here.

Theorists in experiential education have identified a number of 'villages' of activity – conservative, liberal, progressive and radical (Weil and McGill, 1989; Saddington, 1992). Developments in feminist pedagogy I would set within the radical village which has at its core a view that oppression is the most serious problem, that social change is the main aim, and sets the educator the task of conscientisation to encourage in the learner reflection, thought and action. In the above account I have tried, by drawing on experiences, to say something in relation to this about my own development, and something of the development and work of students I have encountered across a number of years. In doing so I hoped to expose the 'tutor as student', who is privileged to learn alongside the 'student as active learner' in a process of shared or negotiated learning.

I would place experiential learning at the centre of this active learning process for all participants, in that the *gathering of one's own experiential learning exemplars*, and the setting of these in a *wider structural context*, serves to engage and transform the group in a meaningful learning process. Theorists concerned with the politics of education such as Freire and Negt have argued however that the *process* at the core of such learning, and the grasp of issues gained as new insights, is not something a learner can expect to have once and for all, but is something to be actively grasped many times over – this is argued, for example, in Negt's perspective on class consciousness, and in Freire's concept of conscientisation. In both instances it is suggested that when new knowledge is not usable for practical organisation, this knowledge can dissipate and be lost. Developing understanding of a more stable, permanent kind, it is suggested, comes from participation in activities directed towards change, and in linking new learning coming from the subjective experiences of learners with theory. Theory in this context becomes theory *building*: developing a view of social reality in which interpretation of social positions and relevant interests is not tied to the concrete situation.

To some extent the combined forces of experiential theory and theory underpinning feminist education serve to provide a context within which learning might be insightful and stable in the sense of being long term – the latter has the potential to offer a theoretical backcloth against which the experiential learner is able to 'see' how their individual experiences can become learning exemplars which go beyond the concrete to reveal social positions and inherent, deep seated relevant interests. Learning and relearning, grasping and regrasping issues would take students from local to global through examples facilitating a growing understanding out of the evaluation of competing explanatory frameworks.

There is a third area of theoretical activity, though – *collaborative research*, which is a method supportive of both experiential and feminist perspectives. Indeed, one might locate the collaborative research method between the concrete and particular of the experiential perspective, and the broader, collective explanatory framework of the feminist perspective in education.

In my own work, and that of colleagues, collaborative research surfaces as a *method* to overlap with concerns outlined by experiential learning theorists and those concerned with political and women's education. In looking across these three dimensions of thought, I have identified a certain dovetailing. When combined, the three views suggest a broader perspective capable of developing dialogue. As far as I know, however, the three views have not been examined together in anything like a systematic way. The latter, discussed in detail elsewhere (Shuttleworth *et al*, 1994), is an approach to practical, group-based activity which is to do with sharing and working together, to generate and to keep new knowledge stable, longer term and alive through participatory action.

Working collaboratively is a research method used in an educative sense bringing together participants with a range of skills and knowledge. In the active task of investigation or problem solving, participants become learners engaged in a creative combining process, synthesising, as Freire suggests, their own minimally systematised knowledge (ie the more concrete, experiential or particular) with knowledge which has the capacity to be maximally systematised (ie the generalised, theoretical or explanatory). In collaborative projects with which I am familiar, learning groups have tended to investigate issues to do with the workplace – low pay, health and safety, aspects of legislation relating to working conditions; or have examined stereotyping or aspects of gender in education. In all cases, students have engaged with a process of finding things out. Collaborative research as education, is as much about this process of learning as it is about research findings and outcomes. Indeed, at the core of the collaborative approach is the notion that engagement in this process is itself an outcome – thus the concept *process as outcome*, takes shape.

Conclusion

Using women's lives as the curriculum is nothing new. *How* to do this and build a view of *what is happening* is something still to work at.

I said in the introduction that this would be an attempt to develop a more systematised, conscious, understanding of how lives and the curriculum interconnect by considering the possibility of learning drawing on experience. I have attempted, in setting out something of experiences encountered in working with adult students, to consider aspects of those interconnections. I also said that *the engagement with experiential frameworks can be seen as a methodological device in a process of negotiation.* In this process the learner comes to recognise the particular in relation to a wider historical and social context. Examining what this means has been related to three specific areas of educational activity and theory – the *experiential* as a first learning stage, the *collaborative* as a method with educative potential, and the *feminist* as an explanatory framework.

This paper has been put together with the inspiration and help of students I have encountered across a number of years teaching. A particular acknowledgement goes to Margaret Larvin and Bill Sheavyn.

References

Brown, J (1994) 'A paradox of experiential learning in fostering social change', in Keeton, M T (ed), *Perspectives on experiential learning*, The International Experiential Learning Conference, Washington, USA.

Elden, M and Chisholm, R (1993) 'Emerging varieties of action research', *Human Relations,* February, 46(2), 121–142.

Forrester K and Thorne C (eds) (1993) *Trade unions and social research*, Aldershot: Avebury.

Freire P (1985) *The politics of education: culture, power and liberation*, London: Macmillan.

Negt O (1975) *Sociological Imagination in Exemplary Learning* Roshilde: RUC forlag.

Reagon B J (1985) 'Are my hands clean?', developed from, Cavanagh J (1985) *The journey of the blouse: a global assembly*, Institute For Policy Studies.

Saddington J A (1992) 'Learner experience: a rich source for learning', in Mulligan, J and Griffin, C (eds), *Empowerment through experiential learning: explorations of good practice*, London: Kogan Page.

Shuttleworth S J, Somerton M F and Vulliamy D L (1994) *Collaborative research for social change: shared learning between workers and academics* HEFCE Research Report ISBN 0–85958–099–7, University of Hull Press.

Shuttleworth S J, Somerton M F and Vulliamy D L (1995) 'Learning from working together: experiencing collaborative research as education', in Hamilton, M and Withinall, A (eds), *Innovations in continuing education provision, teaching and learning: research perspectives*, UACE, SCUTREA & SRHE Seminar Series, University of Lancaster Press.

Weil S W and McGill, I (1989) *Making sense of experiential learning: diversity in theory and practice*, Milton Keynes: SRHE and OU.

Chapter Ten

New choices for women from mining areas

Mair Francis

Introduction

This chapter will explore the experiences of women in the Dulais valley of south Wales since the miners' strike of 1984–85 and relate these experiences specifically to the political, social, economic and political development of women in mining communities. This contribution will examine the influence that the participatory role of women in a mining community and their European partnerships have had on the provision of the part-time degree programme, the Community University of the Valleys (CUV) provided by the Department of Adult Continuing Education (DACE) of the University of Wales Swansea. The miners' strike became the catalyst that spearheaded initiatives by women for women and their families and served as a public platform where women were able to voice their concerns and their hopes for the future. It enabled women to learn the necessary skills to establish the DOVE (Dulais Opportunity for Voluntary Enterprise) Workshop, its education and training programme and community co-operative at the Banwen Community Centre in a remote mining community. With a spirit of expectation and anticipation a group of women from the miners' support group met in 1984 to discuss the implications of setting up a women's workshop to teach women both traditional and non-traditional skills. There was a feeling within some of the support group that the strike was soon to end in defeat, but this defeat was only in terms of the loss of male jobs and the closure of the local collieries. For women these changes signalled a different future where their role could be more public either achieving in further or higher education or successfully seeking work. To assert this position within a traditional patriarchal community the workshop developed as an 'alternative' organisation that could challenge patriarchal formal networks and to feminise the education and training provision by providing a flexible and open approach to the needs of women and their families.

During the past decade there have been three predominant developments in the history of the DOVE Workshop that have been specific to the political, social, economic advancement of women in the Dulais valley. These are the miners' strike of 1984–85, the establishing of a women's community co-operative in 1989 and the setting up of a collaborative strategy with the higher and further education sectors. These developments can be seen as strategic indicators on a continuum linked to the experiences of women coping with industrial change, an insight into their personal needs and the improvement and enhancement of their opportunities within a wider context of enriching a community. Each episode has been linked to the other and it is precisely this holistic approach that has given strength to the initiatives that have taken place.

The founder members of the DOVE Workshop shared a common objective even though they represented dissimilar backgrounds. Before the strike some of them had politically active experiences within the formal political structures of the local political parties and the trade union movement; others had been politicised though their involvement in new social movements such as the peace movement; some had little or no formal political attachment; and some became involved in environmental campaigns. This has since brought to centre stage three main issues. One was the visibility of women during and after the strike and the awareness raising of feminism and difference; the second was the changes in traditional gender roles within a patriarchal class conscious community; and third these experiences became a catalyst for change. The main difficulty is to evaluate that change and measure it against the education and training opportunities available to women and the need to create quality employment. During the past decade the decline in the traditional coal, steel and agricultural industries, the increase in the number of women part-time workers, the expectation of women requiring quality work, all point to the evidence of occupational changes and the changing demand for skills. Here it is important to recognise that this re-structuring of employment is not a British phenomenon but also a European one. Referring to the changes in employment patterns the European Commission stated that:

> the nature of work is in continuous transition – with, for example, an increasing need for inter-personal communication skills rather than physical dexterity – all under the pervasive influence of information technologies which are now an integral part of much of modern economic activity. (European Commission, 1994, p 159)

To meet these changes effectively and to equip women with the necessary skills to participate in the workforce, to become multiskilled, to widen cultural, economic and social horizons it was necessary to develop a holistic approach to education and training provision. This would include the implementation of equal opportunities measures, improved child care provision, family friendly work practices, home-based working opportunities and career breaks and opportunities for women to take up (or return) to education and training courses. Whether these measures have benefited and will empower the majority of under-represented women in mining communities, is yet to be evaluated and quantified. However, what must be recognised is that significant cultural changes will need to take place in order for women to be in positions where they are able to make economic, social and personal decisions affecting their lives. This independent and feminist approach leading to women's autonomy has presented challenges in changing attitudes of both men and women within a patriarchal mining community. This approach has questioned the traditional role of women within the home and challenged the cultural barriers facing women who want to return to education or training. More importantly it asserts the concept that women should be given the opportunity to be decision makers within the public sphere.

It was within this spirit of taking control in 1984 that women of all ages from a cross section of the community – teachers, factory workers, nurses, miners' wives, mothers and homemakers came together to become politically active in a struggle to protect and to 'save their communities'. Through this dynamic social and political activity they identified that their organisational and managerial homemaking skills could be transferred to proactive work, as political activists sharing political platforms with local and national politicians, on demonstrations and at picket lines. As a result of these experiences their lives took a new direction. In an area where job opportunities for women are limited to low paid, low status and part time work and where women predominantly work as unpaid domestic workers, together with an inadequate and expensive transport service and a total lack of affordable child care, the women met, and established the following aims and objectives:

- To provide facilities and an opportunity to teach women new skills, thus enabling them to seek quality employment.
- To provide child care facilities for mothers of young children making it possible to attend day time courses.
- To provide a flexible learning environment.
- To provide transport to enable women to participate in such activities as were available.

An organising committee was set up and in March 1985 the group received a grant of £600 from Opportunities for Volunteering funded through the Welsh Office. An Urban Aid Grant was received from the Welsh Office and Neath Borough Council and in 1986 the Valley Initiative for Employment of Women, VIEW, was established as a limited company and charity. In 1987 the DOVE Workshop became tenants of the Open Cast Executive offices of the National Coal Board (NCB) in a small remote village on the edge of an open cast mining site. These offices were vacated by the NCB during their 'rationalisation' programme and were given to the Onllwyn Community Council to use as a community resource. Renamed the Banwen Community Centre it became a community education and training centre with adequate space for a creche, seminar and meeting rooms.

In 1989 the workshop established a community co-operative to improve the creche facilities, to offer a community-based desk top publishing service at affordable rates and to provide in-house technology training with a declared commitment to women-specific training. Apart from the South Glamorgan Women's Workshop, based in Cardiff, the DOVE Workshop has become the model for women specific community based training in industrial south Wales.

DOVE and its collaborative strategy

The education and training provision in the community needed to develop a strategic link with community development. They did this by drawing on the good practice of the strike's local support group and by liaising, not only with women with grass roots knowledge, but also including women with effective social and political skills. This group recognised that by developing a collaborative approach towards a specific objective the "survival" needs of the community could be effectively met. In 1987 the Department for Adult Continuing Education (DACE) of University College Swansea was seeking partnerships and new venues in the valleys. DACE was committed to developing an informal learning programme and designed a community-based programme meeting the needs of the 'non-traditional' learner in consultation with the DOVE Workshop. At this time negotiations were also taking place with the local further education college and the Workers' Educational Association to provide traditional and non-traditional courses. It was the establishing of the Women In Technology courses that was to be the main thrust of the work that enabled women to improve their skills so that they could compete effectively in the local labour market and seek quality employment. During the past ten years this has become a burning issue for the workshop. Women in mining communities have always worked in low paid, low status and part time work particularly in the gender segregated areas such as the services sector and on the assembly line in local factories. The provision aimed to offer women hope.

The decline of the 'heavy' industries of coal and steel since the mid 1980s has been paralleled by the growth of the service sector. According to Teresa Rees this has led to a decrease in skilled full-time male employment and a growth in semi-skilled and unskilled female work in the service sector. Rees argues that the development of training is a key issue and training women in particular 'warrants urgent attention' (Rees, 1994, p 95). In south Wales this shift and change is reflected in female employment patterns that represent a fluctuation between full and part time work. Women as young girls have aspired and still aspire to full-time factory work and part-time 'swing shift' employment in the clock and instrument factory affectionately called the 'Tick-Tock'. This tradition created not only a wages gap with men but also a skills gap. The political and social experiences of women during the Strike raised their awareness of the opportunity to upskill. Of course this is not merely a Welsh experience but also a European experience to which I will refer later.

DOVE continued this practice and brought together the skills of the democratically elected representatives from the community and district councils, the local trade union branches, (miners' lodges), women working as unpaid domestic workers, part time and full time working women, the professional skills of tutors and teachers and some financial support from small businesses. This was the social partnership in action (with women in positions of decision making) within a mining community. It is significant that throughout the European Union the concept of the social partnership has been acknowledged as the most effective way forward to regenerating the European economy. Indeed Cynthia Cockburn, the feminist sociologist, asserts that there is a need for gender democracy within the European social dialogue since this will enable women to meaningfully take part fully in this 'new international forum', as long as 'women are present among delegates and staff of the social partner organisations in proportion to their presence in the constituencies they represent' (Cockburn, 1995, p 1).

Within this collaborative partnership women became visible and proactive in equal opportunities issues. In this context, the need to collaborate equally with higher and further education sectors was deemed to be necessary in order to support the education and training needs of the community. DOVE's role as a 'grass roots' organisation and its ability to progress adults into accredited provision and employment by way of informal learning provision became an example of good practice of working in partnership. This has been successfully developed in other communities in south Wales with the support of the European Community Initiative programme, RECHAR.

This 'bottom-up' approach facilitated the negotiations with both voluntary and other sector organisations to relocate their resources and provision in the valley communities. What is interesting is that in the 1980s DOVE was perceived by the statutory sector as an 'outreach' centre, outside the mainstream provision both geographically and socially, and to some extent this labelling still exists not only among the more traditional providers but at local authority level as well. Women are challenging this perception of education in the community by asserting their independence and autonomy, and above all giving the community a sense of ownership in developing their education and training needs. By establishing a women's agenda the women's remit has been widened, changing the image of women from being merely Welsh to Welsh Europeans.

DOVE and its European links

The experiences shared with women from other mining regions in Europe has influenced the relationship of women and their connection to Wales. Raymond Williams remembered that such a change started to happen for him from the late 1960s and wrote:

> *There was a continuity in a quite overwhelming feeling about the land of Wales; as feeling and writing that stays through. But then I began having many more contacts with Welsh writers and intellectuals, all highly political in the best tradition of the culture, and I found this curious effect. Suddenly England, bourgeois England, wasn't my point of reference any more. I was a Welsh European, and both levels felt different. (Williams, 1979, p 295–6)*

Williams continued by stating that from the intricacies of the politics follow the alternatives that connect him to the sense that he is 'necessarily' a European and continues:

> *that the people to the left and on the left of the French and Italian communist parties, the German and Scandinavian comrades, the communist dissidents from the East like Bahro, are my kind of people; the people I come from and belong to (ibid)*

In ten years the activities at the DOVE Workshop have recognised that Welsh women share this radical and cultured outlook and by working collaboratively with European women will learn the connections identified by Raymond Williams. By disseminating good practice the realisation was that Europe was becoming the reference point where exciting initiatives and projects were taking place. By the beginning of the 1990s contact was made between DOVE and women's organisations in other mining communities in Belgium, Italy and Spain. This period of "apprenticeship" helped develop links with women's training organisations in Europe.

In 1991 DOVE became a member organisation of the European network, IRIS, whose mission statement declared:

> *to increase the general levels of skills and knowledge, community co-operation and integration and at improving the status of women as a group which suffers systematic discrimination and unequal treatment on the labour market.*

In April 1992 IRIS organised an exchange visit to the Istituto Formazione Orientamento Lavoro Donne (IFOLD), a training organisation in Sardinia, Italy. DOVE was selected to represent the United Kingdom on this delegation and identified similarities between the aims and objectives of IFOLD and DOVE that practised a holistic approach to training with particular reference to the embedding of guidance and counselling within all training courses. This innovative holistic approach was adopted by DOVE and DACE: DOVE by way of its Information Technology provision and DACE's commitment to guidance and counselling. This proved to be the embryo of the CUV: the negotiating and delivery of higher education in a community location.

The collaboration between the voluntary sector and a higher education provider represented innovative practice in Britain and attributed to the direct exchange of ideas with our European sisters.

Women in south Wales and Sardinia were for the first time able to compare both socio-economic, environmental and political similarities in their persona and working lives through the delivery of education and training provision for women. The Sulcis Iglesiente region in south west Sardinia had been experiencing industrial changes within its small mineral and coal mining industries. Miners and their families were involved in political struggles against their Government. Strikes, 'stay down' strikes and television programmes conducted not only at the pit head but underground as well, marches and demonstrations in Rome led to the subsequent victory when the miners secured private and state sector support. In spite of the defeat of the British miners, this experience came close to our own experiences in south Wales in 1984–85. Similarly, in 1987 the Belgian coalfield was to undergo complete economic and social changes by implementing the Strategic Limburg Plan involving provincial authorities, regional and national governments and the European Community. The aims of this plan were to:

> *stimulate employment, reduce unemployment, increase the participation of the Limburg population in education and training provision and reconvert initiatives in communities where mines had closed. (Francis, 1993, p 4)*

By 1995 the Dulais Valley Partnership, with DOVE as a founder partner, was established to facilitate and co-ordinate the development of an integrated regeneration strategy for the Dulais valley that would include economic, environmental, educational and social elements (Dulais Valley Community Needs and Opportunities Analysis, 1995, p 4).

Guidance and counselling (Orientamento) and progression routes

Guidance and counselling has become a crucial and significant prerequisite to ensuring that an informed choice is made by potential learners. Mainstream guidance and careers counselling services have been narrow and specific to school leavers and insensitive to barriers facing women. This traditional provision continues to fail to meet the needs of women, in particular those needing creche support, transport support and a flexible, family friendly learning environment. The task of the DOVE Workshop was therefore to raise the awareness among women that an alternative approach to adult education and training provision could offer opportunities. The Belgian, and in particular the Italian model of guidance and counselling, was to be the innovative method most suitable for the south Wales experience. IFOLD's and KEERPUNT's (A woman's training organisation based in Hesselt, in the former Belgian coalfield) objectives of informing trainees of the need to give value to existing skills raises awareness of the legal, social and political implications affecting women's lives, thus giving priority to women's employment. This is the 'cutting edge' where gender segregation is challenged, where the position of women as low paid employees is questioned. The Sardinian 'Orientamento' guidance model is based on equal opportunities information offered to women to offset their subordination. This is an overtly political act and at the heart of their guidance and counselling. Trainees are not encouraged to become more like men in order to succeed in the labour market but to recognise their differences as women and to develop an approach which values sharing, partnerships, co-operation and assertiveness. These ideas were brought to a seminar, Women in the Workforce, supported by European funding at the DOVE Workshop. Participants included IFOLD, KEERPUNT, women from the Yorkshire coalfield and from the Derry Women's Centre in Northern Ireland.

The overwhelming success of the provision at the Banwen Community Centre can be attributed to the relative ease with which adults progress on to further education or training provision, supported by the guidance and counselling facilities that are available to learners. The Community University of the Valleys (CUV) is one such route. With financial support from the European Commission, the Banwen Community Centre was converted in 1993 to accommodate a library, improved creche provision, seminar and lecture rooms. The programme is flexible and modular and accepts learners from the existing provision.

Critical reflections

Since 1986 the easy task was providing education and training courses developed from grass roots knowledge. Building on experiences and social, economic and political knowledge enabled DOVE to effectively meet the needs of the community. However, sustaining this provision during a time when the Conservative Government was systematically attacking mining communities and destroying the economic base was difficult. There was pressure to adhere to a framework of accreditation, for example, that was anathema to the needs of the 'non-traditional' student. Training skills had to relate to the needs of a market economy, business executives were dictating the curriculum, further education colleges were being incorporated and taken out of the democratic control of the locally elected councils, and child care provision was seen to be the right of those who could pay and not those in need. To overcome some of these difficulties DOVE needed to be focused on the explicit economic needs of the community. This agenda prioritised women. It would have been so easy to change the curriculum and respond to the demands from the Training Enterprise Council's culture, but we refused and became the founder members of the Open College Network in Wales. Recognising students' achievements instead of penalising them and erecting barriers, accessing EC funding to provide free courses and free child care enabled the Workshop to continue to build the confidence of the community. Working within a system that became funding-led rather that student-led posed serious difficulties. With the constant support of the local authority it was possible to continue to develop the curriculum but since local government reorganisation in 1996 the financial situation has deteriorated with serious results. A significant cut in core funding, parochial in-fighting and a misconception of the importance of women's issues as a priority could lead to a grim future. The main hope will be to establish a National Assembly for Wales so that the democratic rights of women and men, particularly within the older industrial areas, will be effectively represented and recognised.

Conclusion

The community partnership continues to grow and encompasses a wider representation. From the initial partnership involving the University, a local FE college and the WEA, the collaboration extends to the local Training and Enterprise Council (TEC) and the community groups. The many developments taking place at Banwen Community Centre are as a result of women's experiences within a wide political spectrum. Decision making that has historically been gender specific and owned by men is now very much part of the organisational aspect of DOVE's work. Undoubtedly the progressive thinking of DACE, the inherited working class education classes through the South Wales Miners' Union and the National Council for Labour Colleges (albeit provision for men and implicitly excluding women) has all contributed to the success of the provision at the Banwen Community Centre. However there have been examples of best practice taking place in Europe that have influenced DOVE, in particular within coalfield areas in Belgium and Italy. With the support from IRIS the European Network for Women's Vocational Training DOVE has been proactive in establishing provision that has been recognised as a model of best practice in Europe. In future we will disseminate our ideas not only with women's groups but with trade unions, the private sector and voluntary and community groups. The initiative has possibly come full circle and the 'social partnership' established in the crisis of 1984–85 has developed in such a way as to provide a learner-centred education and training provision for future decades.

References

Cockburn, C (1995) *Women and the European social dialogue: strategies for gender democracy,* European Commission, DG V.

Dulais Valley Community Needs and Opportunities Analysis (1995) *Final Report,* Community Development Foundation and BP.

European Commission (1994) *Employment in Europe,* DG V.

Francis, M (1993) *Women in the workforce: alternative choices for women from coalmining areas: report on the DOVE workshop partnership visit to Belgium 12–16 October 1993.*

Francis, M (1995) *Women and the aftermath of the 1984–85 miners' strike: a south Wales analysis,* MSc Dissertation.

Istance, D and Rees, T (1994) *Women in post-compulsory education and training in Wales,* Equal Opportunities Commission Research Discussion Series No. 8.

Rees, T (1992) *Women and the labour market,* London: Routledge.

Rees, T (1994) 'Women and paid work in Wales', in Aaron, J, Rees, T, Betts, S, and Vincentelli, M (eds), *Our sisters' land: the changing identities of women in Wales,* Cardiff: Cardiff University of Wales Press.

Williams, R (1979) Politics and Letters, London: New Left Books.

Section Three

_____

Shifting paradigms: researching women and
women researching

Chapter Eleven

Women researching in continuing education: voices, visibility and visions

Pat Whaley

Introduction: mapping the field

I want to use this chapter to explore issues and aspects of women researching in Continuing Education (CE), using my own experience as a focus, and linking it to the experience of others and to the substantial epistemology on women, on research and on CE. Given that these three fields have been tilled for some time and that there are many important issues in the rather less well hoed territory of women researching in CE, whose boundaries stray into all the other three, I have chosen to concentrate on a few issues of significance in my life in continuing education research.

I intend to explore a series of simple questions: who are the women researching in continuing education and where, when, why and what do they research? Some of the most simple questions are also the most profound and in this case can be used to explore important and complex issues – of control and power; of distinctiveness and difference; of value and status; of experience and theory; of identity and partnership; of practice and praxis.

I aim to offer some insight into what counts as research for women in continuing education; what is distinctive about that research and what contribution women in continuing education can and do make to the academic canon and practice and perhaps more importantly, to their own lives and those of others. 'What had the many-metre-deep pile of publications . . . added to the sum of human happiness or wisdom?' asked a member of the CE subgroup to the Education Panel of the 1992 Research Assessment Exercise (RAE) (Duke, 1995, p 14). What difference can we make?

THE WHO: A question of identity: can you identify (with) this woman?

There is a certain discomfort in focusing on self, even if it is used to explore issues, develop insights, address theory. I would argue that there is a strong and proven tradition of autobiographical reflection in all three themes – women, research and CE – and one from which other parts of the academy can learn. The issue of 'the self' as substantive or methodological position is not unproblematic. I have always believed that there is a certain vulnerability in teaching and researching in this way but that this is a strength in terms of process and output. It is not, however, without its dangers. There are tensions around inclusivity and exclusion, empathy and alienation, intimacy and detachment.

I have spent most of my working life teaching, counselling, managing and researching in continuing education, mostly in pre–1992 universities but also in the post-1992, for the Workers' Educational Association (WEA), and for the longest time of all, for the Open University (OU). This last was my first university job as a young mother, one that continued, with varying degrees of commitment, while I worked part- and full-time for other institutions. It was the OU that gave me my first opportunity for research in the 1970s, on student motivation and advice and guidance (see eg Whaley 1978; Richmond and Whaley 1979).

My paid work has always had to be fitted in and around my domestic responsibilities as wife, mother, daughter and sister. When I used to teach students 'how to study' and we looked at books which suggested identifying yourself as an owl or a lark in order to maximise learning, I used to wistfully wonder if I would ever find out my own ornithological identity, since my time, energy and output seemed always to be controlled by something/one else.

At any rate, it has meant that my research experience covers full-time and part-time; academic and 'applied'; scholarly and 'popular'; funded and unfunded; individual and collaborative; as staff and student. Curiously, the three years spent as a full-time paid researcher on a well funded and subsequently published piece of sponsored research was also the time when – to continue the animal imagery – I felt neither fish nor fowl. I not only had permission to devote myself to research, I was paid to do so. Yet the role of researcher in the university was an enigma to many people – was I academic or academic- related? Young and upwardly mobile or wise and already there (in which case I would surely be a Fellow!)? To which 'comfort station' should I be given the keys? An exaggeration of course; yet there is a real enough hierarchy, ambiguity and confusion in research roles and status. 'Whose voices are heard in a piece of academic writing?' (Brookfield, 1993, p 77).

> Most people associate the word 'research' with activities which are substantially removed from day-to-day life and which are pursued by outstandingly gifted persons with an unusual level of commitment. (Howard and Sharpe 1983, quoted in Newton, 1993, p 67)

The frantic transfer market before the 1996 Research Assessment Exercise would seem to endorse this view. There is also no doubt that research can present a frightening prospect to many of us. 'I really believe that research can seriously damage your health' (Marshall, 1994, p 121). For those of us in the university sector, research is a contractual obligation, leading to what Miller and Jones call 'a desperation to publish' (1993, p 5). Just how much pain, pleasure and pursuit there is depends on who we are.

So what of women's research identity? There is no space here to debate the crucial issues of essentialism and difference (see for example, Preece, Zukas in this book) but clearly the issue of identity is a challenging one. O'Rourke illustrates one aspect of the 'identity crisis' in pointing to the tensions in community writing between feminism and class (O'Rourke, 1996).

In writing about national identity, Ascherson talked about:

> a classic old model of identities, It was a concentric model. It was seen from the central dot of all those concentric rings – the individual . . . The model was a statement about the self 'I am the centre of creation'. But it was also a list of overlapping memberships – identities if you like . . . The question which the model does not answer is this: which of these identities, if any, has priority? By which ring does the central dot wish to be identified by others? (Ascherson, 1996, p 82)

How might women researching in CE be defined? How do we define ourselves? Which identity has priority? Do we feel greater affinity with CE or with women? With our academic subject or with andragogical issues? With feminism or with Freire? Do we have to choose one identity over another? We may not want to share Ascherson's vision for future generations as 'Lords of all the rings, the heirs to an infinity of identity' (p 95). We do need to learn from the important debates on essentialism, on difference and diversity, on class, sexual identity, race and ethnicity, on mothers and others, to identify again the category women and draw up a visionary map of CE research with women's distinctive contribution confirmed.

We need to take account of the enormous sea-change in higher education (HE) over the last decade which has had major implications for those working in CE (see, for example, Robertson, 1996; Waterhouse,1996, and the numerous debates on lifelong learning). Any mapping of women researching in CE must be set within a number of boundaries ' . . . the changing boundaries in the moorland of lifelong learning presents an ongoing set of challenges' (Edwards *et al*, 1996 p 6). I mapped the boundaries for myself by seeing the intersections in my own interlocking circles. I realised how important networks, largely though not exclusively, of women, have been in my work (and the subject of my research in the 1980s) and indeed how much of my research has grown from and been encouraged by informal and formal contact and collaboration.[1]

It would be interesting to see whether women or men do more collaborative research, in or out of the field of continuing education. Quantitative data alone would not, however, reveal the gender narrative of collaborative research. My own experience encompasses quite different kinds of joint research. The Breakthrough Charter For Access began with a conference paper (Whaley, 1987a) and was taken forward by a cross-sectoral group of committed, enthusiastic and sensitive women.[2] This last quality was very important as we struggled to respect each others feelings as well as ideas, with a strong commitment to acknowledging each woman's efforts. Researching and writing in this way was not easy in terms of the practical – it took a lot of time, patience and multiple communications – 'are you sure it's OK with you?' – before we reached the stage where I could take responsibility for its eventual publication (Whaley, 1989). But it did work and it was a very happy experience. It was also supported financially and in other ways, by REPLAN[3] which allowed me to develop the research following a high profile launch of the Charter, for a further year.

A contrasting experience of joint research was my two years working as part of a hierarchical team in a mainstream department with a different culture and tradition to that of CE. The roles and relationships were of a different kind to ones I had previously experienced and in the eventual publication my role was acknowledged in an opening appreciation rather than by shared authorship.

It is clear that collaborative research can embrace the very best of women's ways of working (see, for example, Kelly *et al*, 1994; Shakespeare *et al*, 1993; Shuttleworth *et al*, 1995; Unwin, 1995). Based on trust, it can encourage the timid as well as individual and collective confidence and inspiration. But collaborative research also rests on an understanding of the issues of control and power which are so much a part of any story of women's research in CE. There are major questions and tensions to do with research ethos, assessment and rules, resources, recognition, roles (perceived and actual, as West and Alexopoulou (1993, p 106) discuss), ownership and authority, subjectivity and self. As Kelly says in relation to Community Education:

> Status determines the position the individual or group has within the hierarchy of power: the more status an individual or group has the more access they have to resources. What receives public recognition reflects the distribution of power and control in society. (Kelly, 1996, p 101)

Clearly this is a gendered issue:

> Who are the initiators of action within the institution, the controllers of the space and the agenda? . . . All decisions made are value laden and gender determined, for example, the growing emphasis on research and the downgrading of teaching skills are clearly not neutral in their effects. Traditionally men have had more access to research and publishing networks, more domestic support to facilitate research and better promotion prospects, whilst women have been encouraged into caring pastoral roles within the University, which can give little time or opportunity for self advancement. (Davies et al, 1994, p 3)

What of women in CE then? I believe that the ethos of CE happily embraces women's ways of working. However, CE can be and is a wide and changing space (see, for example, Anderson and Gardiner, Law in this book; Duke, 1996; Taylor, 1996). Depending on view(ing) point, the landscape is beautiful or bleak, clear or clouded, familiar or threatening.

THE WHERE: There's a place for us, somewhere a place for us

So how can we map that space? Is CE a place or an idea? An examination of the kinds of published research by women in CE (see Benn in this book) will reveal something of the variety of contexts which CE now encompasses. There is the opportunity (although only briefly in this chapter) to examine these contexts to see what is shared and what is different. Are some places safer and more comfortable for women who want to do research? Do some jobs make research easier? Where do the greatest opportunities lie? One important place where women's voices are not being heard directly is on the Dearing Research Working Group – all nine members are male (*Guardian* 1996). For many of us in the pre-1992 university sector the recent years have been fully focused, although not from personal choice, on the need to develop a successful accredited programme in order for the CE Department to survive. Unfortunately, full time academic staff are still judged by the research criteria that applies to the mainstream, where so very different conditions operate.

However, opportunities do exist precisely because continuing education is different. My work brings me into regular and significant contact with a variety of continuing education providers – WEA, Training and Enterprise Councils (TECs), national and regional committees, voluntary sector groups, community education and development agencies and providers as well as colleagues in HE and FE. Partnership has been both the subject and process in my research in the 1990s, including the relationship between the WEA and the University of Durham.

I collaborated with a colleague from the WEA. Northern Region and another from my University's Community and Youth Unit to submit a research outline to the Economic and Social Research Council (ESRC) (Banks *et al*, 1996). A similar collaboration was with a colleague from a FE college in a bid to Joseph Rowntree

Foundation. Some of my 'work in progress' is in the voluntary sector and linked to concepts of lifelong learning, training and enterprise. I look forward to joint research with a number of practitioner colleagues, including the WEA and a number of community and voluntary sector groups in Teesside. I share Field's view that 'an approach to research which is informed by the ideas and goals of the learning society demands an active engagement between researchers and practitioners' (Field, 1997, p 106).

'Collaboration is now the name of the game in the North East "out of necessity and choice" says Tony Robards, York Pro Vice Chancellor (*Times Higher*, 1997). Collaboration strikes one of the key notes for continuing education in the future, and it is one in which women's voices sing out.

THE WHEN: **Bedlam! Bedlam! Bedlam!**

If collaboration is a keynote, time itself is the key to successful research; not merely having the time but seizing it; meeting the deadlines; knowing the timetables; actually being aware that the opportunity is arriving and knowing when and where to catch it (You know how it is, there isn't one for three years and then six arrive together!).

There are a number of problematic issues here. We operate in different time zones and our body clocks have great difficulty in responding – there is the personal, the institutional, the political, the financial and, for many of us the dreaded reaper of the RAE. Furthermore, research time is quality time; I find that while some aspects of research can be done fairly mechanically, spasmodically, whenever, and irrespective of mind, mood or motivation, much of research is just not like that.

As well as numerous time constraints imposed from without, we construct our own from within. I cannot be the only woman who has felt selfish and guilty by 'indulging' in research when there's things to be done . . . This is a feeling recognised by a number of our women students, regularly articulated in research I did on New Opportunities for Women (NOW) students (see Whaley, 1987, 1987b).

I was struck by recognition of a theory expounded in an American text I was using for my MA students. This was an impressively outlined thesis . . . and I already knew it! I had laughed at Ben Elton's joke (BBC TV *c* early 1990s) that the only people who watch Songs of Praise are schoolchildren with homework for Monday morning; I cut out and kept the Posy Simmond's cartoon (*Guardian c* 1980s) where Wendy Weber has a WHOLE DAY ALONE to write her assignment, only to progress from sharpening quite redundant pencils through dusting window sills to hysterical breakdown as partner and children return home without a meaningful paragraph to show them. In my own case, my partner was doing postgraduate studies as well as working full time for several years after we married. He happily withdrew for a period each evening and left the domestic responsibilities to me. When it came to my turn he suggested we follow that successful pattern. I would sit at my desk upstairs and then – bedlam! bedlam! – down the stairs, partner is placid, children are not. What was I doing? He could cope; I could not.

For those of us without children there will be a similar attack, from within, on our research. We need to take ourselves seriously so that others will do so too. But we also need to be unafraid to show and share what it costs us and other women, in a society which makes us (feel) responsible for the happiness and well-being of so many others.

THE WHAT: **What matters?**

- What matters; what are the subjects of continuing education research?
- What matters; what counts as research? – to ourselves? to the Academy? to the Funding Councils? to the nation?
- What matters; how is it measured? valued?
- What matters; does it matter differently to women than to men?
- What matters; pedagogical, disciplinary, multidisciplinary or interdisciplinary research? What about methodology?
- What matters; what do we want to know?

An awful lot of questions from two words, but then the issue of what CE is, has been debated since the adoption of the term in the 1970s (Fieldhouse, 1996). It took over without pause from the previous long conversation about adult education. The question of what CE research is, is no less problematic. Duke expressed the view that

> 'Until the merger [of UFC and PCFC][4], continuing education research, in so far as it existed and was recognised at all, belonged formally in the University sector, but its existence, identity (in the multi-disciplinary extra-mural tradition), rationale and legitimacy were ambiguous and disputed' (Duke, 1995, p 5).

The importance of being able to point to a distinctive research rationale in the light of the great changes in post-compulsory education, and its implications for CE, is made by Taylor:

> If you are committed, as I am, to continuation of an academic continuing education department structure, then it seems to me that the development of a research culture and performance in continuing education is a very high priority. In the end, subject specialists in continuing education departments may have to make an uncomfortable choice: do they transform themselves into continuing education specialists, albeit with ancillary, subject-based research interests? . . . or is their commitment to their subject paramount . . . ? (Taylor, 1994, p 103)

I feel fortunate that for most of my working life my research has been a happy marriage of the subject-based/disciplinary and the generic/inter-disciplinary, this latter covering a variety of aspects of adult and continuing education, from concepts to contexts to cases. An example of the way my historical research interests were successfully combined with my commitment to continuing education is the project I undertook in 1987, while NOW Course Director at the University of Leeds.[5] The series explored and promoted community history and CE. The making of the series, the transmission (and its repeat two years later), the publication and literally years of feedback and follow-up demonstrated to all involved the excitement and power of both history and learning in people's lives. It was in many respects a woman's story and the framework was of feminist scholarship and analysis. It was also entirely in keeping with the best of CE values and ethos and the project's rationale and making was supported throughout by my colleague, Malcolm Chase, who contributed a chapter to the publication (Chase and Whaley, 1987). I think he and I would agree that it illustrates a successful synergy of CE and subject-based research.

The sibling links between oral history and feminism, born out of a concern to uncover and recover different pasts to the traditional narratives, are well established

(Stuart, 1994). Mary Kennedy *et al* suggested similar 'familiarity' between adult and CE and women's studies (Kennedy *et al,* 1993)

It is slightly less easy to classify my doctoral research into women mature entrants to teaching (Whaley, 1997). It is a historical and feminist analysis with women's experience at the core. Although none of the women returners were students of CE, I would argue that the thesis addresses many of the issues and arguments that preoccupy us as adult educators. Moreover, while the case for dedicated, distinctive CE is compelling, we must not conflate this with a plea for a narrow and monolithic tradition:

> *We must not fall into a kind of andragogical exclusivity. Certainly in the USA and in some European societies, there is a growing convergence of interest among those involved in the systematic study of learning . . . Recognition of common thematic and theoretical interests does not necessarily imply a loss of identity, but it does mean that those who are interested in post compulsory education and training have the opportunity of shaping the agenda for educational research. (Field, 1997, p 106)*

In methodological terms both my subject and CE research are based on the same ethics, values, considerations and questions. Just one of these is a concern for language. 'The language that we speak structures the reality that we know' (Rowe, 1988, p 20). The fascination of language, both as a subject of research as well as often its means of dissemination, is one which seems to me to be significant in both feminist scholarship and in CE research. Both remind the mainstream of the importance of a gender agenda in substance and process, of reflexivity, of ethical considerations, of (under) representation and (in)visibility.

In Taylor's analysis of the contemporary ideological context of CE he notes the significance of the women's movement. (Taylor, 1996, p 185). Whether or not the new and rapidly shifting world of CE will acknowledge and accept women's contribution remains uncertain; the old liberal adult education CE had a somewhat problematic relationship with women's experience and scholarship. We have, I think, to value and evaluate it ourselves. There is much to learn from the work on reflective practice, from instrumental research in areas like health care (see eg Shakespeare *et al*, 1993; Fairbrother and Hibbert, 1996) and from collaborative studies which link women from different sectors and in different situations (see Benn and Gerver 1996, pp 25–26). We will at the same time have to explore critically the relationship between distinctiveness and inclusion, with its tensions and confusions.

There is something else that matters very much: our students (two thirds of them women). CE has always had a major contribution to make to the Academy in pedagogical and pastoral terms. The promotion of research should not be at expense of teaching. Our students (actual and potential) are at the heart of CE. Our research and teaching should be in interaction.

'The Butterfly and the Snake in the Grass' is a metaphor I use in both my teaching and research. The butterfly is an enchanting image. I have heard it used to convey the adult or mature student experience – the caterpillar emerges from the chrysalis transformed by education into a beautiful butterfly which flies away into a brave new dawn. This has always seemed to me to be flawed. The adult student, especially a woman returner, does not fly away leaving the chrysalis/baggage behind. She does not slough off her old skin like a snake does. She travels on, adding layers and learning to accommodate to the experience as well as to whatever subject she has chosen. If we do not recognise this and its implications for adult educators, we overlook one of the distinctive features of CE and a profound link with the holistic approach of women's studies and feminist analysis. This is not to say that learning does not transform, or that in the process people leave things behind. But for some the adding on of layers or the rupture of chrysalis or skin is as much pain as gain; poets like Charlton and Harrison speak with respective poignancy and anger of a sense of loss as well as opportunity experienced by working class boys after a grammar school education (quoted in Williamson, 1990, pp 207–8). Their words struck a resounding chord with many of my adult students.

Conclusion: THIS IS MY VOICE: How was it for you?

I decided to leave the 'why' question to the end, largely because it demands fuller treatment that I can give here and opens a dialogue that others may wish to take up. Why do women do research in CE? Whose decision is it? Who is it for? What do we want for ourselves?

It seems to me that we should learn from what we teach our students. To question; to explore; to use experience to create, test and challenge theory and theory to explain and endorse experience; to demystify the extraordinary and to value the ordinary; to see learning as liberating and life-enhancing – these are all powerful motives for research. We should question the prevailing ethos that often makes research an oppressive burden that drives us instead of offering us a lift. We should have the courage to affirm the importance of research while challenging the way it is defined and operates in the academy. What do we want for our students? A place of safety where the experience of learning is positive and empowering, encouraging independent learning by support. What do we want for women and men who do not yet imagine they might be our students? Access to that same place and whatever they need to claim it as their own.

I was once challenged by a fellow academic on the wisdom of the NOW programme. It does not do the women any favours since they have got to face 'the harsh real world' eventually. It seems to me he might as well have suggested I subject my children to cruelty from day one in order to prepare them for the pain that undoubtedly faces them one day. I prefer the view of Helder Camara:

> 'Teach your child from infancy
>   To love open spaces,
>   widen his [sic] mind
> He will be glad of this,
>   especially if later
> he must endure
>   a life confined
> by a slit window's littleness
>   to one small patch of sky'

We can provide a model from CE for a new 'real world' that values our values, shares our purpose. Research and publication can be one way in which this is achieved. Women's contribution from the margins can transform the centre. We do know.

That's why.

I am very grateful to Mary Kennedy for sharing her wisdom and experience in our initial discussions of this chapter.

Notes

1. I have been/am involved with UACE, FACE, Women's History Network, Women Returners Network, Women and Training Network, Adult Learners Network, REPLAN Networks and a number of community education and voluntary sector networks.
2. Women Returners Network in the North East
3. REPLAN: a Government-funded educational programme to extend opportunities to unemployed adults (see Fordham, 1992).
4. Universities Funding Council (UFC). Polytechnics Funding Council (PFC).
5. 'At the Works', a nationally networked seven part television series.

References

Adamson, F and Kennard, R (1992) *A study of mature entrants to the teaching profession,* Sunderland: University of Sunderland.

Ascherson, N (1996) 'National identity', in Radice, G (ed), *What needs to change: new visions for Britain,* London: HarperCollins, pp 82–95.

Banks, S, McGee, P and Whaley, P (1996) *The learning community,* unpublished research proposal.

Benn, R and Gerver, E (1996) 'Dividing by more than two; shifting paradigms of gender in continuing education research', in Zukas, M (ed), *Diversity and development: futures in the education of adults*, Proceedings of the 26th Annual SCUTREA Conference.

Brookfield, S (1993) 'Breaking the code: engaging practitioners in critical analysis of adult educational literature', *Studies in the Education of Adults,* 25(1), pp 64–91.

Chase, M and Whaley, P (1987) *At the works,* Newcastle: Tyne Tees Television.

Davies, S, Lubelska, C and Quinn, J (eds) (1994) *Changing the subject: women in higher education,* London: Taylor and Francis.

Duke, C (1995) 'Footprints in the sand? The legacy of the University Funding Council's support for research in continuing education', in Hamilton, M and Withnall, A (eds), *Innovation in continuing education provision, teaching and learning: research perspectives,* Lancaster: University of Lancaster, pp 5–14.

Duke, C (1996) 'The Leeds department in the 1960s and the 1990s: and the impact of current trends in university continuing education' in Taylor, R (ed), *Beyond the walls: 50 years of adult and continuing education at the University of Leeds 1946–1996.* Leeds: University of Leeds.

Edwards, R, Hanson, A and Raggatt, P (1996) *Adult learning, education and training 1: boundaries of adult learning* London: Routledge in association with the Open University.

Fairbrother, P and Hibbert, C (1996) 'Back to the future: development and diversity of reflective practice in nurse education', in Zukas, M (ed), *Diversity and development: futures in the education of adults*, Proceedings of 26th Annual SCUTREA Conference, pp 70–73.

Field, J (1997) 'Judging research quality in post-compulsory education and training: lessons of the 1996 assessment exercise', *Studies in the Education of Adults,* 29(1), pp 101–108.

Fieldhouse, R and Associates (1996) *A history of modern British adult education,* Leicester: NIACE.

Fordham, P (1992) 'Comment 1: Replan 1984–1991', *Studies in the Education of Adults,* 24(2), pp 225–228.

Guardian, (1996) 11 October.

Kelly, L, Burton, S and Regan, L (1994) 'Researching women's lives or studying women's oppression? Reflections on what constitutes feminist research', in Maynard, M and Purvis, J (eds), *Researching women's lives from a feminist perspective,* London: Taylor and Francis. pp 27–48.

Kelly, M B (1996) 'Women, credit, status and power', in Smyth, A (ed), *Politics and community*, Papers from the Women's Education Research and Resource Centre Annual Conference, University College Dublin, pp 92–107.

Kennedy, M, Lubelska, C and Walsh, V (eds) (1993) *Making connections: Women's Studies, women's movements, women's lives,* London: Taylor and Francis.

Marshall, A (1994) 'Sensuous sapphires: a study of the social construction of black female sexuality', in Maynard, M and Purvis, J (eds), *Researching women's lives from a feminist perspective*, London: Taylor and Francis. pp 106–124.

Miller, N and Jones, D J (eds) (1993) Introduction, in *Research: reflecting practice,* papers from the 23rd Annual SCUTREA Conference. pp 5–6.

Newton, R (1993) 'Reflecting research practice – from concrete experience to abstract conceptualisation', in Miller, N and Jones, D J (eds), *Research: reflecting practice,* Papers from the 23rd Annual SCUTREA Conference, p 67.

O'Rourke, R (1996) 'Gendered local culture of writing', unpublished conference paper, University of York.

Richmond, A and Whaley, P (1979) *Information for adult education advisors,* Register of Institutional Research and Development, Buckingham: The Open University.

Robertson, D (1996) 'Policy continuity and progress in the reform of post-compulsory and higher education', in Edwards, R et al (eds), *Adult learning, education and training 1: boundaries of adult learning,* London: Routledge in association with The Open University, pp 276–294.

Rowe, D (1988) *The successful self,* London: Fontana.

Shakespeare, P, Atkinson, D and French, S (eds) (1993) *Reflecting on research practice: issues in health and social welfare,* Buckingham: Open University Press.

Shuttleworth, S, Somerton, M and Vulliamy, D (1995) 'Learning from working together: experiencing collaborative research in education', in Hamilton, M and Withnall, A (eds), *Innovation in continuing education provision, teaching and learning: research perspectives,* Lancaster: University of Lancaster, pp 103–111.

Stuart, M (1994) 'You're a big girl now: subjectivities, feminism and oral history', *Oral History,* Autumn, pp 55–62.

Taylor, R (1994) 'The changing role of the professional in university continuing education', in Armstrong, P, Bright, B and Zukas, M (eds), *Reflecting on changing practices, contexts and identities,* papers from 24th Annual SCUTREA Conference, pp 102–104.

Taylor, R (1996) 'The future of university continuing education: "what is to be done?"' in Zukas, M (ed) *Diversity and development: futures in the education of adults,* proceedings of the 26th Annual SCUTREA Conference, pp 183–185.

Times Higher Education Supplement (1997) 4 April.

Unwin, J (1995) 'Group research projects in adult continuing education', in Hamilton, M and Withnall, A (eds), *Innovation in continuing education provision, teaching and learning: research perspectives,* Lancaster: University of Lancaster, pp 25–31.

Waterhouse, R (1996) *Lifelong learning – a European perspective,* FACE Occasional Paper No. 2.

West, L and Alexopoulou, F (1993) 'On keeping a diary: a new approach to reflective practice' in Miller, N and Jones, D J (eds) *Research: reflecting practice,* papers from the 23rd Annual SCUTREA Conference, pp 104–106.

Whaley, P (1978) *Interest course index evaluation,* Register of institutional research and development, Milton Keynes: The Open University.

Whaley, P (1987a) *Access to Education,* unpublished paper, Women Returners' Network in the North East Conference, 20 March 1987, Gateshead.

Whaley, P (1987b) 'New opportunities for women: Cath's story', *Women in touch,* 2, March. Newcastle: Replan pp 12–16.

Whaley, P (1989) *Breakthrough charter for access: quality provision for women in education and training,* Newcastle: Replan/ FEU.

Whaley, P (1997) *Wise women wanted? A study of mature women entrants to teaching 1940–1990,* (ongoing doctoral thesis).

Williamson, B (1990) *The temper of the times: British society since World War II,* Oxford: Blackwell.

Chapter Twelve

Researching difference

Julia Preece

Method is significant in relation to the what of knowledge sought (Weiner, 1994, p 141)

This chapter explores some of the ethical and methodological issues for researching difference in relation to age, disability, race and class. I draw on life history research methods and issues, referring to feminist, post-structuralist theories, their applicability to the notion of difference and their identification of experience as contributing to theory and new knowledge. I then outline my own efforts to research three groups of new adult learners. The majority are women, but identified as 'different' by virtue of their race, class, disability and age. I describe my attempts to accommodate issues of difference in the interview process particularly in relation to my position of privilege as a white, professional and non-disabled researcher. I discuss how far I have succeeded in providing a valid interpretation of the researched voice.

The theory

Post-structuralist thought claims that identities are multiple and fragmented, while knowledge is contextual and situated within a constantly changing set of experiences. People's interpretations of truth and their own identity are contingent on how they are positioned in discourses. Discourses are the all-pervading systems, language and strategies for sustaining cultural values and regimes of truth. Discourses, are also influenced by events in time, often resulting in reconstructed logic which rationalises the new state of being and justifies why things are done in a certain way. The extent to which people's own definitions of truth or knowledge are recognised – or how far they resist oppressive definitions of themselves – depends on how they relate to dominant power structures (Foucault, 1972; Weedon, 1987). For people most on the margins of dominant power relations their own subjugated knowledges create a platform from which they see themselves as outsiders looking in to the centre discourse fields (Hill Collins, 1990; Morris, 1992; Shakespeare, 1994; hooks, 1984). Feminist post-structuralist models of analysis explore gender power relations and their social construction. This framework for interpreting gender difference is increasingly being recognised as applicable for deconstructing other aspects of difference, such as class, age, race and disability, particularly as a research tool (Morris, 1992; Preece, 1995; Skeggs, 1994; Holland and Ramazanoglu, 1994; Sanger 1995).

By simply acknowledging people's difference of class, race, gender, age or disability in the research process, however, two issues arise. First there is a danger of ignoring the differential power relations within these categories and between individuals and society (Maynard, 1994). Consequently descriptive interpretations tend to submerge analysis of oppositional discourses or resistance to power. By the same argument

Gorelick (1991) suggests that the researcher has a responsibility to do more than simply revoice the voice of those on the margins. She argues for a methodology which deals with the 'blindness of privilege' in the researcher – that is the researcher must attempt to move the statements and experiences of the researched beyond where they are by building the research into a historical and social explanation for how difference is both sustained and suppressed, as well as acknowledging the situatedness of the researcher in that explanatory process. In other words the researcher must take a reflexive approach to interpreting the data.

The empirical study tried to identify discourses (language, behaviours, attitudes) of alternative truths and realities by allowing marginalised groups to speak on their own terms. For researchers, however, who are trained in one dominant academic mode to analyse others against given norms, research can be an insidious means of reinscribing, and not recognising appropriately, the cultural difference of 'others'. The feminist post-structuralist stance, therefore, is to maintain the notion of situated knowledge, where the 'oppressed' or unrecognised voices can have 'epistemological privilege'. In other words oppressed knowledge can be superior, but specific and local to the condition of its production (Weiner, 1994; Stanley and Wise, 1993). Experience forms the basis of such knowledge.

The aim, therefore, is to represent the multiple and contradictory realities and resistances of those on the margins in ways which allow their explanations of themselves and their experiences validity in their own historical context. Experience alone is not taken as a given truth, but used to explore, within the context of power relations, alternative knowledge perspectives and as a means of challenging dominant textual versions of truth or normative values. As Skeggs argues on behalf of women:

> *Women's experience carries with it special knowledge and that this knowledge is necessary to challenge oppression. It is because women are placed in a position to struggle against the force and powers that oppress that experience provides them with different understandings and knowledges (Skeggs, forthcoming).*

While Skeggs' standpoint recognises the epistemological privilege of working class women's experience, women with disabilities, women of colour, women of working class origin (and also men from marginalised social groups) would take this view further and claim experience as representing privileged forms of knowledge beyond the category of woman (for example, Morris, 1992; hooks, 1984; Mac an Ghaill, 1994). This feature of epistemological privilege became central to my research; it also provided me with several ethical concerns when I entered into the research process. A particular ethical concern of many researchers is that research is commonly conducted on, rather than by, marginalised groups and that women of difference are denied a central position in the academic research world (Lather, 1991). Morris (1992) takes a pragmatic view to these issues. She details specifically the responsibilities of an able bodied researcher researching people with disabilities. The researcher must use the research first to inform and question her own attitudes; second to question the academic institution's absence of disabled researchers and third as a platform to challenge oppression. She also emphasises the need for differences to be seen in relation to each other, rather than isolation. For post-structuralists, these concerns must be viewed in connection with the shifting and fragmented nature of class and power relations as well as other differences that separate role model researchers from the least powerful.

One final point at stake relates to the status and intersection of 'hired hand' research. That is, face-to-face data collection which is returned by field workers to the research manager for analysis. Gorelick (1991) highlights the potential ambiguity of a strategy which introduces a third human agency in the research process, resulting in 'two subject populations'. She emphasises the oppositional privilege of powerlessness which the situation can create, in that while 'hired' interviewers rarely have access to influencing data analysis or published outcomes, they may have, in Foucauldian terms, a power-resistance or gatekeeping role which may distort what forms of data are selected and passed on. The issue of hired hand research was a feature of my own study and I shall return to this point later.

It is with the above theoretical framework and its contingent issues in mind that I now turn to my engagement with difference as a white, able bodied, professional in the position of privilege over my research subjects, and how I set about collecting and interpreting my data.

The research study

I am responsible for developing learning opportunities for adults who are marginalised from the education system's mainstream by virtue of their educational background which is often linked to their ethnicity, culture, age or disability. Some have experienced educational disadvantage since their school days and many are now in socio-economic or cultural circumstances which further distance them from accessing existing formal educational activities. Participation is contingent on provision which is sensitive to different cultural, linguistic and practical needs — in terms of curriculum, recruitment, additional support and timescales (Preece and Bokhari, 1996). A particular feature of the programme in which I am involved is its employment of role model link staff who liaise directly with community groups and frequently teach on the courses. The rationale behind this strategy relates to the 'standpoint' and epistemological arguments in this chapter. That is, an 'outsider's' connection of 'otherness' with the learner will help to facilitate relationships which might otherwise be missed by the privileged insider looking outwards to different marginalised sectors.

I set out to explore the educational values and historical circumstances which might need to be addressed if differences are to be acknowledged and integrated into dominant practices. While the total research has also involved interviews with other professionals I shall concentrate here solely on issues surrounding contact with the learners and their role model tutors.

For me there are five concerns for my research:

- the need to raise the profile of outsider standpoints;
- the concern to start from and explain the interviewee's position in relation to her wider social context and in particular the world of adult education;
- a commitment to challenging dominant discourses which marginalise and exclude such learners;
- a commitment to making the link of epistemological privilege with my learner groups through the use of tutors and interviewers — but an awareness of the double-sided issue of hired hand research in denying the interviewers their central position or in filtering the data;

- a need to guard against my position of privilege in terms of power and reinscribing the data.

The research process

I set about addressing these concerns in two phases. In the first phase I followed my instinct based on my existing experience of working with disenfranchised adults. For instance, the sole purpose of my research was grounded in a commitment to challenge dominant educational practices by demonstrating the unrecognised values of marginalised adults and ensuring that at least some outsider voices were heard. My purpose in involving the role model interviewers was to encourage just that. They could draw on some shared experiences with the learners as well as a more informed understanding of academic discourses. I was actively allowing opportunities for 'self disclosure' which might facilitate more open discussion with the respondents (Lather, 1991; Reinharz, 1992). Role models were typically, of Asian heritage, a working class background or with experience of disability, depending on the learner group. The notion of role model 'bias' was not to me a particular concern, since views in opposition to dominant theories were what I was seeking to exploit. I also felt that by remaining true to the interview voice I would avoid as much as possible the dangers of reinscription, while being aware of the 'selectivity' process of any research.

I chose three adult learner groups who had remained with the programme for some months. They were also selected for their contrasting representation of 'difference'. They were ten white, working class adults age 36 to 70 years from an urban town; ten white, working class disabled adults aged 35 to 55 years who attended a social services day centre and ten Asian women aged 20 to 30 years who had arrived in England from Pakistan or India in order to get married. The latter consisted of two completely separate learner groups, one Hindu, the other Muslim. In all, 23 out of the 30 people interviewed were women. My intention was to interview each individual once, then again after a twelve month time gap. This gap would serve two purposes for me. I wanted time to absorb and analyse the data and share my findings with the role model tutors with a view to developing a more focused approach for the second round of interviews. I also wanted to explore any long term outcomes or issues which the learners might attribute to their involvement with the programme.

I decided to use a life history approach, around the theme of educational experiences, for the first set of interviews. Life histories seem pertinent for post-structuralist research. Life history enables the interviewee to describe experience not as it is, but how it is seen and interpreted (Usher, 1995). This allows the speaker's voice to be historically and culturally situated and provides clues to how identities are shaped from images other than the historical text version (Aldridge, 1993; Sparkes, 1994). Factual accuracy is not what the researcher is seeking. Rather it is the individual interpretation of change as culturally constructed within its own set of rationalities (Preece, 1996a). Life history can be a medium for validating the notion of difference, fragmentation and multiple identities (Norquay, 1990). The interviewees' stories would provide a source for culturally contextualised versions of education which might reflect their differences from dominant discourse positions. In view of the number of women taking part in the research, the findings were also well placed to highlight gender not as one category of difference but as a complex interface with a range of differences and power relations, influenced by time, place, experience and cultural representation.

By employing role model link staff or tutors as interviewers I hoped to avoid one layer of communication difficulties which have already prevented the majority of these adults from participating in a system which I clearly represented. In addition I was keen that the Asian women would feel free to talk in the interview through their first language to avoid unnecessary language inhibitions. In the event the two role model disabled tutors who had been involved with the day centre both proved unavailable to do the interviews. As I had also been a course tutor over some months for many of the respondents I chose to take on the interviewer role, but still interviewed the two tutors.

Other questions arose around the nature of the samples. I used Glaser and Strauss's grounded theory approach for generating theory from the data, and comparative analysis across the samples (Glaser and Strauss, 1968; Layder, 1993). The intention was to produce illuminative data to generate interest in further research. I chose the three groups as theoretical samples with only a vague notion, based on adult education participation theories (for example, Cross, 1981), that each group would provide me with information that might be of generalisable value. The relationship of the research to feminist methodologies and feminist standpoint epistemology as a theoretical framework to explain the epistemological privilege of the research groups was not yet a gleam in the eye. With only ten people from each sample it was possible only to suggest commonalties of difference within the groups, though some cross comparisons relating to educational values were possible.

There were a number of strengths in my method. Morris's declaration of the importance of researching differences in relation to each other was accommodated. Furthermore, the life history approach highlighted a number of power relationships, perceived realities and struggles for alternative perceptions of truth against often conflicting discourses. The role models in particular became advisors as well as demonstrated layers of difference within their own cultures. In their interviews with me they helped me to focus the analysis on issues which were important for their cultures or experiences. They also read my initial descriptive data analysis and commented on my interpretations so far. In view of my own situatedness they perhaps had more influence than most hired hand researchers, which fed, to some extent back into the final outcomes.

I made assumptions that by remaining true to the learner voice the interviews would speak for themselves. I checked my initial analysis with the role model interviewers and satisfied myself that I was validating their experiences on their terms. Such an approach has been criticised by Lather (1991), Skeggs (1994) and others as not being sufficiently interpretational for the ethical responsibilities of feminist research – describing 'as it is' rather than describing beyond what is. They emphasise that the researcher and her access to academic discourses already influences what is perceived to be reportable knowledge. The process of selection and interpretation, therefore, has already begun. By simply attempting to validate the respondent voices I was placing them in a position of no change and already reinscribing their knowledge. In order to present their experiences in opposition to dominant practices I had to move their voice beyond self validation and into the language of the power holders. By not doing this I was already abusing my position of privilege as researcher by acting as gatekeeper to the opportunity for their differences to be acknowledged beyond how they saw themselves. By adopting a more theoretical approach to the data, of course, I was also moving the researched into a field which lay outside their own (and at this point my own) discourses. The process of further translation was a risk which I felt uneasy about.

At this stage my position as a woman seemed a very tenuous link to both the life realities of those I had interviewed and to the research relationship I had created with my 'hired hand' researchers. The issue of 'ownership' or gender mutuality was fraught with varying expectations and values which perhaps had less to do with my gender but more to do with my status as a white, Western university representative, the location of university people in the minds of the interviewees and their own understanding of why people interview them in the first place.

Explaining my choice of theory

These insights, however, only emerged in theoretical form during the second phase when I was able to ground them in concepts of difference, fragmentation and shifting identities. Although gender was a constant category across all three groups, this in itself was not sufficient. I needed a theory which acknowledges a multiplicity of positions and above all recognises experience as a legitimate construction of the situated knowledges which were emerging as a result of the interviewees' class, disability, religious and cultural backgrounds. While post-modernism challenged the essentialist notions of woman (for example, Nicholson 1990 and Zukas in this book) I also needed a theory which legitimated new ways of seeing and knowing, which didn't reduce all knowledge to non-comparable situations but which allowed the flexibility of shifting positions of knowledge within culturally identifiable discourse frameworks. Black feminism challenges the concept of gender as a single source of oppression but also challenges post-modernism for its rejection of all 'grand narratives' – that is, all ultimate definitions. I felt that a feminism which allowed the 'strategic essentialism' required by writers of different oppressions (for example, Brah 1992), but which analysed how oppression works and how resistance is possible, would provide me with a sufficient range of perspectives to both define and leave open the layers of discourse and situated values for each interview sample. The feminist post-structuralist framework helped me to see how power is exercised through discourse and the role people play in their own power relations. I decided to apply the feminist model of post-structuralism, drawing on feminist standpoint epistemologies, to help me form equivalent models of analysis for disability, class and race.

Armed with these new forms of analysis, the consequent power relations between interviewer and interviewee seemed to operate at many levels. These levels included a mixture of gender, class, status and specific cultural or physical issues. My role as interviewer to the adults with disabilities, for instance, created a number of reactions. The participants were accustomed to responding in varying degrees, to carers. Social care status is often conferred on women, and both the men and women respondents would have frequent experience of interacting with professionals in this capacity. Their responses to me often reflected their feelings about professional social workers, or of people who had some form of interventionist status – both regarding their disability and with regard to their previous life experiences of professional figures.

A number, for instance, refused to let me interview them in their homes. Indeed one woman who did, stated she felt very uncomfortable about it because the situation was too similar to a social worker's visit. The interaction in these interviews could also be plotted on a continuum of responsiveness in proportion to how well they trusted me as a course tutor. For this group their disability circumstances were closely intertwined with working class educational and social and family backgrounds. My position, as researcher, seemed to be viewed without reference to my gender, but more in relation to how well I understood and respected each individual as a person and someone with ability to learn: 'You made me feel comfortable – you didn't treat me as if I was thick,' (from one male interviewee). Linguistically, however, my position as someone who controlled the data, was unassailable. The responsibilities of respecting class, language, a range of disability experiences and perceptions of power in relation to themselves and their interactions with me, were great.

While I felt constrained to be the interviewer for this group, I felt more secure in the knowledge that the other interviews would be conducted by (female) peers with shared experiences of their town, language and culture. These interviews were preceded by discussions over interview technique and appropriate question wording, as well as some pilot interviews. The Asian women confirmed the value to them of bilingual and same-sex interviewers and one interviewer confirmed that many cultural and religious questions would not have been answered so frankly to a white questioner. For the working class interviews, the responses from wives about their husbands suggested to me that a woman interviewer had secured information from the women, at least, which might otherwise have been withheld. Equally, I felt that the interviewer's ability to understand and therefore to prompt local experiences and attitudes produced class-specific data which might also have been withheld from me, irrespective of my gender or age. My hired hand researchers then became crucial extricators and participant interpreters, as well as representatives, of difference which is multiple and complex, particularly when intertwined with the higher education interface. Their role in the research process became in itself a feature of the analysis.

Conclusion

My conclusion from these varying issues is that gender was only one determining factor in all the interviews. Indeed the responses from men and women were influenced by class, age, religion, culture and shared experiential backgrounds. Each interview produced information that was particular to that interview relationship. This does not mean the data was not valid but it confirmed the complexity of truth and reality.

By simply reproducing the interview voice, then, I was inhibited from exploring the power relationships during and prior to the interview which had helped each individual to build their own identity and position themselves now in relation to adult education. I took heart from Gorelick's (1991) emphasis on the need to make theoretical connections between differences and the value of theory in helping the marginalised voice to see beyond what is already apparent. The one common factor for all these (men and) women was their difference and distance from the centre discourse practices for adult and continuing education.

The research issue no longer became 'whose voice am I using?' – but about exposing assumptions about gender as a definitive category, as well as other relations in research. It became focused on a concern to present difference as something which must be continually redefined but also integrated into dominant discourses. The analysis is about exposing how all people on the margins, irrespective of gender, remain unnoticed because the dominant language ideology fails to recognise their existence as a category with sub-categories and, therefore, their discourses as providing new sources of knowledge.

Research is always value-laden – I have tried to recognise this by acknowledging the values of those involved in the research, using a theoretical framework which explores people's changing positions and knowledge perspectives in relation to their own lives. – I also drew comparisons across and within the groups concerning the common experience of managing their difference. Role model tutors and hired hands provided additional guidance in interpreting the cultures of the study groups. They also demonstrated the effect of their own experience and identity on drawing out, as well as influencing, the interview data.

The problems of my role as researcher, therefore, were multiple. As the groups were already situated in an unequal power relationship, even with role model researchers, the value-load of any research findings would still apply. I felt that the extent of their marginality justified the use of role models where these were available. Where they were not, the data could be seen in the context of a different power relationship, but which would still serve as a valuable archive of discourses which are rarely portrayed in research. The research will always be embraced by my voice, but by collecting examples of less researched values I could see contrasting issues more clearly. Helped by the theory I could make the necessary connection beyond just representing their experiences. It enabled me, for example to analyse marginalised discourses in respect of power relations, hegemony and styles of resistance, which both formed and were informed by alternative knowledges. These findings are the subject of other papers (Preece, 1996a; 1996b; 1997). They have implications for how continuing education is packaged and presented to a range of social groups of both sexes. My bridging role in the research becomes equally a bridging responsibility to ensure appropriate learning opportunities for different sectors of society. This latter feature places the research within a feminist ethic which aims to 'make resistant discourses more widely heard . . . to . . . interrupt the power imbalances' (Weiner, 1994, p 141).

References

Aldridge, J (1993) 'The textual disembodiment of knowledge in research account writing', *Sociology*, 27(1), pp 53–66.

Brah, A (1992) 'Difference, diversity and differentiation', in Donald, J and Rattansi, A (eds), *'Race', culture and difference*, London: Sage, pp 126–148.

Cross, K P (1981) *Adults as learners: increasing participation and facilitating learners* (2nd ed), California: Jossey Bass.

Fairclough, N (1989) *Language and power*, London: Longman.

Foucault, M (1972) *The archaeology of knowledge*, London: Routledge.

Glaser, B and Strauss, A L (1968) *The discovery of grounded theory*, London: Weidenfeld and Nicolson.

Gorelick, S (1991) 'Contradictions of feminist methodology', *Gender and Society*, 5(4) pp 459–477.

Hill Collins, P (1990) *Black feminist thought*, London: Routledge.

Holland, J and Ramazanoglu, C (1993) 'Women's sexuality and men's appropriation of desire', in Ramazanoglu, C (ed), *Up against Foucault*, London: Routledge, pp 239–264.

hooks, b (1984) *Feminist theory: from margin to centre*, California: South End Press.

Jones, A (1993) 'Becoming a "Girl": poststructuralist suggestions for educational research', *Gender and Education*, 5(2), 157–166.

Kelly, L, Burton, S and Regan, L (1994) 'Researching women's lives or studying women's oppression? Reflections on what constitutes feminist research', in Maynard, M and Purvis, J (eds), *Researching women's lives from a feminist perspective,* London: Taylor and Francis, pp 27–48.

Lather, P (1991) *Getting smart,* London: Routledge.

Layder, D (1993) *New strategies in social research,* Cambridge: Polity.

Mac an Ghaill, M (1994) *The making of men,* Milton Keynes: Open University Press.

Maynard, M (1994) 'Race, gender and the concept of difference in feminist thought', in Afshar, A and Maynard, M (eds), *The dynamics of race and gender,* London: Taylor and Francis, pp 9–25.

Morris, J (1992) 'Personal and political: a feminist perspective on researching physical disability', *Disability, handicap and society,* 7(2), pp 157–166.

Nicholson, J (1990) *Feminism/postmodernism,* London: Routledge.

Norquay, N (1990) 'Life history research: memory, schooling and social difference', *Cambridge Journal of Education,* 20(3), pp 291–300.

Preece, J (1995) 'Discourse and culture', in Bryant, I (ed), *Vision, invention – celebrating adult education,* Proceedings of the 25th Annual SCUTREA Conference, pp 154–159.

Preece, J (1996a) 'Class and disability: influences on learning expectations', *Disability and Society,* 11(2), pp 191–204.

Preece, J (1996b) 'Positions of race and gender: excluded discourses in continuing education', in Zukas, M (ed), *Diversity and development: futures in the education of adults,* Leeds: SCUTREA, pp 158–161.

Preece, J (1997) 'Deconstructing the discourse of community education and development for women of Muslim Pakistani Heritage: alternative solutions?' in Apitsch, U (ed), *International year of lifelong learning,* Bremen: ESREA, pp 1–12.

Preece, J and Bokhari, R (1996) 'Making the curriculum culturally relevant', *Journal of Further and Higher Education,* 20(3), pp 70–80.

Reinharz, S (1992) *Feminist methods in social research,* Oxford: Oxford University Press.

Sanger, J (1995) 'Five easy pieces: the deconstruction of illuminating data in research writing', *British Education Journal,* 21(1), pp 89–98.

Shakespeare, T (1994) 'Cultural representation of disabled people: dustbins for disavowal?', *Disability and Society,* 9(3), pp 282–300.

Skeggs, B (1994) 'Situating the production of feminist ethnography', in Maynard, M and Purvis, J (eds), *Researching women's lives from a feminist perspective,* London: Taylor and Francis, pp 72–92.

Skeggs, B (forthcoming) *Becoming respectable,* London: Sage.

Sparkes, A (1994) 'Life histories and the issue of voice: reflections on an emerging relationship', *International Journal of Qualitative Studies in Education,* 7(2), pp 165–183.

Stanley, L and Wise, S (1993) *Breaking out again,* London: Routledge.

Usher, R (1995) 'Telling the story of the self/deconstructing the self of the story', in Bryant, I (ed), *Celebrating adult education,* Southampton: SCUTREA, pp 178–183.

Weedon, C (1987) *Feminist practice and poststructuralist theory,* London: Blackwell.

Weiner, G (1994) *Feminisms in education,* Milton Keynes: Open University Press.

Chapter Thirteen

A fair hearing for the fair sex

Roseanne Benn

When I read in this book and elsewhere about women being oppressed I am very conscious of my privileged position of being a white well-educated middle-class woman. This reflects the ever-present ambiguities of difference and diversity in the concept of woman clearly expressed by Zukas in this volume. As a researcher and one whose research is often concerned with gender and gender difference, I certainly recognise and do not contest the oppression in many women's lives. But in the context of research, I feel a sense not of being oppressed but of being ignored. I feel that my words and those of other women staff and learners in adult education are not being properly listened to and heard. This is particularly galling in a discipline where the majority of students are women, there has been a substantial increase in the number of programmes aimed specifically or mainly at women (Access provision, for one, comes to mind), and a high proportion of staff are women (even if usually at the less well paid end of the profession) (Benn and Zukas, 1993; McGivney, 1990). It is particularly important in higher education where the medium for being heard is publication and the outcome of publishing is crucial not only for career progression but indeed for job security.

This chapter is the outcome of my attempt to understand whether women are being heard in the 1990s in adult education research. Are women's voices being heard as writers – is women's research being published? Are women learners and women's ways of learning being considered in research studies and in particular are they being researched as individuals located in specific social, economic, historical and political environments? It will also touch on the contribution that feminist thought and the feminist voice has to make to adult education provision and research.

Gender difference: myth or reality?

Before moving on to the empirical results, I will first briefly justify why I consider in research on the adult classroom, gender is always a significant research variable. There is still a common assumption that the teaching offered to men and women is experienced in the same circumstances. This view assumes that equivalence of outcome is assured if difference is ignored. It is typified by comments such as 'I concentrate on the student and ignore their sex (or race, etc)', offering the same resources to all, and declaring an equal opportunities intent without considering the implications of this on the institution, staff and students. This is to ignore the deeper issues involved in learning outcomes of students as opposed to provision by teachers and institutions. Learning opportunities are orientated to the dominant values in society. These are reflected in the education system as a whole and are concerned with helping individuals to adapt to dominant educational and cultural structures without questioning the modes by which education controls differential access to knowledge and power. This ensures that the rhetoric of 'equal opportunities' and 'individualism' obscures the way in which terms like 'individual need' and 'student centred' are socially constructed and located in ways that make knowledge more readily available to certain groups (Keddie, 1980). However, a constuctionist approach to learning suggests that it is impossible for any two learners to construe the same learning experience in the same way. In particular, the different messages carried for males and females by social, political and economic contexts are part of the circumstances in which learning is set and hence are strongly influential on the outcomes. Learner expectations, societal expectations and tutor and institutional behaviour all sit in and are influenced by this context. The formal learning setting is a socio-political setting within which different messages are given to and received by different groups of students (Burton, 1990). As a report on gender and schooling concludes, 'Girls may follow the same curriculum as boys – may sit side by side with boys in classes taught by the same teacher – and yet emerge from school with the implicit understanding that the world is a man's world, in which women can and should take second place' (Stanworth, 1983, p 8). I would argue that the same can be said for women and men learners.

Researchers and research are always located in a socio-political and historical framework. The attitudes within society affect the attitudes of researchers. An example of this is the evolving attitude of researchers interested in girls learning mathematics. In the 1960s it was generally believed that girls were mathematically less able than boys and research concentrated on 'why girls can't do mathematics?'. By the 1970s, biological determinism had been largely discredited and, supported by the growing belief in social explanation for gender differences and the re-emergence of the women's movement, researchers were concentrating on achievement rather than ability. So 'why girls don't do mathematics?'. Today it is becoming clearer that girls do achieve as well as boys in mathematics but choose to participate less. The question now is 'why girls won't do mathematics?' (Benn, 1997; Willis, 1989). There are many in our society, including but not confined to feminists, who share a basic recognition that the position of women in society is one of disadvantage and see education as one of the ways of challenging that disadvantage. They recognise the experience of individual women but locate that experience in the wider structure of society and the recognition that other women have shared or do share the experiences of the individual woman (Coats, 1994). I will seek to identify whether adult education research and publications exclude and marginalise women and if so, place the marginalisation within a broader canvas.

Research and power

Carr and Kemmis (1986) suggest that research is undertaken to 'deepen and extend our knowledge of why social life is perceived and experienced in the way it is'. But underneath this seemingly straightforward statement it needs to be seen that what is researched, who researchers are, who submits and gets accepted for publication, how research is carried out, and what methodologies are used, all these are deeply political questions. There is a close link between power and knowledge, between power and whose voices are heard, between power and the concept and ownership of a discourse. As Foucault so powerfully expresses it, through research we can 'rediscover the silent murmuring, the inexhaustible speech that emanates from within the voice that one hears' (1986, p 28).

I shall look at the concept of discourse relating this to the discourse of adult education research. One aspect of the term discourse is that of the social process through which collective understandings are constructed by groups of people with a common interest. A specific discourse consists of a loose knit collection of concepts, terms, assumptions, explanatory principles, rules of argument and background knowledge which are shared among the members of that discourse community (Northedge, 1994). The term discourse is used in this context to emphasis the social nature of reading and writing practices.

A discourse has the power to create reality by naming that reality and giving it meaning. It is not just a matter of words but real power with the discourse able to deem what is 'real' and 'true' and hence what is included and what is excluded. What is not named may not even be noticed. The result can be that the social and cultural life of some groups in our society go un-named and un-noticed and hence the 'silent murmurings'. We all belong to a multiplicity of discourses, some informal such as gardening or tennis, some more specialised and elaborate such as law or medicine. Some formal discourses require considerable training to enter but bestow corresponding prestige and status. Who controls the discourse of adult education research, the dominant groups in adult education society (white middle-class middle-aged males?), or groups less well heard (including women, ethnic minorities, the disabled)?

Notions of common sense and rationality are expressed by the dominant culture through culturally specific discourses. The dominant rationality in society is based on narrowly defined boundaries measured against particular norms which ignores alternative discourses, languages and practices. It also ignores power relations and influences of historical circumstances on the different discourses, their practices and constructions of reality (Preece, 1995). Hence certain patterns of human development become 'natural' or the manifestation of progress while other cultural values and forms of knowledge are not recognised. The narrative of development forces convergence to the 'same' because difference is either marginalised or treated as a threatening 'other' (Usher, 1995). There are alternative realities, truths and discourses which are not recognised by dominant cultures and this causes the marginalisation of certain groups in society. Within education as in society in general, postmodern thought postulates alternative discourses but again some of these are not valued or represented in Western academic discourse. To hear these discourses, we must 'rediscover the silent murmuring'. Postmodernist deconstruction echoes this desire for rediscovery by focusing on that which may be missing from or hidden in the text and celebrating diversity, a plurality of perspectives and the partiality of all knowing. Does this appear in adult education publications? It is clear that within the construction of discourses lies power and the ownership of knowledge. The construction of the adult education discourse lies to a great extent on the adult education literature. To identify who controls the discourse, we need to examine who controls and who participates in the literature.

Many adult educators are committed to empowerment of their students through the educational process so in adult education, if no where else, the silent murmuring should be heard. But, as Gramsci's ideas of contradictory consciousness suggests the discourses of adult educator researchers draw upon many influences and fragments of many ideologies (discussed in more detail in Benn and Burton, 1995). These discourses may find themselves at odds with the dominant or hegemonic research discourses. Fragments of ideologies or ideas may be absorbed by researchers to create a 'mosaic' which may be unsystematic, lack coherence and subject to influence. It may even be contradictory. The resultant consciousness in individuals may prove frustrating and allow the domination of other more powerful ideologies, cultures or discourses. Hence researchers may be seduced by the hegemonic research discourse to greater or lesser degree. Forces ranged on the side of conformity to the dominant discourse are formidable.

Alternative research discourses

Woman-centred research questions basic assumptions and paradigms while looking for alternative approaches. It investigates both women as individuals and their role in society. Gender-aware research would lead to a review of adult education learning theory, a focus on women's experience of learning and education and an investigation of the gender implications on both the learning and teaching process (Hayes, 1992). It would lead to research that was for women, not about women (Zukas, 1993). Feminist research would promote women's perspective; through action research and hence to praxis; be based on standpoint theory; acknowledge power relationships between researcher and researched; and be aware of authority and power in research and the written representation of research. It would endeavour to clarify how adult education provision benefits, disadvantages or otherwise, different groups of women. Feminist reconceptualisation of theory and research would counteract the potential male biases that perpetuate exclusion and misrepresentation of women. Culture and our way of thinking was shaped by a male perspective which applied even when the life identity and thought of women were considered. This still leads to omissions, blind spots and biases which destroy reality and may invalidate a research project and its findings. Researchers, both male and female, consciously or unconsciously transmit their own interests and socio-economic conditioning (see Zukas's critique of Belenky *et al*, 1993; Preece this book).

Methodology

To investigate whether women are obtaining a fair hearing in the 1990s in the adult education research world, five outlets for publications were considered. *Studies in the Education of Adults* is the foremost refereed British adult education journal published biannually. The *International Journal of Lifelong Education* is a refereed journal attracting both international contributors and subscribers. Both these journals are theoretically based with a target group of researchers and scholars in the field. The *Journal of Access Studies (JAS)* is refereed, attracts mainly British contributors and subscribers. It concentrates on one aspect of adult education, namely access, and is aimed at practitioners, researchers and scholars. *Adults Learning* contains shorter, non-refereed articles very much aimed at keeping practitioners in the field up-to-date on new initiatives and developments. I have also included the conference proceedings of *The Standing Conference on University Teaching and Research in the Education of Adults (SCUTREA)*. The annual SCUTREA conference is the main forum for researchers and scholars in adult education to meet and share ideas. As such its proceedings are a major outlet for the dissemination of research and developments in adult education. Although historically membership was restricted to university staff, it has now widened to a broader constituency. The abstracts are carefully refereed but not the papers themselves.

The period considered is January 1990 to August 1997. To examine if women researchers' voices are being heard, the proportion of women to the total number of contributors has been calculated. The emphasis on women-specific issues has been assessed by finding the percentage of the number of articles with an explicit focus on women as providers; learners; women's education; women's programmes; male/female roles; and gender difference or bias in any process or activity or outcome of adult education to the total number of papers. Power over whose voice is heard lies with the editor(s) and the editorial body so the gender balance of these roles is also considered.

In a very small number of cases it has not been possible to identify the gender of an author. Whether a paper is on a women-specific issue or not has sometimes been a subjective judgement and I have not included in this category the very few articles specifically on men's provision. This chapter has not considered quantitatively whether articles in the 1990s are gender-aware or otherwise though a subjective comment will be made in the analysis.

Findings

Interestingly the *JAS*, publishing in an area of adult education where women staff and students form an even larger proportion than the rest of adult education, has as we might expect the highest proportion of women contributors but, at about a half, this does not represent proportionally the number of women working in the area. Very surprisingly, with over two-thirds of Access students being women, only ten per cent of articles are on women's provision, courses, etc (Benn and Burton, 1994). Many more articles include gender as a social variable of disadvantage alongside eg class or race but are not gender-aware in the manner defined earlier in this chapter. The editors and editorial body have a gender balance that favours men. The annual conference of the Forum for Access Studies which had close links with *JAS* did not publish proceedings, but because of its informal nature did provide a safe training ground for women (and men) who wished to disseminate their research findings.

Table 13.1.　CE publications 1990–1997

Journal	Number of papers	Authors			On women as %	Editors % women	Ed. body % women
		Total	Women	% women			
Access Studies	129	183	97	53.00	10.00	31	45.80
Adults Learning	203	253	131	51.78	11.80	7	n/a
IJLE	194	267	71	26.60	4.60	0	7.70
SCUTREA	344	464	232	50.00	13.10	44.40	45.20
Studies	102	120	31	25.83	10.80	53.30	43.70

AL has a strong emphasis on reporting provision, it is not refereed and contact with the editor is in my experience friendly, helpful and not intimidating. Nevertheless still only about a half of contributors are women. Articles on women which are about twelve per cent are very much concentrated in special editions on women's provision. *AL* has had a very small number of guest editors as women mainly for such occasional editions.

The *IJLE* has only about a quarter of its contributors being women and less than five percent of its papers on women's issues. The *IJLE* has never had a female editor (though this I believe is due to change shortly) and it has never had more than a tiny proportion of its editorial body being women

SCUTREA conferences are attended by roughly equal numbers of men and women with the same number of each writing. SCUTREA conferences allow a high freedom of choice in topic. Abstracts are refereed stringently but rejection is rare with authors being encouraged to rewrite. Over the years examined, the proportion of women authors was less than a third in 1990; increasing to just under a half for 1991, 1992, 1993, 1994, 1995; moving to almost 60 per cent in 1996 and 1997. The proportion of papers on women has fluctuated with a very high 20 per cent in 1997, the year of a large international conference. Many of these 1997 papers came from overseas contributors and many other articles from non-UK contributors were highly gender-aware. The editors and editorial body are both slightly balanced towards men. The better-than-average performance by SCUTREA in the area of gender has not been the result of a deliberate gender policy but might be attributable to a concerted effort to make SCUTREA more accessible to a wider range of contributors both in Britain and overseas. The papers on women in the SCUTREA proceedings are highly gender-aware and many written from very well-informed theoretical feminist perspectives.

Studies has only a quarter of its contributors being women with just over ten per cent of articles being highly gender-aware theoretical pieces. For the first half of the period considered the editor was a woman and for the second half the number of women has exceeded men on the editorial body. As Hayes (1992) suggests, *Studies* publishes theoretical work which can be characterised as conceptual analysis opinion pieces. This would suggest a journal receptive to social critique.

There are of course other outlets for women's voice in adult education to be heard. The WEA produced a series of pamphlets between 1984 and 1989 entitled *Breaking our silence* as well as a Women's Studies magazine. There are also a few books published on women and adult education, particularly by the National Institute of Adult Continuing Education (NIACE), the Open University Press and Taylor and Francis.

Discussion

Apart from SCUTREA conference proceedings there is no discernible trend that contributions by women are increasing, nor that women are more likely to be editors. However, women more likely to be equally represented (SCUTREA) or in the majority (*JAS, Studies*) on editorial bodies. *IJLE* lags a long way behind in this respect. Perhaps women are publishing elsewhere in which case we need to bring this writing into the adult education mainstream. Many adult education writers espouse social justice. Can this be a legitimate aim when so many adult education tutors and students are women yet their voices still remain perhaps not silent murmurings, but certainly not the loud shout that their numbers would justify? The number of articles on or about women has stayed approximately constant over the period.

The findings lead to the conclusion that fundamentally women's voice is not heard as clearly as men's; positions of power in decision-making in publications still mainly rests with men; and gender and gender issues still remain very much a minority interest in the field. There are, as is to be expected in our fragmented post-modern world, many factors contributing to this state of affairs. These include *inter alia* the profile of feminism and feminist thought in society in the 1990s; the mental maps of adult educators, researchers, providers where other issues such as funding, post-modernism itself have become dominant; the move from collectivism to individualism; the concern to ensure adult education as a 'respectable' field of study; funding council attitudes to gender studies; the impact, often silent and hidden, of the refereeing process; issues of presentation ie oral or written. Issues of time – those publish who ruthlessly carve out time to do so. Are women conscientiously running their programmes rather than writing? These and other factors and attitudes need to be considered and changed if the proportions given in Table 13.1 are to reflect a fairer representation.

Hayes and Smith (1994) identify articles in adult educational journals from both sides of the Atlantic which position women in one of five ways: women as adult learners – learners who happen to be women; women as deficient in personal attributes such as confidence or study skills; women coping with new social roles such as increased participation in, for example, higher education or workforce; women as marginalised or under-represented; women as collaborative learners where gender is seen as the base for preferred learning styles; and women as feminists. The last category are very much the minority in 1990s publications. In general, these articles take little note of the social, economic, cultural and political conditions of being female with a tendency to use stereotypes rather than feminist scholarship (Blundell, 1992). There is limited awareness of sex as a social variable with the associated recognition of the need for a pluralist perspective in research, appropriate language and a layered recognition of difference and diversity (Eichler and Lapointe, 1985).

The importance of gender as a significant research variable was argued in the first section of the chapter. In addition feminist thought has much to contribute to adult education research. Feminists challenge much of existing structures and locate theory at the point of lived experience. They argue that all knowledge is subjective and partial and that the establishment in adult education has 'preferred' knowledge exercising conscious or unconscious partiality. Feminist thinking challenges curriculum design. For example, Parsons (1990) takes curriculum thinking in a new direction and suggests new areas of enquiry which may redraw the map of traditional academic disciplines. Lack of articles from a feminist persuasion may reflect adult education's insecurity as discipline, seeking the safety of conventional and traditional research paradigms in order to protect the still fledgling area of study.

The extent to which gender issues remain a minority interest in the field shows the extent to which all adult education and women's education is or is not informed by theory or itself does or does not inform theory (Malcolm, 1992). It is impossible to form coherent strategies for women's education if it is not clear what is being attempted, lessons learned from experience are not available in an appropriate form and there is a lack of theoretical base for practice. Providers need the scholarship. The lack of systematic research makes it impossible to say with any certainty what effect provision has on women's lives.

If gender awareness were to be there in all adult education research, one outcome might be a reconceptualisation of the field of study, a re-examination of assumptions and empowerment for both researchers and researched. As Parsons (1990) argues, the challenge of feminism is the critical questioning of present paradigms, and the search for justification and/or change. Gender-aware research and theorising can link to the curriculum through attitude, language and power and hence the identification of new possibilities. Whether the feminism used is liberal for equality of treatment and status or radical for different opportunities which reflect the uniqueness of women, it can enrich adult education writing and, by encouraging a greater understanding of the majority of students, might lead to a more liberatory adult education provision.

References

Benn, R (1997) *Adults count too: mathematics for empowerment,* Leicester: NIACE.

Benn, R and Burton, R (1994) 'Participation and the mathematics deterrent', *Studies in the Education of Adults,* 26(2), pp 236–49.

Benn, R and Burton, R (1995) 'Access and targeting: an exploration of a contradiction', *International Journal of Lifelong Education,* 14(6), pp 444–58.

Benn, R and Zukas, M (eds) (1993) *Women and gender issues in continuing education,* Warwick: UACE.

Blundell, S (1992) 'Gender and the curriculum of adult education', *International Journal of Lifelong Education,* 11(3), pp 199–216.

Burton, L (1990) 'Passing through the mathematics critical filter – implications for students, courses and institutions', *Journal of Access Studies,* 5(1), pp5–17.

Carr, W and Kemmis, S (1986) *Becoming critical,* Basingstoke: Falmer.

Coats, M (1994) *Women's education,* Buckingham: SRHE and Open University Press.

Eichler, M and Lapointe, J (1985) *On the treatment of the sexes in research,* Ottawa: Social Sciences and Humanities Research Council of Canada.

Foucault, M (1986) *Power/knowledge,* Brighton: The Harvester Press.

Gilligan, C (1982) *In a different voice,* Cambridge, MA: Harvard University Press.

Hayes, E (1992) 'The impact of feminism on adult education publications: an analysis of British and American journals', *International Journal of Lifelong Education,* 11(2), pp 125–38.

Hayes, E and Smith, L (1994) 'Women in adult education: an analysis of perspectives in modern journals', *Adult Education Quarterly,* 44(4), pp 201–221.

Keddie, N (1980) 'Adult education: an ideology of individualism', in Thompson, J *Adult Education for a Change,* London: Hutchinson.

Malcolm, J (1992) 'The culture of difference: women's education re-examined', in Miller, N and West, L (eds), *Changing culture and adult learning,* Boston: SCUTREA, pp 52–55.

McGivney, V (1990) *Access to education for non-participant adults,* Leicester: NIACE.

Northedge, A (1994) 'Access as initiation into academic discourse', in Lemelin, R (comp) *Issues in Access to Higher Education,* Portland: University of Southern Maine, pp 145–51.

Parsons, S (1990) 'Feminist challenges to curriculum design', *Studies in the Education of Adults,* 22(1), pp 49–58.

Preece, J (1995) 'Discourse and culture', in Bryant, I (ed), *Vision, invention and intervention – celebrating adult education,* Southampton: University of Southampton, pp 154–59.

Stanworth, M (1983) *Gender and schooling: a study of sexual divisions in the classroom,* London: Hutchinson.

Usher, R (1995) 'Telling the story of self/deconstructing the self of the story', in Bryant, I. (ed), *Vision, invention, intervention: celebrating adult education,* Southampton: University of Southampton, pp 178–83.

Willis, S (1989) *Real girls don't do maths: gender and the construction of privilege,* Victoria: Deakin University Press.

Zukas, M (1993) 'Feminist issues in adult education research: links and conflicts', in Miller, N and Jones, D (eds), *Research: reflecting practice,* Boston: SCUTREA, pp 38–41.

Section Four

Engaged to the institution

Chapter Fourteen

Women staff and equal opportunities

Elizabeth Bird

In this chapter I will be drawing primarily on my own experience and from four perspectives: as a sociologist; as a trade union activist; as a 'manager' or Head of Department; and, finally, as an advocate. I have been involved in adult education all my working life as the first money I earned as a graduate was in respect of teaching an evening class in A level Sociology at Brighton Tech in 1968. My experience has been in pre-1992 universities, so my perspective is inevitably confined to that sector, but I will try to draw parallels and comparisons with other providers.

Universities in the United Kingdom, from the perspective of a sociologist, are essentially large scale bureaucracies, situated in the public sector but not wholly publicly funded, and subject to employment law and practices under both UK and European legislation. While it might be thought that large public sector institutions would be in the vanguard of 'best practice' in the field of equal opportunities, in fact, as is well known, academia has been marked by profound gender inequalities in respect of the employment and promotion of academic staff (Acker and Piper, 1990; Jackson, 1990; Hansard, 1990). As employers, universities are obliged to comply with the law relating to sex discrimination, which falls primarily under the Sex Discrimination and Equal Pay Acts. The policy of the institution may range from minimum legal compliance to a more proactive commitment to best practice and to the positive promotion of equal opportunities, perhaps in areas where there are no legal requirements, such as sexual orientation or child care provision.

The effect of being a member of the European Union has been to increase the extent and reach of the law such that, being a large bureaucracy, a university may well use its personnel or legal staff resources to advise on and monitor employment practices in the light of judgements under the European legislation. Universities may be well informed but not necessarily well intentioned, or, they may be well intentioned but not necessarily well informed. Although it is difficult to generalise, in relationship to gender and equal opportunities, universities have been rather less well informed and less well intentioned than many other public sector large bureaucratic employers, such as local authorities (*Equal Opportunities Review*, 1995; Farish et al, 1995). The causes of the deep seated gender inequalities within universities, however, are not easy to discover and are therefore difficult to challenge and probably even more difficult to eradicate. For the most part, neither legal challenges nor best practice policies can tackle the inbuilt biases of academia.

Universities as institutions – the formation of equal opportunities policies

When I was appointed to my present post in 1976, eyebrows were raised in the staff dining room, as I was the second woman to be appointed to the then Department of

Extra-Mural Studies within six months and we both had red hair. My previously appointed colleague assures me that she was asked at her interview whether she would be able to carry the book boxes (a book box is a kind of mobile library taken by tutors to classes held in areas remote from library provision). Whether because the Sex Discrimination Act, passed in the previous year of 1975, had influenced my (all-male) interview panel, or whether my colleague had demonstrated the redundancy of the question by showing herself well able to heft the heaviest of book boxes, I do not think I was asked a similar question. As a committed feminist and trade union activist, what would I have done if I had been asked such a question? I tell this story in order to illustrate the difficulty of establishing the causes of gender inequality. I am fairly certain that, in 1976, the panel would not have been influenced by any thought of being accused of sex discrimination. If challenged they would no doubt have thought it a perfectly reasonable question.

Not so now, twenty years later, when at least one of the panel would have been required to have attended a 'Fair and Effective Recruitment' Training Day, where they would have had to consider whether the requirement to carry book boxes was a legitimate requirement, and, been advised on the legal pitfalls of indirect discrimination should it be included as a necessary requirement. It is likely, but not absolutely certain, that there would be at least one woman on the panel, this being recommended but not required.

Awareness of the law relating to discrimination, and the issuing of good practice guidelines, are part of the progress made by the institution in which I work, in trying to fulfill the equal opportunities policies to which it is publicly committed. The process of arriving at those policies over the twenty year period since the 1975 Act has been described elsewhere by two of my colleagues (West and Lyon, 1995). In her rather depressing account of the way in which equal opportunities policies are frustrated by male institutional resistance, Cythnia Cockburn (1991) concludes that the only effective strategy is for women to work together at the grass roots level in building a collective spirit. In some institutions the trade union cannot provide a site for such communal action for it is itself dominated by male resistance. In my current university I have found that trade union activism and feminist consciousness have no difficulty in cohabiting. The local executive has nearly always been 50 per cent female, and steady progress has been made on the ground in raising awareness. This has not been easy. In 1984/5, I was the elected President of the local Association of University Teachers (AUT) branch when I went to see the (interregnum) Vice-Chancellor about widowers' pensions. He thought that I wanted to talk about widows' pensions and it took some time even to get him to understand the concept of a widower's pension.

As well as the documenting of gender inequalities in academia (Acker and Piper, 1990; AUT, 1992, 1993; CUWAG, 1988; EOR, 1995; Hansard, 1990; Jackson, 1990), much has also been written on its possible causes (Acker, 1992; Aziz, 1990; Davies *et al*, 1994; Edwards, 1994; Morley and Walsh, 1996; Thomas, 1996; West and Lyon, 1995). The implicit assumption, demonstrated by my two examples, that university academics are men, no doubt stems from the unconscious. This makes it very hard to document, to prove, to challenge, or to shift. On the other hand, universities are institutions in which discussion is encouraged, containing ample numbers of people skilled in research, argument and debate. This makes it relatively easy to raise issues and awareness, at all levels. Within my institution the AUT has worked within the committee structures which have characterised universities and other educational institutions. Pre-1992 universities to some extent differ from post-1992 universities in that their management structures tend to be less centralised and all members of the institution can actively participate in policy formation if they wish.

In my case, an early involvement in trade union activism, coupled with election to Senate within two years of joining the institution, has given me the experience of being involved in its governance at all levels, through presidency of the local AUT to membership of the employing body, the Council. Often I have been the only woman on key committees. It is impossible to prove a negative, but I suspect my presence has been sufficient to lead other committee members not to make sexist remarks and to think before they speak. Attitudes have changed in imperceptible ways. To tell another story, in 1982 I was an elected member of Council but had been away for a term's maternity leave. I returned to a meeting at which Council was being asked to lower the age at which children could attend the university nursery. A retired medical professor objected: 'The best place for a child under three is with his mother.' I had to speak out, saying that I was now back at work and my child was fine. The amendment was agreed and afterwards two male colleagues approached me and said: 'Of course, what he really meant was that you shouldn't be at work.' I was intrigued by the reaction of my male colleagues and aware that they had firmly categorised the professor as a mysogynistic reactionary rather than an expert in child health.

Nationally, universities have been slow to accept the evidence of gender discrimination and again, within the pre-1992 university sector, the AUT has played a prominent role in both raising awareness and doing the research to provide the evidence (Aziz, 1990; AUT, 1992, 1993; Hart, 1993). The main body that represents the management side of universities, the Committee of Vice Chancellors and Principals (CVCP) (CVCP, 1991) has set up a Commmission on University Career Opportunity (CUCO) (CUCO, 1994) which aims to encourage and help universities as employers to realise the value of diversity and to 'emphasise that diversity includes age, colour, disability, ethnic or national origin, gender, marital status, nationality, race, religion and sexual orientation' (EOR, 1993, p 20). The AUT has a national Women's Committee (founded in the 1980s) the Chair of which is a member of the AUT Executive and I was encouraged to take on the local branch presidency by the fact that at that time the General Secretary of the AUT was a woman. NATFHE has had a lower profile but it has an Equal Opportunities Officer and has issued guidelines on employment (NATFHE, 1994). There has been a steady growth in universities which have joined the Opportunity 2000 (a voluntary group of employers committed to increasing the numbers of women at senior levels in their organisations). A recent article in *Equal Opportunities Review* concludes that 'the reliance on voluntary action . . . means that universities currently vary greatly in the priority given to equality initiatives'. (EOR, 1995, p 30).

Implementing equal opportunities on the ground

I have been Head of a large Department (70+ staff defined as being on the establishment pay role plus up to 800 part-time tutors) of Continuing Education for three years. The process by which I became head is in itself interesting as an example of institutional change. In 1985 the pre-1992 universities received the Jarratt report (Jarratt, 1985) which recommended that the role of academic leadership should be separated from the role of managing resources. What this meant in effect that was that 'The Professor' was no longer necessarily 'The Boss'. In my institution Jarratt led to the Parsloe Report, (Parsloe after Professor Phyllida Parsloe, the chair of the committee, who, at the time she was appointed to the Chair in Social Work in 1979, was the only female professor in the university) which was in its way revolutionary. It ended the *ex officio* headship of departments and separated appointment to a chair (professorship) in a subject from the duty/right to be head of the subject department. Henceforth all headships were to rotate, and the staff employed in the department had to be consulted as to whom they wished to see appointed. By such a process I came to be appointed as a (non-professorial) head.

Having considered the general issues around gender and equal opportunities in academic institutions, I should like to focus on continuing education, looking at four areas where equal opportunities intersect in a specific and particular way with continuing education, and discussing them from the perspective of a manager in a large bureaucratic institution: part-time employment; promotion and professors; sexual harassment; race, disability and equal opportunities.

Part-time employment

Although other university departments hire part-time staff for teaching purposes, the scale of employment of part-timers in a continuing education department is such that the question of the employment rights of part-time staff is one which cannot be ignored. Following the House of Lords ruling in 1995 that to treat part-timers less favourably than full-timers was to discriminate on the grounds of sex, teaching institutions that rely heavily on part-timers have reacted to the need to comply with the law (with effect from April 1996) in different ways. Potentially the ruling gives all part-time staff rights to sick pay, maternity pay and maternity leave and holiday pay and entitlement. My own institution has recognised a claim made by one of our part-time tutors to maternity pay (albeit a minimal amount) but, no doubt in common with other academic institutions, it is anxious to avoid part-time temporary or casual staff acquiring full employment rights.

Given that many devices, such as signing waiver clauses, (whereby staff are required to waive their rights), may prove to be ineffective in preventing part-time staff from acquiring full-time employment rights, some institutions have taken the view that it is better to wait for cases to be brought to industrial tribunals where employment rights will be determined by case-law. In the case of the approximately 800 part-time tutors employed by my department, we are moving to a situation where some are being placed on *pro-rata* full-time contracts, but the majority are being treated as casuals. If more men than women are placed on contracts which are deemed to be more favourable, or *vice versa*, then the university could be open to a sex discrimination charge. In such a situation, all one can do is to keep an eye on the statistics. (See EOR (1995) and Hart (1993) for details of pay differentials between full- and part-time staff.) Overall, increased awareness of the employment rights of part-time staff has resulted in better conditions of service for all part-time tutors, about one third of whom are women. Additionally, the fact that the courses on which they teach are now validated by the university, means that the majority of part-time tutors are now 'recognised teachers', giving them library borrowing rights. This change was perceived by one woman part-time tutor as a significant improvement in her status and she counted this among the benefits of the accreditation or 'mainstreaming' of liberal adult education in an article published in a national daily newspaper.

Promotion and professors

The various campaigns around gender and equal opportunities mentioned above have drawn attention to the fact that, although women make up an increasing proportion of lecturing and research staff in universities, in common with other institutions, such as the civil service or large corporations, they remain concentrated in the lower grades. The question I posed myself in relation to women and continuing education was – is it harder or easier for women in university continuing education departments to get promotion? This is a question which has proved very difficult to answer – harder than for women in other university departments or harder than for men? How many universities have separate continuing education departments? What kinds of grades are the staff who work in them employed on: lecturing – so called 'academic', or, administrative – so called 'academic related'? Post-1992 universities are very different from pre-1992, in both the nomenclature of grades, and the structures of promotion. Although promotion procedures are not subject to national conditions of service, all pre-1992 universities were subject to an agreement to make such procedures more open and accountable. At the institution in which I work, this has resulted in a prolonged period of reform where the procedures are certainly more open and accountable but it has not, as yet, resulted in an appreciable improvement in the proportions of women being promoted from Lecturer to Senior Lecturer grade. For continuing education departments, if they are included in the same procedures, then the chances of women in continuing education are no different from those of all women. Promotion to Senior Lecturer grade is the most competitive stage in pre-1992 universities, and, when compared against one's peers, the criteria are all-important (see West and Lyon, 1995 and Thomas, 1996). There is an inbuilt tendency, which in my institution is proving very hard to shift, to make comparisons solely on the grounds of excellence of research, as exemplified by publications.

Some quantitative exercises have been attempted, some of which demonstrate that women publish less than men (Halsey, 1992), but others show that even where women publish at least as much, they are still less likely to get promoted (Thomas, 1996). For women in continuing education departments, the opportunities to carry out research are often severely curtailed – for example, administrative tasks are relatively greater; vacations are spent in teaching or organising leaving no time for prolonged research; sabbaticals or study leave are not available; research is not given a high priority; access to facilities such as laboratories or computing systems may be inferior. If the institution recognises that the work is of a different kind, and has a system of rewards for teaching or administrative excellence or service to the community, promotion chances may be good. If not, they will be very poor. By and large, men working in continuing education departments will be subject to the same relativities.

For the pre-1992 universities, the Universities Statistical Record (USR) records for 1993–4 (the last year for such data) provide separate figures for departments of Adult Education. These show that for such departments, women made up 40.5 per cent of lecturing staff (compared to the average for the whole sector of 23.7 per cent); 13 per cent of reader/senior lecturers (compared to 10.6 per cent for the whole sector) and 21.4 per cent of professors (compared to 5.5 per cent for the whole sector). As is well known, UK academic subject departments vary enormously in their gender composition, with engineering having very few women, and nursing studies, social work and education having relatively many more women. As one would expect, adult education departments are not significantly different from education departments (in which women are 39.7 per cent of lecturers, 20.6 per cent of readers/senior lecturers and 14.1 per cent of professors). As regards professors in adult education departments the numbers are very small (22 men and 6 women) (cited in Edwards, 1994).

More recent data (THES, 1996) for the unified sector shows that there has been a fairly dramatic increase in the total numbers of women professors. This is certainly the case for my own institution, where the proportion of women professors has grown dramatically, but the proportion of women appointed to 'personal chairs' (ie internal promotions) and to readers/senior lectureships has remained static. This would seem to indicate that the high value placed on research holds women back in internal promotions, and, that it has proved possible to attract some high profile women researchers to vacant chairs.

Sexual harassment

Although sexual harassment cases which reach industrial tribunals have attracted considerable publicity, few such cases are brought. As far as women staff are concerned, were harassment to lead to a woman feeling that she had little choice but to resign, it would be possible to seek compensation for constructive dismissal. Most institutions are aware of this and have issued guidance on appropriate behaviour towards other staff and have implemented internal disciplinary procedures to deal with complaints and allegations. Increasingly, bullying is being seen as another form of harassment to which the same procedures apply. Universities, however, are also the site of 'unwanted attention' towards non-employees, namely students. Although the code of guidance will also cover students, they do not have recourse to industrial tribunals and it is claimed that even fewer cases are ever reported, usually because of the relative powerlessness of the student. In the case of continuing education, the guidelines on permissible behaviour are problematic. While continuing education students are still in a position of relative powerlessness, they are all adults, and their studies are usually only a part of their lives. Some years ago, the AUT attracted tabloid publicity when the Council debated 'consensual relations' between staff and students. As a head of department, what kind of line should one take towards such relations? We know that adults are frequently advised to take an evening class if they are lonely and we can assume that some are looking out for sex and romance. What if they find it with the tutor? While employees may be more protected by codes of practice, what about the part-time tutors, who, as we have seen may not be accorded the same rights as full-time staff? What obligations do they have, and what is the responsibility of the institution to safeguard both staff and students from unwelcome attentions in either direction? These are all grey areas and during my time as head of department, I have had to deal with some difficult cases.

Race, disability and equal opportunities

Equal opportunities law and practice includes much more than gender discrimination. In universities, the role of the continuing education department is often both to provide access for disadvantaged groups, and to put pressure on the whole institution to be aware of these issues. While race discrimination in employment is covered by legislation which is similar in scope and operation to that of sex discrimination, the employment of people with disabilities is less regulated. The old system of quotas has been abandoned as unworkable and replaced by the new Disability Discrimination Act (1995). It remains to be seen whether this will have an impact. At present there is no available national data on the employment of academics by either race or disability, so it is difficult to know the extent to which continuing education departments may be more or less representative of the whole. In some universities, equal opportunities units are contained within continuing education departments. My own department has run a programme of courses for adults with sensory loss for ten years, and in the last three years has employed two deaf women to work on this programme. Additionally the university has employed a visually impaired man to provide student support services. In terms of race, neither the department nor the university has employed any significant number of people from ethnic minorities. While we may provide courses on employment and equal opportunities, we have a long way to go in putting our own house in order.

Conclusion

As the reader will by now be aware, I have viewed my post within the university as a base from which I have been able to promote equal opportunities, primarily in relation to gender, but I have an equal commitment to opening up access to working class students. While the department in which I work may be relatively open to such ideas, it is only in the context of an institution which is relatively closed. The main business of universities is to develop, discuss and disseminate new ideas but they remain profoundly conservative institutions, fearful of change and reluctant to engage in radical activities. For a university such as mine, a department of continuing education which provides a service to the local community to some extent serves as its conscience. Its existence means that it can claim that it provides opportunities for part-time study and for part-time employment. However, in both cases the opportunities are severely limited and confined. Maintaining an active role in promoting equal opportunities is also hard work. In the past three years I have inevitably found a conflict between the role of manager and that of trade union activist, but, so far, and touch wood, I have not experienced a conflict with my feminist consciousness.

References

Acker, S (1992) 'New perspectives on an old problem: the position of women academics in British higher education', *Higher Education*, 24, pp 57–75.

Acker, S. and Piper, D. (eds) (1990) *Is higher education fair to women?*, Society for Research in Higher Education/Nelson.

Association of University Teachers (AUT) (1992) *Sex discrimination in universities*, AUT Research Department.

AUT (1993) *Results of the 1993 AUT survey of professional and equivalent staff*, AUT.

Aziz, A (1990) 'Women in UK Universities: the road to casualisation?', in Stiver Lie, S and O'Leary, V E (eds), *Storming the tower: women in the academic world*, London: Kogan Page.

Cambridge University Women's Action Group (CUWAG) (1988) *The CUWAG report on the numbers and status of academic women in the University of Cambridge*, Cambridge: CUWAG.

Cockburn, C (1991) *In the way of women: men's resistance to sex equality in organisations*, London: Macmillan.

Commission on University Career Opportunity (CUCO) (1994) *Report on university policies and practice on equal opportunities and employment*, CUCO.

Committee of Vice-Chancellors and Principals (CVCP) (1991) *Guidance on equal opportunities in universities*, London: CVCP.

Davies, S, Lubelska, C and Quinn, J (eds) (1994) *Changing the subject: women in higher education*, London: Taylor and Francis.

Edwards, M (1994) *Women breaking the glass ceiling: are we prepared to count the cost?*, Paper given to the Women in Higher Education Conference, Preston, Lancashire.

Equal Opportunities Review (EOR) (1995) 'University academics: the equality agenda', 59, Jan/Feb, pp 20–30.

Farish, M *et al* (1995) *Equal opportunities in colleges and universities: towards better practices*, Buckingham: SRHE and Open University Press.

Halsey, A H (1992) *The decline of donnish dominion: the British academic professions in the twentieth century*, Oxford: Oxford University Press.

Hansard (1990) *The report of the Hansard Society commission on women at the top*, London, Hansard Society for Parliamentary Government.

Hart, A (1993) *Part-time, poor deal: a survey of part-time staff in traditional universities – an AUT report*, AUT.

Jackson, D (1990) 'Women working in higher education: a review of the position of women in higher education and policy development', *Higher Education Quarterly*, 44, pp 297–324.

Jarratt Report (1995) *Report of the steering committee for efficiency studies in universities*, London: CVCP.

Morley, L and Walsh, V (eds) (1996) *Breaking boundaries: women in higher education*, London: Taylor and Francis.

NATFHE (1994) *Equal opportunities: a best practice guide for negotiators*, NATFHE.

Thomas, R (1996) 'Gendered cultures and performance appraisal: the experience of women academics', *Gender, Work and Organization*, 3(3), pp 143–55.

The Higher (THES) (1996) 'Chipping away at the glass ceiling', No 1238, pp 16–17.

West, J and Lyon, K (1995) 'The trouble with equal opportunities: the case of women academics', *Gender and Education*, 7(1), pp 51–68.

Chapter Fifteen

Women's career progression: A case study

Jean Gardiner and Rebecca O'Rourke

In 1996 we were asked to contribute a women's perspective to the fiftieth anniversary celebrations of the continuing education department in which we work (Taylor, 1996). This was a challenging task as Leeds, like most comparable departments (and, indeed most universities) has a rather chequered history where women are concerned. It was founded in the immediate post-war period, and staffed in its early years largely by men with a forces background.[1] The resulting particular culture of masculinity was consolidated by a major commitment to institutional loci of education and training for the armed forces, the prison service, the police and trade unions, particularly the National Union of Mineworkers and the Iron and Steel Trades Confederation, which were heavily inflected not only towards men, but also by a particular version of masculinity. We did not want to gloss over this history, nor to include women tokenistically. Neither did we want to be crones at the feast: muttering against the celebrations.

We concentrated on how women had experienced working for Leeds and it is the data we collected for that purpose which forms the basis for this chapter. It provides both a documentary map of work patterns in one institution and a more personal account of the sense women made of their working lives there. We drew on two main sources: documentary records and interviews with past and present academic and academic-related staff. Clerical staff were not interviewed, a major lack given the centrality of their work to the department and their exclusively female composition. However, early drafts of the research findings were circulated to several clerical staff and their comments were incorporated in the final version (Gardiner and O'Rourke, 1996). A more comprehensive study would also need to take account of the experience of fixed contract research and development staff, among whom women have been well represented, and of part-time lecturers.

This discussion of our research findings incorporates two new aspects which we hope will interest a wider audience. First, we contextualise our work within the developing literature on research into women's employment. Second we suggest ways in which research of this kind could be continued, in our own and other workplaces.

The context for this research

Until recently, research issues concerning women and education have tended to concentrate on student experience of provision, policy and participation. However, a new type of research work is beginning to develop which takes the workplace as its object of enquiry. Two factors have contributed to this. First, feminist concerns have been extended to management and organisation theory, for example by Fiona Wilson (1995) who challenges the gender neutrality of both organisational behaviour and the sociological, psychological and management theories which claim to account for it. There is a growing literature which both explores and offers ways to subvert the checks on women's professional advancement popularly known as the glass ceiling effect (Walsh and Morley, 1996).

Second, within the education sector specifically, a more visible and concerted professional interest in advancing women's employment opportunities has emerged. For example the Universities Council for Adult Continuing Education (UCACE) established a Women and Gender Issues Working Party which found in a survey of 35 universities that around one-third of academic staff were women and 'the higher the salary scale, the worse the ratio of women to men; the lower the salary scale, the better the representation of women' (UCACE Women and Gender Issues Working Party, 1993, p 6). Concern for staffing issues is also evident in the development of training programmes for women, such as those sponsored by the Association of University Teachers or the work at the University of Strathclyde in developing personal and professional development courses for women holding middle level academic and academic-related posts (Brown, 1996). These concerns have been given a historical dimension by Carol Dyhouse (1995). The work discussed here adds a qualitative dimension to the statistical findings of the 1993 UCACE Report into women's employment in Continuing Education. It is suggestive rather than conclusive in what it has to say about women's experience of work. Certainly, the size of our sample (twelve women in all, of whom there were seven lecturers and five administrative/library staff) is not large enough to support statistical conclusions. Nevertheless, the study has begun to articulate important aspects of women's experience which suggest directions for future research. The next section provides a brief overview of women's employment in the Department of Adult Continuing Education (DACE) at the University of Leeds since its establishment in 1946.

'The influx of female members of staff'

During the first 15 years of the Department, only one woman appeared in the lists of academic staff (from 1948 to 1951). Women were not only marginalised as teachers in the early years, but also had very little access to the formal and informal institutional influence associated with serving on the committees which directed the work of the Department.

In the 1960s, the development of applied social studies (probation and child care), was to increase significantly the employment of women staff and recruitment of women students. Without these programmes, female academic staff would have continued to be virtually absent from the department between the mid-1960s and the mid-1970s. In the liberal adult education division only one woman lecturer stayed for longer than two years during that period. She happened to be married to a senior member of the university's academic staff. Although many of the women in applied social studies were initially seconded from senior posts in established professions, none of them became a senior lecturer and no woman ever headed the division of applied social studies which was created in 1969.

The period from 1976 to 1982 saw the first sustained increase in women staff in the liberal adult education division. Over this period six women lecturers were appointed and all except one stayed for a significant period. The annual report for 1979–80 refers to the 'influx of female members of staff' (Department of Adult Education and Extramural Studies, 1980, p 10). In that year the number of women academic staff reached its all-time peak with ten lecturers, six of whom were in applied social studies. Women were then 24 per cent of the academic staff.

The fact that an increase in female academic staff to less than a quarter was perceived as an 'influx' demonstrates how strong the traditional masculine culture of the department remained. Perhaps it illustrates some nervousness about how far feminisation would proceed. At any rate the 'influx' soon came to a halt. The 1980s saw both a slight decline in the proportion of women academic staff in the Department as a whole, reflecting the phasing out of applied social studies work, and an increase in the proportion of part-time staff among women academics. While the adverse financial climate had also taken its toll on male academic staff, the relative decline was slightly less from 31 in 1979–80 to 18 in 1989–90. Part-time appointments were uncommon for men but a rising proportion of male staff found themselves on temporary contracts (see Table 15.1). The proportion of female academic staff (counted as full-time equivalent staff) declined to only 16 per cent in 1989–90. Two women transferred from part-time to full-time posts during this period but no new full-time academic appointments, of which there were six, went to women. Only one black woman was appointed to an academic post and this was part-time and temporary. The 1990s saw a renewed increase in the proportion of women academic staff in a context of overall cuts in staffing. By 1995–96, 32 per cent of the academic staff were women (28 per cent of the full-time equivalent staff) (see Table 15.1).

The overall proportion of women academic, related and research staff had increased earlier. The role of administrative staff had become more significant with changes in funding and women had increased their share of administrative posts. Likewise there was an increase in fixed-term research appointments from the early 1980s and women were well represented in these appointments. In 1995–96 for the first time ever, women exceeded men in academic and academic related posts as a whole. However, as Table 15.1 indicates, within these posts women were concentrated in fixed-term posts in administration, research and development and only one of the six senior academic staff was a woman.

Clerical staffing has always been exclusively female. In spite of the increased administrative workload there was a large reduction in clerical staffing in the 1980s from 29 in 1979–80 to 16 in 1989–90 and the ratio of clerical to academic and related staff actually fell during this period. However, clerical staff in the main administrative centre increased in numbers and became a more cohesive group, the only staff group in that centre to establish an institutionalised morning coffee break.

In 1991–92 only 22 per cent of academic staff in DACE were women compared with a national average of a third in university continuing education (UCACE Women and Gender Issues Working Party, 1993, p 6). In 1993–94 women were 21 per cent of academic staff in the pre-1992 universities as a whole, having increased their share of academic jobs rapidly from only 13 per cent in 1983–84 (*AUT Woman*, 1995, p 3).

There have been very few women in senior academic posts in DACE. The first appointment of a woman to senior lecturer was in 1987. In 1991–92 there were two male senior lecturers and one male professor. In the same year about 20 per cent of

Table 15.1. Gender composition of academic, related, research and clerical staff in the Department of External Studies/Adult Continuing Education, University of Leeds, 1987–96

	1987–88		1989–90		1991–92		1993–94		1995–96	
	M	F	M	F	M	F	M	F	M	F
FT Senior Academic	1	1	1	1	3	–	5	–	5	1
FT Lecturer Permanent	11	1	8	1	6	2	4	2	2	1
PT Lecturer Permanent	–	2	–	2	–	1	–	1	–	1
FT Lecturer Rolling					2	–	3	1	5	2
PT Lecturer Rolling					1	2	1	1	1	1
FT Lecturer Fixed	5	–	8	–	6	–	2	–		
PT Lecturer Fixed	1	2	1	1						
Total Acad FT Equiv	17.5	3.75	17.5	3.25	17.5	3.25	14.5	3.75	12.5	4.75
FT Ac/rel Perm	2	2	2	3	–	3	–	3	–	3
FT Ac/rel Fixed							–	2	–	1
PT Ac/rel Fixed					1	–	1	–	–	1
Research Fixed	–	2	–	2	5	3	5	7	–	1
Development Fixed									2	4
Total Ac/ Ac.rel/Res	20	10	20	10	24	11	21	16	15	16
Technical									1	–
Clerical	–	18	–	16	–	18	–	16	–	17

Note: The figures in the table are taken from annual reports and exclude staff fully seconded out of the Department and temporary staff employed for 6 months or less. Totals for research, development and support staff exceed full-time equivalent staffing since no allowance is made for part-time posts.

professors/heads of department in University Continuing Education were women and 27 per cent of readers/senior lecturers were women (UCACE Women and Gender Issues Working Party, 1993, pp 23–24). In the pre-1992 universities as a whole, 6 per cent of professors and 12 per cent of readers/senior lecturers were women in 1993–94 (*AUT Woman*, 1995, p 3). There were two further senior lectureships among the female staff of DACE in the mid-1990s, bringing the proportion of women among the senior academic staff to 25 per cent and in 1997–98 the newly reorganised School of Continuing Education will have its first woman head of department.

The next section discusses women's career progression using evidence taken primarily from the interviews. It considers first administrative and then academic staff perceptions.

Perceptions of career progression

Although evidence from the interviews in the early 1990s suggested that DACE was a good place to be a female administrator then, this does not seem to have been the case during its earlier history, when, for example in the 1960s, exceptionally high turnover rates of female administrative staff were common. In the late 1960s and 1970s, the Department was still experienced as a hostile and unwelcoming place by women administrators.

For at least a half of DACE's history there was a clear division in terms of career paths between administrative and clerical posts with the former normally defined as graduate appointments, on the same salary scales as academic posts and hence termed 'academic related'. This separation was not always so clear and some clerical staff in earlier generations are known to have progressed from senior clerical to administrative posts, on the strength of proven administrative ability and not necessarily graduate status. However, there appear to be only three cases of promotion from clerical to academic related grades in the Department's history.

Posts, rather than their incumbents, have more often switched backwards and forwards between clerical and administrative grades. The Middlesbrough Centre administrative assistant post was converted to a clerical post in the mid–1970s and, as such, was filled by a sequence of women. The last of these was considering a claim against the University under the Equal Pay Act when she got another job and left. When her replacement, a man, was appointed the post had again reverted to an administrative grade. There was also sometimes an overlap in the actual work done by administrators and clerical staff. Clerical staff, especially the centre secretaries at Bradford and Middlesbrough, showed new administrative staff the ropes and deputised for wardens during periods of illness or absence.

By the early 1990s, DACE emerged in a more favourable light, offering job security, training opportunities and promotion to its women academic related staff. Restructuring created an assistant director (administrative), as well as an academic assistant director, and this senior administrative post was held by a woman. Academic related staff commented on the support received from senior male staff but also highlighted the important informal mentoring role played by other women staff.

> One of the strengths of the Department is that it has got women on the staff who are respected and who have responsible positions. I feel quite strongly that my development in the job has been on the strength of relations with these women and not at all in relationship with men.

Nonetheless, the opportunities for career progression within administration are inevitably limited within the confines of a single department. It is interesting, in this respect, to note the different career path taken by most of the men who came into the Department initially as administrative staff. Out of the twelve men appointed to administrative posts since 1946, seven subsequently became lecturers in the Department, three went on to senior lectureships and two eventually to head of department and professor. This pattern of career progression for men was particularly common from the 1950s until the mid 1960s, when only one of the male administrative assistants did not make the move to staff tutor or lecturer. None of the nineteen women administrators who worked in the Department followed this route. This was partly a matter of choice. Two of the women administrators we interviewed saw themselves, first and foremost as administrators and did not want to teach. Conversely many men appear to have gone into administration not as an end in itself but as a route into a university academic career.

The roles and aspirations of men and women administrators were also perceived differently and hence different opportunities flowed from this. For example women administrators in the past were often expected to play more of a servicing role than were the men. On the other hand reference was made to a departmental culture of equality since the 1980s which set Leeds apart from other similar departments. A more intractable problem was the way women are perceived and perceive themselves, each reinforcing the other. On the subject of career progression:

> *Men regard themselves as serious and weighty in a way that women do not. Because they do, other people do too. I will think about something but I don't automatically assume it's an important statement and of interest to other people.*

Perhaps more of the men have had a strategic approach to their career:

> *Males and females have a different approach to getting things done. The female approach focuses on the task itself whilst the male approach is more likely to be concerned with how completion of the task will reflect on them. Men are good at building those stepping stones and having them mapped out.*

Moreover, women lack the domestic support systems that have enabled some men to take on large amounts of teaching and research on top of their administrative jobs.

> *If somebody has that career path, if that person is male, they are more likely to succeed, more likely to have a good domestic support system, more likely to go home to tea cooked for them, not to washing up and hoovering.*

For academic women a more mixed picture emerges with respect to career progression, especially when linked with working part-time. Four of the seven women interviewed had worked part-time for a significant period. For these women, even when their jobs had expanded and developed, career progression, in the sense of higher status and recognition had not followed during their years on part-time contracts. In some cases working part-time and remaining on the margins was a definite choice but still uncomfortable.

> *I was full of ideas and very frustrated. I didn't want to sit there and say 'we should do this or that' because I would not have been able to carry it out.*

Moving to a part-time post is often perceived as a definite step back in career terms. Several women had worked part-time, not from choice but because there were no full-time jobs available and some mentioned a desire to take on a major teaching or administrative responsibility which they felt they could have managed within their part-time post. However:

> *People assumed that I wasn't interested in getting involved in anything more responsible or central to the department because I was part-time.*

The domestic constraint is often a factor making it difficult to move around in search of jobs. For some the very reasons that brought them into adult education make career progression difficult.

I tend to face out rather than in, more than other people in the Department. I'm much less involved in the goings on with the University and there are penalties attached to that.

If career advancement was based more on a collective view of how staff could best be used to achieve organisational objectives rather than on the relationship of the individual to management women would undoubtedly find it easier to gain promotion:

Women are generally poor at putting themselves forward if the outcome is a gain for 'self', but very good at identifying their own and colleagues' ability to act for the collective good.

Among the women academic staff we interviewed who felt that their careers had progressed, one woman mentioned the crucial informal mentoring role played by women administrative staff.

I had this real sense of being brought on or mentored, both in terms of the structures and politics of the department and in terms of the work I was doing and how it was going to develop.

Some women mentioned that the new managerial approaches introduced in recent years (work profile meetings with the head of department and staff reviews) had been very helpful. Where formalised support and decision making systems are lacking, informal structures and friendship networks come into play and can have an undue influence on key decisions and career development. There are boundaries set around cross-gender friendship and these have been particularly difficult to negotiate in the generations that were moulded by single sex education. Male friendship networks were perceived to have had a strong influence on the culture of DACE.

Several women commented on the absence of any support or encouragement to do research prior to the late 1980s. This absence, combined with the heavy administrative workloads common in continuing education, meant that only single-minded and self-directed individuals, with the confidence and vision to carve out space for themselves and delegate time-consuming tasks to others, managed research at all. It is no accident that these individuals were men, although even among men they were a minority.

The women all had absolutely enormous administrative loads. The assumption was – this was what we were good for – and, of course, the men could get on with their research. It was partly our own collusion. We also doubted our own capacities.

There is a sense that individual women struggled to get an understanding of the department they were in. It was a large and disparate organisation and for much of its history there was no induction for new staff.

Nobody ever took the time to explain to me how adult education was run, about joint courses and the WEA. Gradually you had to pick it up. At the staff conference I enjoyed meeting other people but it was a bit of an ordeal, I used to feel very much an outsider there.

There have been few opportunities for gender issues related to staffing to be openly discussed. A women's assertiveness course organised for all the women administrative, clerical and academic staff in the early 1980s is recalled as a turning point. It gave some women the awareness and strategy they needed to work together to tackle their own invisibility in meetings.

After that we worked out a technique. Two people were not enough. Three of us were needed, X and two others. You needed one person saying 'I don't think we've heard X's view yet' and a second person to repeat 'I don't think we've heard X's view yet' and then X would have a chance to speak. This was so effective that we only had to use it a couple of times. It wasn't a big confrontational issue, it was just our own and the men's ignorance of what was happening.

Assertiveness is identified as a particularly crucial quality by those academic women who have been successful in advancing their careers. They also mention the need at times to resist an implicit, sometimes explicit, assumption that certain men had a prior claim for promotion. Single women and lesbian women experience a particular pressure to assert their own need for financial independence. They also benefit from the autonomy which comes with a domestic life not organised around supporting men. Assertiveness is more possible in this context but its transgression of femininity carries other risks.

The women academic staff have been fragmented in their areas of work and often geographically dispersed across the extramural region, which stretches from Teesside to Calderdale. Women have been divided by material factors such as race, class, sexuality and motherhood, just as much as, or more than, they have been united by gender identification. In each of these cases, those women experiencing a minority status, whether socially, in the Department, or both, have felt distanced from other women. And women have had contrasting degrees of job security. The workplace culture has made it difficult for these different experiences to be expressed. For example the silence of women who have children about their children is striking to some of those who do not.

If women brought their kids into work, people might think 'they're not being professional'. Men don't have this problem and, if they are involved in child care, they are more likely to take their children into work with them. People just think, 'aren't they cute?'

Women have to learn to cope with enormous time pressures when babies are born. One woman recalled marking scripts while breastfeeding. Another took urgent correspondence with her to hospital when she went into labour and recalls: 'finishing a chapter in twenty minute bursts, coinciding with the attention span of the baby'.

The women who have had children place great value on the ways motherhood has helped them in their jobs as enablers, teachers and managers. Yet there is a sense in which a major aspect of women's achievement and abilities for those who have children is written off, unmentionable: 'In this job being a mother is not seen as enriching you but as pulling you away.'

For some women job insecurity has been an overriding problem, making them feel outsiders and out of the running for career progression. Very few women academic staff initially appointed on fixed term contracts have stayed beyond their initial term. This contrasts with the experience of a number of men who succeeded in progressing their careers in spite of, or even because of, the temporary and insecure nature of their posts. Men who feel insecure are likely to redouble their efforts to gain promotion and assume they can count on the support of colleagues in this project, while insecurity often makes women feel powerless and excluded.

There are also inequalities inherent in an adult education programme that relies so heavily on part-time tutors. The success of DACE in surviving the cuts and policy changes of the 1980s and 1990s was largely based on the shift of full-time staff from teachers to programme managers and the increased proportion of teaching done by part-time tutors, about half of whom are now women. Part-time tutors have no job security and every appointment is conditional on adequate recruitment of students. By comparison even part-time lecturers on fixed term contracts feel privileged.

Even feminists found it hard to highlight gender issues from the mid-1980s onwards. There was a legitimate concern that race inequality was as great an issue as gender. While white women had improved their position significantly as staff in DACE, by the mid 1990s there were still no black academic or administrative staff and black people continued to be under-represented as students. The women who were the most active on equal opportunities found it hard to attend to important gender issues while promoting their concern about race, which was the central focus of the equal opportunities committee set up in the mid 1980s. Gender inequality is also harder to pinpoint and to challenge in a department whose culture and reputation is egalitarian by comparison with the institutional context in which it is located.

When I think about the rest of the University I wonder how much comfort we should be drawing from the thought that we are better than them.

Gender inequality cannot be tackled effectively either without addressing the inequalities of class status which are so deeply embedded in the culture of the institution:

Thinking about the University reminds me of 'All things bright and beautiful', everyone in their proper place – the lecturer in his study, the secretary at her word processor.

For clerical staff, assertiveness has as much to do with status as with gender. Certainly, in the 1970s, the Department was experienced as a very hierarchical and formal place. Being on first name terms with senior staff was 'A privilege only accorded to academic and administrative staff'. Clerical staff spoke of a definite improvement in the attitude towards them in the last twenty years and attribute this partly to the increased use of information technology. This has given clerical staff an expertise which academic staff need and particularly male academic staff often lack.

Although small-scale and limited, this research identified some issues that are likely to have wider relevance to women's career progression. Support and informal mentoring by women in responsible and senior positions can play an important role in the career progression of other women. Difference, for example in relation to race, employment contract, sexual orientation, occupation and status, shapes women's experience in very different ways. The culture of the organisation and style of management can inhibit or facilitate women's career progression. It is to be hoped that there will be further opportunities to investigate these issues as discussed in the next section.

Extending the research

There are two main directions in which we might extend this research. One involves developing a more comprehensive study of gender and employment in a single institution, the other entails constructing a comparative study of different institutions in this sector of education. In both instances, it would be important to examine the impact of differences in organisational culture between continuing education and mainstream university departments on the evolution of gender relations. Similarly, our initial focus on women's experience and testimony would be enhanced by accounts of how men perceive the construction and operation of gender relations, both as they apply to women and to men. For example, in identifying the role played by male friendship networks in influencing departmental culture and career development, the situation of men who are excluded from these networks and their benefits, has not been considered. It would also be interesting to explore further some of the difficulties women encounter in their working relations with other women staff as they struggle to establish themselves as equals with their male colleagues. This could be taken further by researchers drawn from outside the particular workplace.

Other methodological issues identified in the course of this study would need to be addressed. In using archival sources, which in some instances related to incidents and events in which we had been directly involved, we were conscious of the extent to which they produce an official version of events, often skating over or leaving out the complex contestations that attend change and development. In further research, this evidence would be the starting point for further exploration and analysis which would draw on a wider range of documentary and other source material.

However, the main source material would remain the oral testimony of those whose working lives are at the heart of the project. While it is true that arguments about the validity of such testimony continue to exercise oral historians and ethnographers alike, it is also the case that a considerable amount of work relating to good practice in this area now exists (Stanley, 1990; Stuart, 1994). Subsequent work would need to engage more consciously with this material. Developing a comparative study would ameliorate the most powerful constraint upon the interviews we conducted, namely the impossibility of anonymity. This affected what questions we felt able to ask in the interviews and the degree to which we probed and followed up the replies. An interviewer drawn from outside the workplace, who did not share its assumptions, collective history or current working relationships, might have circumvented the deliberate discretion with which some questions were answered. However, as with all feminist research it is likely they too would be told: I want to tell you this, but I don't want to see it in print.

There are gains as well as losses from researching in one's own workplace. The research project recorded here facilitated and legitimised conversations between women staff that would otherwise have been unlikely to take place. It politicised the personal and raised awareness of both particularity and commonality in women's experience in a specific workplace. It provided a means of voicing and negotiating difference among women, otherwise experienced as unspoken division and distance. This raised the profile of gender as a workplace issue and helped to foster informal networks of support which are so important for survival and for progression in the workplace.

Note

1. We are grateful to Malcolm Chase for supplying this information.

References

AUT Woman, 1995, no. 36, Autumn.

Brown, R (1996) 'Scaling the towers of academe', *AUT Woman,* No 37, Spring, p 1.

Department of Adult Education and Extramural Studies (1980) *Thirty-fourth Annual Report 1979–80*, Leeds: University of Leeds, Department of Adult Education and Extramural Studies.

Dyhouse, C (1995) *No distinction of sex? Women in British universities 1870–1939*, London: UCL Press.

Gardiner, J and O'Rourke, R (1996) 'Less lucky, less stroppy or what?', in Taylor, R (ed), *Beyond the walls: fifty years of continuing education at the University of Leeds,* Leeds: Leeds University Series in Continuing Education, pp 270–282.

Stanley, L (ed) (1990) *Feminist praxis*, London: Routledge.

Stuart, M (1994) 'You're a big girl now: subjectivities, feminism and oral history', *Oral History*, Autumn, pp 55–62.

Taylor, R (ed) (1996) *Beyond the walls: fifty years of continuing education at the University of Leeds,* Leeds, Leeds University Series in Continuing Education.

UCACE Women and Gender Issues Working Party (1993) *Report on women and gender issues in continuing education*, Universities Council for Adult Continuing Education.

Walsh, V and Morley, L (eds) (1996) *Breaking boundaries: women in higher education*, Basingstoke: Taylor and Francis.

Wilson, F M (1995) *Organizational behaviour and gender*, London: McGraw-Hill.

Chapter Sixteen

Juggling for a living: the working lives of women adult education tutors

Jan Sellers

I would like to begin by expressing my thanks to the 177 women who have contributed to this research by completing questionnaires, and to the seven whom I have interviewed. This chapter is dedicated to them. To ensure anonymity, quotations have been edited.

Part–time tutors in adult and continuing education, most of whom are women, have become expert at putting together a working week. Juggling work, travel, carer responsibilities and other commitments, they make an (often precarious) living, frequently working for several employers and sometimes combining teaching with other types of employment. Some work briefly as tutors and move on to other fields; others build careers in education spanning twenty years and more. In 1992, I had myself been working as a part–time tutor for five years; I had three such jobs at that time, and was also a student on the MA in Continuing Education programme at the University of Kent at Canterbury. For my dissertation, I set out to find out more about the careers and working lives of women part–time tutors, about whom little has been written except in relation to training. The project grew, and has become a doctoral thesis – in part, because of the enthusiasm of the women who responded to my question-naire. In this chapter, I will draw on their responses and on interviews with current or former tutors. I will examine their experiences as tutors, the complexity of their working lives and their reflections on the possibilities ahead for adult and continuing education.

Myself in my research

Where do I stand in relation to the research? Clara Greed, carrying out research on women quantity surveyors, comments: 'I am studying a world of which I myself am part, with all the emotional involvement and accusations of subjectivity that this creates' (Greed, 1990, p 145). This is, to a large extent, true of me. For much of the duration of the research, I worked as an adult education tutor, and have written from within that experience, that shared perspective. In common with a number of women who completed my questionnaire, I have taught adult education classes in many different settings, and have suffered job losses due to cutbacks in adult education. I work part–time in order to have time for study and for creative work. I have experienced disable-ment. My gender, race, class origins and sexuality contribute to particular understandings of the world and of my work, that give me common ground with some tutors and place me on foreign territory with others. While acknowledging the need to be open to the views and ideas of all responding tutors, I must also acknowledge the particular shapes – patterns, concepts, feelings, ideas – that my personal experiences enable me to see, to the possible exclusion, detriment or misunderstanding of other 'shapes' not part of my own experience or culture.

I have been moved by the words of women reflecting on their lives, sharing their experiences; often women who are struggling to keep going, to do the best work they can in very difficult circumstances. I have tried through the questionnaire design and through the writing that follows to give room for women's own voices, their own thoughts and ideas and feelings about their work and careers in adult and continuing education.

Methodology

In 1993–94 I carried out a small-scale survey, distributing questionnaires to women tutors and ex-tutors in a limited number of educational institutions in London and the south east, the north east and the north west of England. I gathered responses from women tutors working for local authority-funded adult education services; for university and college adult and continuing education departments; and for voluntary sector organisations employing tutors on a similar basis (due to significant differences in conditions of service for part-time tutors, I did not include the Open University). A second phase of distribution included efforts to obtain responses from women under-represented at early stages in the survey: Black and Asian women; women who taught in non-traditional subject areas; and former tutors.

In the questionnaire, I asked about current and previous employment, including work other than as tutor; different types of work carried out under tutors' conditions of service (teaching; development and outreach work; special projects; centre management); and future plans. I asked about entry to, and departure from, work as a tutor, and the main satisfactions and dissatisfactions in that work as they experienced it. Other questions covered unpaid responsibilities and interests: voluntary work; political activity; study and creative work (as writer, artist, craftswoman); and responsibilities as carer. Respondents were also asked about factors such as class, ethnicity and disablement, which have been found to affect career development (for example, in work by Susan Boardman and others on class and ethnicity in relation to women's careers (Boardman *et al*, 1987), and in Cas Walker's account of the experiences of black women in educational management (Walker, 1993).)

A number of tutors sent a curriculum vitae, which gave additional insight into the variety and breadth of their experience, frequently gained by simultaneous employment for several employers. A survey of local part-time tutors, carried out by the National Association of Teachers in Further and Higher Education (NATFHE), Waltham Forest Adult and Community Education Branch found:

> *One of the most significant findings of the survey is that 45% of the tutors also teach elsewhere (ie another borough) part-time. In order to understand the working situation of part-time teachers, it is necessary to look at their total working hours (p 2).*

The tutors: who are they?

The tutors and ex-tutors who responded came from a wide range of backgrounds and personal circumstances. At the time of completing the questionnaire, 57 per cent were living in London or the south east, 42 per cent in the north and one per cent elsewhere.

Thirteen per cent of respondents indicated that they were of working class origin. Seven per cent specified that they were of Black or Asian descent, and a number of tutors commented on their experiences of prejudice and oppression:

> *My career was never affected by my race only. It was affected by* gender *problems including problems with* white *women.*

> *I am second generation Irish immigrant . . . I have faced class, gender and racial discrimination.*

Eighty-one per cent of respondents had had carer responsibilities at some point, with several caring for three generations over many years. Thirteen per cent commented on disablement or ill health affecting their careers. Some women expressed considerable frustration that their lives were, or had been, constrained by the illness or the demands of others:

> *Married with children until 1981 where I was expected to know my place (by the kitchen sink) . . . I graduated at 51 and have been looking for work to satisfy me ever since.*

> *Social workers who get 'burned out' on the job are debriefed and advised to take time off sick and/or change jobs. Mothers/wives are not offered that option.*

Pay and contractual arrangements, the insecurity of the work, lack of resources for teaching and child care problems had all contributed to difficulties for tutors. On the other hand, many expressed great pleasure in classroom work and in the achievements of their students (discussed further below and in Sellers, 1995). Tutors found great satisfaction in building their own skills and in working with like-minded colleagues, but raised questions about the amount of unpaid work involved in planning, preparation and meetings.

> *I have found it very satisfying teaching car maintenance to women in a women only environment as I found everyone so keen to learn a subject that has such a mystery around it. I have felt after classes that I have unravelled some of that mystery and boosted women's confidence in their practical ability.*

> *I feel adult education survives very much on the goodwill and commitment of many of its part-time tutors [mainly women] who put in many unpaid hours and provide a good service to the public — would men do as much as this I wonder? And are we [women] taken advantage of or do we allow ourselves to be for our own reasons?*

Seventy-one per cent of respondents were graduates and 50 per cent had some form of postgraduate qualification, predominantly masters degrees or postgraduate diplomas in education, social work and counselling. Seventy-four per cent were current tutors. Of these, 58 per cent also held other posts, mainly in education and training. Of the 45 former tutors, 58 per cent, similarly, held posts in education and training. Some tutors, especially those in adult basic education, had started work in adult and continuing education as volunteers. Teaching part-time was a common route for mothers returning to work when children were starting school. Other starting points were diverse:

> *The truth is I was appalled at the way my daughter was being taught needlework and thought I could do better. To prove to myself that I could, I started at college, gained my City*

and Guilds in Dress and Fashion and went on to gain FE Teaching City and Guilds Certificate in 1977 and have been in part-time work since 1977.

The subjects taught by tutors varied enormously – from Egyptology to Plumbing. While some taught one or two classes a week, others taught a combination of hours amounting to full-time or more, travelling from one town, village or borough to another and from one employer to another, creating a very complex working structure:

> *In addition to teaching literature and creative writing, I am writer in residence for a college and consultant to the local art centre. I also run occasional day schools and weekend courses and write fiction and criticism.*

> *I taught for the County Council (at several adult education centres), the University, the WEA [Workers' Educational Association] and another voluntary sector organisation, all at the same time: evenings and weekends and holidays, approx. 1986–1988, and still couldn't make a living at it!*

In addition to teaching, some are involved in voluntary work, or in cultural activities (paid or unpaid) as writers, artists or craftswomen. Some are involved in part-time study, including research projects, or training part-time for other careers: an embroidery artist, a psychotherapist, a careers adviser and others, gradually building up work in their new fields.

> *Paid work: adult education for the County Council and the university. Study: NVQ [National Vocational Qualification] Registered Assessor, through the RSA [Royal Society of Arts.] Voluntary work: involved in local working mothers group and help at my daughter's school. At times I have felt I have taken on too many paid hours to the detriment of my family. It is a difficult balance to maintain. On the plus side, tutoring in adult education has allowed me to have stimulating, challenging work with hours to fit in with my caring responsibilities.*

Tutors in 1996

I began the research in 1992 at a time of transition in adult and continuing education, with budgetary cuts and both academic and administrative reorganisation beginning to take effect in many places. The process of change has accelerated, with a greatly increased emphasis on accreditation (and associated increases in administrative work) combined with major changes to funding arrangements. In 1996, three years after the earliest questionnaires were returned, I interviewed seven women (six tutors and one ex-tutor), a diverse group with strong and illuminating views. My aim was to obtain current information about their working lives since completing the questionnaire. To ensure anonymity, names and some other details have been altered.

The mathematics tutor

Grace is 50, a black woman living in London with children now at university. She worked for four to five years as a part-time tutor, and is still involved on a voluntary basis with the community development project where she last taught: 'I represent them when they want someone to talk to the Council'. Grace came to Britain in 1965 and graduated as a mature student with an MSc in Mathematics in 1988, after redundancy forced a change of direction. Since then she has taught maths and business skills in adult, further and higher education, and has been involved in development work for young people and women in the black communities including innovative work with a multilingual women's training project. She was teaching up to 12 hours a week, but lost her adult education teaching in 1994. Some classes were cut after her local authority suffered a funding crisis; others were lost when numbers dropped. Guidance before enrolment for classes was inadequate, and Grace advised a number of students to transfer into classes more advantageous for their own career prospects, even though that put her classes at risk of closure.

Grace has since struggled to make a living, but was very badly affected financially by the loss of work. She has not been able to continue working in education, and is currently a freelance dressmaker. She comments that 'whether you specialise or are a generalist, there's still a difficulty in making a living; I don't know how some of these women manage'. Grace describes her efforts to make ends meet, as an unsupported single parent, as part of a greater struggle which also crosses generations: 'I haven't even described the desperation in the black sector; I can only describe my own. A lot of young black women are feeling that'.

Grace regards adult education as a springboard, 'one of the places a lot more funding should go into'. She believes that adult education offers:

> one of the highest 'feel-good factors' out of the whole of the education and training sector, because people are there voluntarily; they're there because they want to do it, because it's vocational, because it adds to their lifelong learning and life skills.

The motor mechanic

Chris is a motor mechanic living in the north west. She has taught her trade since the mid-1980s. In 1995, she was offered redundancy by one college which closed its workshop; she accepted the offer, but continues to teach introductory courses for a college and an adult education service. Chris is considering a career change; she has just begun a Masters degree, and recently started teaching maths. She comments that adult education teaching 'did really suit me, because I was bringing up children on my own'.

Chris has noted many changes in adult education since 1993. With changes in the ways in which adult education is funded, it has become 'almost impossible to get funding for courses which aren't accredited'. She comments that her craft is 'a life skill; some women have gone on and trained, but others have come to save money [so as] not to get ripped off – they don't want anything as formal as accreditation'.

She believes that things are 'going to get more and more difficult with adult education. The needs of adult returners to education are not really being considered any more'. Some courses she has taught, such as 'Do-it-yourself', are difficult to accredit, and colleges are reluctant to put the resources required into workshop spaces. She regrets that now:

> Everything is a battle, there are less and less resources, things coming to an end . . . the colleges are closing down loads and loads of centres that used to be really good for older people and women with children.

Chris has her own analysis of staff changes in adult education. She argues:

Colleges are taking a male approach to jobs rather than a female approach. Adult education worked really well, as there were a large number of women who really wanted part-time work. Now the colleges are taking over, but instead of taking on this 'women's approach' to the jobs, that worked really well, they are taking a male approach with pensions and full-time equivalent contracts, and it doesn't work so well.

The literacy tutor

Annette's experience includes teaching in Latin America, community work and over ten years' experience in Britain as an adult education tutor. She now lives in the north east. Annette and her partner are in frail health; she works part-time through necessity, because of her own limited strength and family responsibilities. Depending on class enrolments, Annette teaches between seven and eleven hours a week on several different sites, all for one employer. Her subjects include literacy, study skills and Spanish.

Annette comments that much local change in adult education has been brought about by cuts in the budget and by new funding methods. A change in management has brought a lighter atmosphere, but other changes have been less welcome. Within the classroom, a series of reductions in the length of terms (from eleven or twelve weeks, to ten) has caused strain trying to fit the GCSE syllabus into less space: 'It is hard to give people what they need in a relaxed way'. In addition, the threatened closure of an old and much loved adult education centre is causing considerable difficulties, not least because of the problems of beginning an academic year with no certainty about a secure venue for the year ahead.

Another change has been in the amount of paperwork required of tutors, as courses are accredited. Annette listed fourteen different sets of records that must now be completed for one course, and commented that teaching is routinely cut short by ten minutes to allow time for form filling and copying. She feels that increased accreditation has brought both advantages and disadvantages: 'It's a way of giving a nationally recognised certificate, to move forward . . . but nobody is allowed to just study something'. Annette suspects that her local adult education service will be abolished or subsumed into the college within the next five years, and sees herself losing her job if this happens; when such a change did take place in a neighbouring town, the posts made available were only half-time or full-time, and Annette does not have the stamina needed for either. She says:

It isn't generally understood how much people gain by having tutors who work short hours and put in lots of preparation. It's valuable having people who can give two hours a week – who can give of themselves, in ways that people can't on a contract requiring them to spend most of their time at the class face.

The dressmaker

Fazanah lives in the north west and teaches dressmaking and textile design for the adult education sections of two colleges. She has qualifications in clothing manufacture, and worked full-time in clothing design before moving into part-time teaching. In addition to her teaching, she does a substantial amount of voluntary work: she is a member of the management committee of a local Women's Welfare Association, arranging functions and negotiating with the local college about classes based in community venues.

Each of Fazanah's classes is based in a different community centre, involving a lot of travel. She works in the day-time and, with four children, does not want evening work. Her part-time income is essential to help with the mortgage. She says:

> I've been teaching for ten years, I can speak several languages; it suits [the colleges] to put me into any group of people who want to learn dressmaking. I love my job, but it's not secure enough.

In an attempt to save funds, some of her classes have been considerably shortened. Speaking of one college, Fazanah commented:

> A twelve week term is now ten weeks – we lost four hours each term. The third term . . . it used to be up to July; they cut it back to May last year and this year is only up to March – two terms. We're told we can't fight for it: that's it.

There is no certainty about which classes will be offered:

> Until we get the contract, we're not sure . . . I have to contact them a week before [the beginning of term] if no contract has arrived, so there is sometimes less than a week's notice that a class is to begin; and sometimes a contract is delayed one or two months.

This uncertainty affects the class, as it takes time to build up a good rapport within the group. Speaking of racism within adult education, Fazanah commented: 'It's there, let's face it. We go by "equal opportunities", all these colleges . . . but racism continues'.

Fazanah was optimistic about adult education till recently, but is very concerned about the future. She believes that her employers want to reduce the number of part-time tutors for financial reasons, and redundancy or early retirement have both been suggested; Fazanah wants neither. One college is cutting down on the number of unqualified teaching staff, and is offering tutors the opportunity to train, though without funding; however, this will not affect Fazanah who is already qualified. Looking ahead, she comments: 'It's the part-time staff who suffer; we only get paid by how many hours we work, we don't get paid for vacation periods . . . If things continue as they have been, things will get worse and worse. Racism is there; there are less chances for me and for Black people, we have to fight for it'.

The counsellor

Jane has been a writer and counsellor, paid or unpaid, for most of her working life. She has worked as a tutor in London for nearly fifteen years, in local adult education services, colleges, universities and voluntary sector organisations. In addition to her teaching, Jane supervises counsellors, has her own private practice and works as a volunteer trainer for the Samaritans.

Jane values her work in adult education and the fresh opportunities it has offered: 'I'm all for adult education; it's been very interesting to be involved in it. If someone goes along with enthusiasm and ideas, they're more than likely to find a slot, as the people who run it are lively and keen'. Most of the difficulties she has experienced have been practical: insufficient rooms for trainee counsellors to use for practice, 'shortage of space, a pressure there; and admin., like having to pay for a car parking ticket'. Jane is close to retirement, and 'getting more reflective'. This year she plans to teach on a diploma course and to run a series of training events. Reluctantly, she has begun to cut back on her teaching load, but says that she 'will go on working for the foreseeable future' and wants to get more involved in community affairs locally, after many years of activism at a national level. She has had plenty of feedback from her students: 'Lots of people write in. They just love to learn; the more of it the better!' She feels that this is 'the particular value of adult education; you can do it later, it's not the end of the world if you fail "O" or "A" levels'.

Tutor in transition

Sally has worked in adult education for over twenty years. She has recently moved from a large town in the north west to a rural area some hundred miles away, and has begun to build up her teaching hours again. Her range of subjects is wide, from history to ecology, and she has begun to develop a new aspect of her work, undertaking research for television programmes. Sally has taught for the WEA, for several adult education departments in colleges and universities, and for local adult education services; she has taught classes at all levels from non-examination to undergraduate.

Until recently, Sally held a management post in adult education, but along with other colleagues was made redundant during reorganisation, one of her main reasons for moving. She now feels she has gone back three or four years, becoming dependent again on part-time teaching hours here and there: 'accepting anything to see what works out'. She has been through a year of considerable difficulty, travelling long distances every week to teach until she was able to find sufficient work locally. Sally has now been offered teaching with the Open University as well as adult education and other university teaching, and is about to relinquish the last of her teaching near her former home. She comments: 'I expect to earn in 1996–97 about a quarter of a full-time salary by doing a lot of travelling for individual contracts!'

Because she has been through so much change recently, Sally is highly aware of differences between the organisations she has worked for, both those she has left and those she has recently joined. Some were well prepared for accreditation to be introduced: 'very well organised, very progressive, very sensible about its interests and willing to try things out'. These employers managed the changes effectively; others were not ready, 'were in a panic' and 'are only just coming to terms with accreditation'. Sally firmly believes that the steep increase in accredited courses has a very positive side: 'It can be introduced as a strength, provided there's some flexibility in the organisa-tion; it's up to the tutor how they present it. Accreditation can be used for the benefit of the class'.

Sally regards adult education as 'something very tough; it's rigorous'. She 'absolutely and totally' believes in it: 'We should be studying till we reach our graves. Adult students are so committed, so stroppy, so delightful! . . . It becomes that voyage of exploration: adults continue to learn, continue to share knowledge, not getting fixed into one's own point of view'. On the down side, she sums up succinctly: 'It's badly paid. It can be exhausting, particularly if you take travel into account. If you're not careful, it can be messy, doing so many different things.'

The linguist

Maria is 35 and has been an adult education tutor for over ten years, in colleges and universities in the south east. She teaches French, Italian and German. Maria worked until recently for a community college which, in 1996, laid off many of its part-time tutors. She lost three evening classes at once, finding out by hearsay through other tutors, 'no letter or anything – I had to ring to find out . . . so after ten years' loyalty we have parted company'. She is eligible for redundancy, thanks to European law, and is awaiting the result of her application, which her union has supported.

Maria's university work continues, teaching language training programmes for employees in local companies. In this area of work, she has been offered additional hours and has recently taken on some coordinating responsibilities, which includes training for colleagues as well as teaching students. Maria has also run a taster course for graduates considering a change of career: 'We had some real success stories. I really enjoyed it. I liked thinking of new ways to teach; they were always interesting people, in their 30s and 40s, in need of a bit of guidance'. Her criticisms of adult education raise questions about a change in ethos, as well as her own concerns about employment: 'What I really don't like about it is that it's just like a business and a money making venture, and the actual teaching seems to be by the way . . . I feel lucky . . . if the [coordinating] work hadn't cropped up I might not be feeling so calm about it'.

Adult education: All change?

The tutors I interviewed, and those who wrote to me through the questionnaire, spoke repeatedly of the joy of teaching, the sense of delight as students gained confidence and moved forward. These 177 women are one small part of the many thousands of part-time tutors across the country. They take enormous pleasure in adult learning, valuing both the work and the contribution they themselves can make to these learning communities. The last few years have seen major changes in the funding of, and priorities for, adult and continuing education at every level of provision: the university; the college; the local authority adult education service; and the voluntary sector.

Reorganisation of adult education provision in many parts of the country, arising from drives to reduce public spending, has led to rapid and confusing changes at local levels. Programmes have been 'streamlined', and class sizes increased with accompanying loss of work for those whose classes do not recruit the higher numbers required. The pressure to 'accredit' many areas of the curriculum has been intense. Within adult education programmes, numerous courses have in fact been certificated for years; these examination classes existed comfortably in tandem with a substantial range of classes for people 'to just study', to learn for the joy of learning – often to very advanced standards – or to develop useful skills (like Chris's DIY students) without seeking qualifications. Now, many tutors are teaching newly accredited courses for the first time, with substantial increases in administrative work (as illustrated by Annette's experience). This teaching is taking place in 'reorganised' adult education institutions, amidst complex changes in the curriculum. The impact of this process on adult and continuing education, and on adult learning opportunity, is and will be immense; only the future will show the outcomes.

These are turbulent times for all who work in adult and continuing education, not least for those whose jobs are the most vulnerable. Part-time teaching is an uncertain way of making a living. Teaching 'the committed, the stroppy, the delightful' has its own particular rewards, but security is not one of them. Gifted teachers, and learning opportunities for students, are being lost as budgets tighten. The question arises, then, as to what gains are being made. Clearly, some tutors have lost much, as Grace's experience shows. Tutors' experiences have varied enormously. This has sometimes been due to organisational factors, made more complex by the impact of race, gender, class and carer roles on women's lives within and beyond the employer institution. These issues are rendered still more complex by uncertainty about jobs and insecurity about the future. Amidst considerable difficulties, those 'at the class face' are endeavouring to assure a sustained and high quality of student learning. The complexity of the working lives of these adult educators, in insecure and changing jobs within organisations which are themselves changing fast, is clearly illustrated here. The implications of this must stand as the agenda for further and deeper study.

References

Boardman, S, Harrington, C, and Horowitz, S (1987) 'Successful women: a psychological investigation of family, class and education origins', in Gutek, B, and Larwood, L (eds), *Women's career development*, Newbury Park, CA: Sage.

Greed, C (1990) 'The professional and the personal: a study of women quantity surveyors', in Stanley, L (ed), *Feminist praxis*, London: Routledge.

NATFHE (1988) *The case for part-time tutors in the Waltham Forest Adult Education Service*, Waltham Forest Adult and Community Education Branch: Part-timers' Working Party).

Sellers, J (1995) 'Walking the tightrope: experiences of women part-time tutors', in *RaPAL Bulletin (Research and Practice in Adult Literacy)*, no 26.

Walker, C. (1993) 'Black women in educational management', in Ozga, J (ed), *Women in educational management*, Buckingham: Open University.

Section Five

Forward to the future

Chapter Seventeen

Gender agenda

Roseanne Benn, Jane Elliott, Pat Whaley

This book was conceived at a time of great change for all post-compulsory education and training. In the opening chapter, we noted the climate and context of change which has shaped the world of CE and the women involved in it. In the 1990s, we have witnessed a national revisiting of the purposes and policies of education and the complex relationship between state, education and work. Issues such as access, accreditation, employability, funding, participation, progression, regeneration and sustainability have been included on the agendas of the major political parties in Britain. The election of a Labour government in 1997 may bring some challenge and redress to nearly two decades of Right wing Tory ideology and policy, which has had a significant impact on education and training. The world-wide interest in the concepts and implementation of lifelong learning has been illustrated in the way the OECD, UNESCO and the G7 nations have prioritised it in major policy announcements and by the setting up of the World Initiative on Lifelong Learning at the first global conference in Rome in December 1994 (see Longworth and Davies,1996). In Britain the debate has been conducted through the consultation process of the Kennedy, Dearing and Fryer Committees (Kennedy,1997; Dearing, 1997; Fryer, 1997). Bodies like the Royal Society of the Arts (RSA) have commissioned cross-sectoral opinion in a number of initiatives and CE as much as any part of the education sector, and arguably more than many, has felt the ramifications of these debates (See for example, Campaign for Learning, 1996). The paper by the University of Leeds Pro Vice Chancellor, Peter Scott, at the 1996 UACE annual conference, suggests a fundamental change in CE and its relationship with HE and the learning society, with possibly 'a growing disjuncture between CE as an organisation formation and as a cognitive domain' (Scott, 1996, p 32). Both Scott and David Watson, the Chair of UACE, note the discomfort and sense of loss incurred by these changes, while also pointing to encouraging and optimistic implications (Watson, 1996, p 33).

For women, too, the 1990s has been a period of change. More than half of all students in HE are mature and a large number of these are women. Nearly two thirds of CE students are women. Yet that seemingly encouraging percentage masks inequalities in women's access to post-compulsory education, as revealed in this book. Nor has the rise in female students led to any rise in the number of women academics and managers (*Guardian*, 1997). Despite large numbers of women staff in CE they are under-represented in terms of promoted posts and positions of responsibility, a pattern repeated throughout the whole education sector, although there has been some welcome change in the traditionally male strongholds of the professoriate and the Committee of Vice Chancellors and Principals (CVPC). Changes in employment legislation for part-time staff have particular relevance to CE (in HE, FE and community settings). The effort to extend pension and insurance rights has caused employers to rethink the policy on the employment of part time staff. We may see more of the instances as in FE where part timers have been forced to register with agencies and their flexibility and terms of employment have been adversely affected.

Importantly, too, in the 1990s there has been a fragmentation of the concept 'woman' and a challenge to feminism from debates on essentialism, race and class, as discussed by several contributors to this book.

Looking forward

In this book we intended to convey something of the spirit and diversity of women and CE at a time of change and challenge. This has meant the inclusion of a number of problems and concerns and the possibility of a bleak and uncertain future. However, it has also been a celebration of what has been achieved; the keynote – for past and present – is that we can make a difference.

In the spirit of optimistic anticipation of 'looking forward', this chapter intends to be positive and persuasive, showing what has been achieved and what is left to do. The future will be shaped by a number of ideas and people. It has to include a gender agenda. What follows are some suggestions related to the key themes of the book. These are not exhaustive but highlight some of the important areas of concern and will hopefully stimulate further debate.

Staffing matters

In the future, CE should be an area where:

- there is an explicit and ongoing review of gender balance and distribution over levels of responsibility;
- if change is necessary it is effected in a way that is mindful of the lessons from the holistic approach common to the best of feminist and CE tradition;
- a culture of possibility, of equality, of support and recognition is the norm;
- job criteria acknowledge the values developed through the women's movement and feminist scholarship, which have strong and familial links with CE;
- account is taken of women's different career patterns and the constraints imposed on them by their other roles;
- staff development is seen as opportunity rather than imposition, employing the best principles of the learning experience we seek to offer students;
- division of labour is not gender–blind, but nor is it predicated on the allocation of pastoral/support roles to women;
- teaching is valued as much as research, and women and men are given equal opportunities to engage with both;
- part-time staff are given the opportunity to have a conceptual overview of the institution and organisation and to listen and be listened to in planning, decision making and delivery;
- new contracts of employment for part-time staff will offer greater levels of security and reward, while securing for the institution more accountability and efficiency;
- there will be a climate in which all administrative, clerical and secretarial staff are encouraged to think in terms of career development and offered opportunities to follow appropriate programmes of study;

- **all** staff including administrative, clerical, secretarial, and part-time and full-time academic staff are given equal recognition for their respective roles in the provision of CE.

Learning lessons

In the future, learners should find CE an area where:

- the gender dimension of barriers is recognised and monitored and ways of extending provision are created mindful of the different situations of women and men;
- financial rules, regulations and eligibility criteria are interpreted in a gender-sensitive way, with awareness that women cannot always qualify for remission and concession by the norms;
- the impact of accreditation is reviewed in the light of women's aspirations and circumstances: with regard to credit accumulation and transfer, timetables for study and for completion of study, access to appropriate advice and guidance and to employment options;
- there is awareness and advocacy, as appropriate, in respect of the effect of job-seeking legislation on learning opportunities, particularly the way in which these affect older women;
- the acknowledged sense of dislocation felt by many women returning to learning as adults is allowed for and addressed by entitlement to a support and resource system;
- there are active efforts to open up opportunities to women from non-traditional and disadvantaged groups.

What counts for the curriculum

In the future a CE curriculum should be one where:

- women are visible and realistically represented in their diversity;
- different cultures are explored and celebrated;
- just consideration is given to gender in book and other text authorship and content;
- teaching and learning strategies consider the gender implications of participation and group work, of subject choice, of experience, of the teacher – learner role and of role models;
- programmes are appropriate to the reality of the learner in terms of preparedness, expectations, aims and interests;
- interdisciplinarity, a corner-stone shared by feminist and CE tradition, is valued;
- methods of assessment recognise that quality can co-exist with innovation and that collaboration and co-operation do not prevent evaluation of individual progress;
- parity does not preclude difference and yard-sticks can incorporate diversity;
- the use of autobiography and life-history are accepted as valid scholarly methods;
- experiential learning is valued in terms of theory and practice;
- academic achievement can be expected and tested without ignoring the needs of non-traditional students for particular provision and support;

- use of reflective practice is encouraged;
- the competing demands of funding and ideology are monitored and resolved in a way that secures the most appropriate programmes and provision;
- AP(E)L incorporates and values women's life patterns and their responsibilities as carers for children and other family members;
- opening up the academy does not close outreach programmes and mainstreaming allows for informal and low-cost entry routes.

In respect of research

In the future, CE research will be an area where:

- there is recognition that a gender dimension exists in all research and is an integral not an extra issue;
- gender is part of the whole research process: opportunity, planning, execution, analysis, publication;
- it is accepted that gender issues relate to subject matter, language and method, to the researcher and the researched, to those engaging in it and those it reaches through dissemination;
- there is recognition of the explicit link between methodology and gender, of research paradigms which incorporate feminist analysis and debates about knowledge;
- there is acknowledgement of women's structural position and of the need for analyses to take account of the broader contexts of power relationships, culture and ideology;
- women's ways of working, drawing on principles from the women's movement and feminist scholarship, are valued, and collaboration, based on these, is encouraged;
- gender issues are a substantive part of research training and teaching, and in evaluation and review;
- there is an ethical code which sensitively respects and involves the voices and perspectives of the researched, women and men;
- empathy and self-reflection are validated in the research ethos;
- research should not assume that all women are the same, the 'other', or are feminist;
- researchers should be reflexive, aware of their own ideological position, sociological status and implicit values and assumptions;
- experience is used to create, test and challenge theory and theory to explain and endorse experience;
- research and teaching are valued equally and combine to create what is distinctive about continuing education.

The ideas for this chapter have been drawn from Network and other workshops; for the last section, from a SCUTREA workshop (Benn & Gerver, 1996).

References

Benn, R and Gerver, E (1996) 'Dividing by more than two: shifting paradigms of gender in continuing education research', in Zukas, M (ed), *Diversity and development: futures in the education of adults*, Proceedings of the 26th Annual SCRUTEA Conference, pp 25–26.

Campaign for Learning (1996) *For life: a vision for learning in the twenty-first century*, London: RSA.

Dearing, R (1997) *Higher education in the learning society*, London: HMSO.

Fryer, R (1997) *Learning for the twenty first century: first report of the National Advisory Group for Continuing Education and Lifelong Learning*, London: Nagcell.

Guardian (1997) 25 March.

Kennedy, H (1997) *Learning works: the report of the FEFC widening participation committee*, London: HMSO.

Longworth, N and Davies, K (1996) *Lifelong learning*, London: Kogan Page.

Scott, P (1996) 'The future of continuing education', in Zukas, M (ed), *The purposes of continuing education*, Proceedings of the 1996 UACE Annual Conference, Leeds, University of Leeds, pp 23–32.

Watson, D (1996) 'Concluding remarks', in Zukas, M (ed), *The purposes of continuing education*, Proceedings of the 1996 UACE Annual Conference, Leeds, University of Leeds, pp 33–34.

Further reading

The references in each chapter in this book provide quite a comprehensive list of further reading, for those interested in developing a greater awareness of these issues. The texts below deal specifically with good and bad practice, problems and solutions, across educational sectors.

Aird, E (1985) *From a different perspective: change in women's education*, London: WEA (Breaking our Silence series).

Benn, R and Zukas, M (1993) *Women and gender issues in continuing education*, Warwick: UACE.

Coats, M (1994) *Women's education*, Buckingham: SRHE and Open University Press.

Coats, M (1996) *Recognising good practice in women's education and training*, Leicester: NIACE.

Farish, M (1995) *Equal opportunities in colleges and universities: towards better practices*, Buckingham: SRHE and Open University Press.

Hughes, M and Kennedy, M (1985) *New futures: changing women's education*, London: Routledge.

McGivney, V (1993) *Women, education and training: barriers to access, informed starting points and progression routes*, Leicester: NIACE.

Spendiff, A (1987) *Maps and models: moving forward with feminism*, London: WEA (Breaking our Silence series).

Whaley, P (1989) *Breakthrough charter for access: quality provision for women in education and training*, Newcastle: Replan/FEU.

Notes on contributors

Viv Anderson is senior lecturer at Leeds Metropolitan University in the school of Professional Education and Development. She has worked in adult education in Leeds for many years, in the first instance as a part-timer, then as an area co-ordinator. Having completed a project with Leeds City Council on a training course for women manual workers, aiming to support them in moving into other areas of work, she began work with the (then) Leeds Polytechnic in 1989 as Access and Equal Opportunities Officer on a job share basis. She is currently working as a full-time lecturer, mainly on short courses, including management courses for women, for black officers and council workers in West and North Yorkshire.

Roseanne Benn has an abiding interest in women's education. She worked at Hillcroft College, the women-only long-term residential college, introducing IT, and Science and Technology into the curriculum. She also developed Access provision to facilitate women's entry into higher education and was a co-founder of the Universities Association for Continuing Education (UACE) Professional Network for Women and Continuing Education. She has written articles, papers and chapters on her research in women and continuing education. She is a Senior Lecturer and Head of Department of Continuing and Adult Education at the University of Exeter.

Elizabeth Bird is Head of the Department for Continuing Education at the University of Bristol and Staff Tutor in Sociology. She began working in adult continuing education at the University of Glasgow in 1974 and has worked full-time ever since in both teaching and managing adult education. She specialises in women returning to study and employment, in gender and social policy and in cultural theory.

Jane Elliott left school teaching in 1986 and worked in the Further and Continuing Education Unit of the Education Department of the then West Glamorgan County Council while completing her MPhil on the impact of gender on student experience of further education. She became a lecturer in Women's Studies in the Department of Adult Continuing Education, University of Wales Swansea in 1992 and is responsible for the development of Women's Studies programmes at non-award bearing, certificate undergraduate and postgraduate levels.

Mair Francis is manager of the DOVE workshop, voluntary sector organisation and charity. It was established during the miners' strike in 1984–85 to provide community based education and training provision. Originally a qualified ceramics teacher, she developed a research interest in women's personal and economic development. She completed her MSc (Econ) in Women's Studies in 1994, her dissertation focusing on women's experience in South Wales during and after the miners' strike. She is currently involved in comparative research looking at the experiences of women in mining communities in other regions of Europe.

Jean Gardiner is a Senior Lecturer in the School of Continuing Education and Deputy Director of the Centre for Interdisciplinary Gender Studies at the University of Leeds. She has worked in adult and continuing education and taught Economics and Women's Studies since the 1970s. She is author of *Gender, Care and Economics* and many articles on domestic labour, women's employment and feminist economics.

Cheryl Law co-ordinates the programmes for Women's Studies and Philosophy at the Centre for Extra-Mural Studies, Birkbeck College at the University of London. She lectures in the history of the nineteenth- and early twentieth-century women's movement and women's rights as human rights. She also works in Central and Eastern Europe on human rights education. Her book, *Suffrage and Power: the Women's Movement 1918–1928*, was published at the end of 1997.

Veronica McGivney is a senior Research and Development Officer at NIACE, the national organisation for adult learning. Prior to joining NIACE, she was Research Fellow at Sussex European Research Centre, the University of Sussex; Tutor in the School of European Studies and Centre for Continuing Education, University of Sussex; Tutor/ Counsellor at the Open University and Lecturer in the Department of Literature and Linguistics, at the University of Nairobi. At NIACE she has conducted a wide range of studies into the different aspects of adult learning and specialised in access and participation issues.

Rebecca O'Rourke has been a lecturer in the School of Continuing Education at the University of Leeds since 1994 and co-ordinates their Adult Education Centre in Middlesborough. Prior to this she held research posts at Goldsmiths' College and the University of Leeds. She spent seven years as a community education worker in East London before combining part-time tutoring with a freelance writing career. In addition to continuing education, she has research interests in women's writing, cultural policy and creative writing, and has published regularly in these areas, including (with Jean Milloy) *The woman reader* (1992), Routledge; *Written on the margins* (1994), University of Leeds; and *Running good writing groups* (1996), University of Leeds.

Julia Preece is a lecturer in the Department of Educational Research at Lancaster University. Among other things she is responsible for a community education, action research project which devises tailor-made courses for community groups. Her current research interests include the cultural values, perceptions and support needs of adults who are under-represented in adult and continuing education. Julia co-chairs the UACE Educational Equality Network and is a member of the UACE Research Sub-Committee.

Jan Sellers has worked at the University of Kent at Canterbury since 1993, developing and running a study skills advice and information service for students. From 1979 to 1995 she worked in adult and community education and in the voluntary sector, as tutor, manager, development worker and volunteer. Her doctoral reseach focuses on the working lives of women part-time tutors in adult and community education.

Sue Shuttleworth is Lecturer in Education and Academic Co-ordinator in Continuing Education in the Centre for Lifelong Learning at the University of Hull. Research interests include: women's education, group working, learner participation and the politics of education. An early focus on student learning in relation to silence and talkativeness in small group discussion has evolved more recently into an interest in participatory collaborative research and how learners become more active by working together, pooling skills and knowledge.

Sue Webb is the course director for Women's Studies in the Division of Adult Continuing Education, at the University of Sheffield, where she contributes significantly to the institutional quality assurance processes. Her research interests are in post-compulsory education, particularly access and equity issues, and women's education. She is currently researching gender experiences and networked learning, and is involved in telematics developments for the University of Sheffield to extend educational opportunities within South Yorkshire. Her recent publications include *Negotiating Access to Higher Education: the Discourse of Selectivity and Equity*, edited by Jenny Williams (1997), Open University Press, which arose out of a national funded project which she co-ordinated.

Pat Whaley is a historian and Director for Community Education and Social Studies in the Department of Continuing Education, University of Durham. She has a long-standing interest in opportunities for women in education and this has been reflected in her work in a number of universities and research projects. Other research interests include issues of access, community education, collaborative and multi-disciplinary research and women's history. She is currently chair of the UACE Women and Continuing Education Professional Network and of the Adult Learners Steering Committee for North East England.

Miriam Zukas became an adult educator in 1978 and joined the Department of Adult Education and Extra-Mural Studies at the University of Leeds in 1980. She is currently Chair of the School of Continuing Education at the same university. Her particular research interests are in the intersection between psychology, adult education and gender.

List of abbreviations

ACACE	Advisory Council for Adult and Continuing Education
APEL	Accreditation of Prior Experiential Learning
APL	Accreditation of Prior Learning
AUT	Association of University Teachers
CATS	Credit Accumulation and Transfer Scheme(s)
CE	continuing education
CNAA	Council for National Academic Awards
CUCO	Commission on University Career Opportunity
CUV	Community University of the Valleys
CUWAG	Cambridge University Women's Action Group
CVCP	Committee of Vice Chancellors and Principals
CVE	continuing vocational education
DACE	Department of Adult Continuing Education
DOVE	Dulais Opportunity for Voluntary Enterprise
EOR	Equal Opportunities Review
ESF	European social fund
ESRC	Economic and Social Research Council
FE	further education
FEFC	Further Education Funding Council
HE	higher education
HEFC	Higher Education Funding Council
IFOLD	Istituto Formazione Orientamento Lavoro Donne
LAE	liberal adult education
IJLE	*International Journal of Lifelong Education*
JAS	*Journal of Access Studies*
LEA	local education authority
NAB	National Advisory Board
NATFHE	National Association of Teachers in Further and Higher Education
NCB	National Coal Board
NIACE	National Institute of Adult Continuing Education (England and Wales)
NIAE	National Institute of Adult Education
NOW	New Opportunities for Women
NVQ	National Vocational Qualification
OCN	Open College Networks
OECD	Organisation for Economic Co-operation and Development
OU	Open University
PCFC	Polytechnics and Colleges Funding Council
PEL	Paid Educational Leave
RAE	Research Assessment Exercise
RSA	Royal Society of the Arts
SCUTREA	Standing Conference on University Teaching and Research in the Education of Adults
SRHE	Society for Research into Higher Education
TEC	Training and Enterprise Council

TQA	Teaching Quality Assessment
UACE	Universities Association for Continuing Education
UCACE	Universities Council for Adult Continuing Education
UFC	Universities Funding Council
UGC	University Grants Committee
UNESCO	United Nations Educational, Scientific, and Cultural Organisation
VIEW	Valleys Initiative for the Employment of Women
WEA	Workers' Educational Association

Index

New books from NIACE

Beyond the boundaries: exploring the potential of widening provision in higher education
Julia Preece (ed), with Cal Weatherall and Maggie Woodrow
ISBN 1 86201 047 1
128pp, £12.95

This book provides commentary and case studies on a wide range of national and international higher education strategies currently being undertaken to strengthen the notion of a learning society. Among the subjects covered are guidance as proactive and inclusive of learner support; regional development as a community partnership; and equity issues from student perspectives. Recurring themes are the embedding of widening participation policy into the institutional mainstream and representing the voice of the socially excluded in the university.

Excluded men
Veronica McGivney
ISBN 1 86201 039 0
1998 forthcoming, approx 80pp, £12.00

Although surveys usually show that more men than women are involved in post-compulsory education and training, this is largely accounted for by employer- and government-supported training. Men with low literacy levels and few qualifications are under-represented in all forms of education and training. Social and economic trends suggest that the issue of male participation is a matter of urgency. This book looks at barriers to participation and implications for targeting and curriculum approaches, with examples of effective practice.

Transforming knowledge: feminism and adult education
Jean Barr
ISBN 1 86201 046 3
1999 forthcoming, approx 160 pp, £14.95

This book suggests that the current social, political and cultural context offers new possibilities for a reconstructed radical agenda for adult education. It seeks to redress what the author argues has been a systematic exclusion in adult education histories and textbooks of the influence of feminism. The author seeks to show that what adult education researchers and practitioners do is located within wider power relations and discourses.

Teaching culture
Nannette Aldred and Martin Ryle
ISBN 1 86201 045 5
1999 forthcoming, approx 176pp, £14.95

This volume reviews the current situation and future directions of cultural studies as an academic field, from the perspectives of teaching and learning. Looking at questions of pedagogy, contributors will examine the changing curriculum of the field and assess how it can be sustained in light of policies, discourses and constraints which dominate higher education.